D0788670

7B

The Theory and Practice of American Literary Naturalism

Selected Essays and Reviews

Donald Pizer

Southern Illinois University Press
Carbondale and Edwardsville

Copyright © 1993 by the Board of Trustees,
Southern Illinois University
All rights reserved
Printed in the United States of America
Designed by Jason Schellenberg
Production supervised by Natalia Nadraga
96 95 94 93   4 3 2 1

Library of Congress Cataloging-in-Publication Data

Pizer, Donald.
    The theory and practice of American literary
naturalism : selected essays and reviews / Donald Pizer
        p.   cm.
    Includes bibliographical references and index.
    1. American fiction—History and criticism—Theory, etc.
2. American fiction—History and criticism. 3. Naturalism in literature.   I. Title.
PS374.N29P48   1993
813.009'12—dc20   92-23398
ISBN 0-8093-1847-4 (cloth)   CIP

The paper used in this publication meets the minimum
requirements of American National Standard for
Information Sciences—Permanence of Paper for
Printed Library Materials, ANSI Z39.48-1984.♾

Contents

v

─┤Preface├──────────────────

As I note in the introduction, my first published essay on
a work of American literary naturalism appeared in 1955. I have
published regularly on this subject since then. The essays collected
in this volume represent one portion of this body of criticism,
that in which specific naturalistic novels are discussed in relation
to general ideas about the nature of American naturalism as a
whole. These essays fall into three groupings, which thereby
constitute the organization of the volume. Some deal with the
full range of American naturalism, from the 1890s to the late
twentieth century, and some are confined either to the 1890s or
to the twentieth century. In addition, further insight into my
views on American naturalism is provided by an introduction in
which I offer a brief historical overview of my interest in the
subject and by a number of reviews of recent studies of literary
naturalism in America. The volume concludes with a bibliography of general studies of American naturalism.

This collection of essays is not intended as a memorial to
my efforts in the field. Rather, it has its rationale in my realization
that the essays in their entirety, as a collection, constitute a full-
scale and coherent interpretation of naturalism in America. Of
course, since the essays have their origin in my efforts to describe
various general characteristics of naturalism rather than in my
desire to give full attention to all major texts in the field, some
works are discussed several times (though from different angles)
and some are mentioned only in passing. But the essays as a
collection are "complete" in the sense that they comprise an

interpretation of American naturalism both in its various phases and as a whole.

A final comment about the contents of the volume. On a few occasions I have borrowed specific passages in one essay for use in another. Since there are only a few such instances and since repetition of this kind also constitutes a form of emphasis, I have not revised these passages. Indeed, other than the correction of typographical errors and the normalization of the style of the notes, I have let the essays and reviews stand as initially published. The date at the conclusion of each essay is the date of initial publication. (The essay on William Kennedy's *Ironweed* appears here for the first time.) For the interested reader, I cite in the acknowledgments the initial publication and, when applicable, earlier republication of each essay and review in the collection.

―┤Acknowledgments├―

"The Three Phases of American Literary Naturalism"
   Twentieth-Century American Literary Naturalism: An Interpretation (Carbondale: Southern Illinois University Press, 1982), pp. ix–xii, 3–10, 13–16, 85–89, 150–52. Reprinted by permission of Southern Illinois University Press.
"American Literary Naturalism and the Humanistic Tradition"
   New Orleans: Graduate School of Tulane University, 1978 (The Mellon Lecture).
"American Literary Naturalism: The Example of Dreiser"
   Studies in American Fiction 5 (May 1977): 51–63; rpt. *Realism and Naturalism in Nineteenth-Century American Literature* (1984). Reprinted by permission of *Studies in American Fiction.*
"Dreiser and the Naturalistic Drama of Consciousness"
   Journal of Narrative Technique 21 (Spring 1991): 202–11. Reprinted by permission of the *Journal of Narrative Technique.*
"Nineteenth-Century American Naturalism: An Essay in Definition"
   Bucknell Review 13 (December 1965): 1–18; rpt. *Realism and Naturalism in Nineteenth-Century American Literature* (1966, 1984). Reprinted by permission of *Bucknell Review.*

"Nineteenth-Century American Naturalism: An Approach Through Form"
> *Forum* (Houston) 13 (Winter 1976): 43–46; rpt. *Realism and Naturalism in Nineteenth-Century American Literature* (1984).

"The Problem of Philosophy in the Naturalistic Novel"
> *Bucknell Review* 18 (Spring 1970): 53–62; rpt. *Realism and Naturalism in Nineteenth-Century American Literature* (1984). Reprinted by permission of *Bucknell Review*.

"Frank Norris's Definition of Naturalism"
> *Modern Fiction Studies* 8 (Winter 1962–63): 408–10; rpt. *Realism and Naturalism in Nineteenth-Century American Literature* (1966, 1984). Reprinted by permission of the Purdue Research Foundation.

"Stephen Crane's *Maggie* and American Naturalism"
> *Criticism* 7 (Spring 1965): 168–75; rpt. *Realism and Naturalism in Nineteenth-Century American Literature* (1966, 1984). Reprinted by permission of Wayne State University Press.

"Self-Censorship and the Editing of Late Nineteenth-Century Naturalistic Texts"
> *Textual Criticism and Literary Interpretation*, ed. Jerome J. McGann (Chicago: Univ. Chicago Pr., 1985), pp. 144–61. Reprinted by permission of the University of Chicago Press.

"American Naturalism in Its 'Perfected' State: *The Age of Innocence* and *An American Tragedy*"
> *Edith Wharton: New Critical Essays*, ed. Alfred Bendixen and Annette Zilversmit (New York: Garland, 1992), pp. 27–41. Reprinted by permission of Garland Publishing Inc.

"Contemporary American Literary Naturalism"
> *Myth and Enlightenment in American Literature*, ed. Dieter Meindl (Erlangen: University of Erlangen, 1985), pp. 415–32.

"Harold Kaplan, *Power and Order: Henry Adams and the Naturalist Tradition in American Fiction*"
> *Journal of English and Germanic Philology* 81 (July 1982): 604–5. Reprinted by permission of the University of Illinois Press.

"John J. Conder, *Naturalism in American Fiction: The Classic Phase*"

> *Journal of English and Germanic Philology* 85 (April 1986): 291–92. Reprinted by permission of the University of Illinois Press.

"Walter Benn Michaels, *The Gold Standard and the Logic of Naturalism: American Literature at the Turn of the Century*"

> *Nineteenth-Century Literature* 43 (June 1988): 113–16. Reprinted by permission of the Regents of the University of California.

"Lee Clark Mitchell, *Determined Fictions: American Literary Naturalism*"

> *Nineteenth-Century Literature* 45 (September 1990): 258–60. Reprinted by permission of the Regents of the University of California.

INTRODUCTION

The Study of American Literary Naturalism

A Retrospective Overview

I did not begin graduate work at the University of California, Los Angeles, in the early 1950s intending to concentrate on late nineteenth-century American literature. For one thing, the doctoral examinations at UCLA at that time permitted only one exam out of the required four to be in American literature, which meant that a good deal of my attention was necessarily focused on English literature. For another, Leon Howard, who directed almost all graduate work in American literature at UCLA during this period, was interested primarily in colonial and antebellum literature. Nevertheless, from my earliest seminar in American literature, during my first year as a graduate student, in 1951–52, I was deeply drawn to the writers of the 1890s and especially to the work of Stephen Crane and Frank Norris. (I was later to write my dissertation on the early work and career of Hamlin Garland, another 1890s author, chiefly because of the availability of his manuscripts at the nearby University of Southern California.)

I did not know why I was attracted to these writers, but in hindsight I believe that it was because the world they depicted in their fiction was closer to my own experience than any other writing I was permitted to work on. At that time, I should note, and especially so in a conservative English department, as UCLA then was, very few dissertations were written on post-1900 literature, and "Modern" was not a fully recognized field within the discipline. But in the fiction of Crane and Norris, and later in that of Dreiser, I found subjects and themes that were "modern" in the sense that they touched upon experiences and concerns that had been part of my own life. I had not suffered, growing up in a New York working-class family during the 1930s and early 1940s, anything like the poverty of a Maggie or a McTeague. Nor had I, as a youth of ten when the Depression ended and as too young by several years to serve in the Second World War, undergone the depth of soul-searching that social chaos and war had brought to a Presley or a Henry Fleming. But nevertheless, as someone who had been raised in a totally urban civilization and who had lived through depression and war, I instinctively sensed the relevance of the lives depicted in this fiction to my own life.

I therefore read the fiction of Norris and Crane initially not because it was required for a course but because it interested me. I did not read it, to put the matter somewhat differently, because it illustrated a body of ideas about this phase of American literature, ideas which I was supposed to learn, but because it gave me pleasure to read it. But I also soon discovered, first through conventional survey courses in American literature and then through my reading of criticism bearing on this period, that a fully developed interpretation of the period was indeed already in place and was almost universally accepted. The novels of Crane, Norris, and Dreiser, I read and was told, were examples of literary naturalism. They therefore derived their essential nature and purpose from the theories and practice of Emile Zola, the foremost spokesman of the movement, and were characterized above all by a desire to demonstrate through fictional characterization and event the thesis that all experience was determined by heredity and environment. The novels of such naturalists as Norris, Crane, and Dreiser could thus best be understood in relation to the ways in which their fictional characters were

shaped, conditioned, and usually destroyed by social and biological forces beyond their control. Moreover, as I was assured by
such standard historical and critical studies of the period as Oscar
Cargill's *Intellectual America* (1941) and Malcolm Cowley's
"'Not Men': A Natural History of American Naturalism" (1947),
the naturalists had failed in this effort to apply a scientific accuracy and detachment to fictional representation. The early naturalists had not only falsely degraded the human condition because
of their commitment to materialistic precepts but had also been
hopelessly confused in their efforts to dramatize a fully deterministic universe. Their novels were therefore both untrue and inept.
Aside from "having opened up American expression to new kinds
of experience" (as the critical platitude was usually put), naturalism was in effect a regrettable false step in the "development" of
American literature.

In general, like most graduate students—at least those of
my generation—I did not quarrel with received opinion. I was,
after all, in graduate school to absorb a body of wisdom, wisdom
which I was then expected, with additional "contributions to
knowledge" of my own, to help perpetuate. But I nevertheless
had considerable difficulty with this particular wisdom. It seemed
to me, for example, that far more was "going on" in a *McTeague*
or a *Red Badge of Courage* or a *Sister Carrie* than the demonstration of a pseudo-philosophical theory of human behavior. The
characters in these novels are weak and inept, and some of them
die in "unpleasant" circumstances, but I did not feel that life was
cheapened or degraded by these conditions and events or that it
had been simplistically and one-dimensionally depicted. More
was occurring in these portrayals than had been allowed, and I
found myself deeply interested in attempting to discover what
this "more" was. It addition, it seemed to me that these novels
were far more successful as fiction than they had been given credit
for. The stories they told—of McTeague's decline, of Henry's
battlefield wandering, of Carrie fumbling her way toward happiness—held and absorbed me more than they were supposed to.
So here, too, I wished to discover the basis for this "more."

My first major attempt to confront these two interrelated
discrepancies between conventional belief about American literary naturalism and my own response to specific naturalistic texts
took the form of a seminar paper on Frank Norris's *The Octopus*

that I wrote for Leon Howard. My training at UCLA had been almost entirely in history-of-ideas criticism, in which a literary work was studied principally as a reflection of the philosophical, political, or social ideas of its time. But I had also, through the influence of a few wayward younger instructors and some undirected critical reading, come into contact with the New Criticism, and especially with issues relating to fictional form and technique. (Mark Schorer's essay "Technique as Discovery," I remember, was a revelation.) So when I said to Howard that I had found many of Norris's ideas about nature and about human perception in *The Octopus* familiar to me from my reading in the American transcendentalists, he encouraged me in this line of inquiry because as a history-of-ideas man he was instinctively in sympathy with an approach of this kind. And when I then said to Howard that I believed that a good many misconceptions about the novel as naturalistic fiction (*The Octopus* was conventionally thought to be completely confused and contradictory in its themes) stemmed from a failure to understand Norris's narrative methods—or, more precisely, his point of view technique—Howard had the good sense not to dismiss this angle of approach because it was foreign to his own methods but rather to recommend a number of useful books on fictional form, books which I then read.

The result was a seminar paper, and later an article called "Another Look at *The Octopus*" (it appeared in 1955 in the journal *Nineteenth Century Fiction*), which represented my first and therefore a tentative yet nevertheless characteristic effort to describe a work of naturalistic fiction as I had found it rather than as I was supposed to find it. What I discovered was that Norris had not been intellectually confused in *The Octopus* and that he had created a largely successful fictional expression of his ideas. His beliefs comprised a late nineteenth-century blend of old and new concepts about nature. Nature was an immense and uncontrollable force, but it was also, when properly understood and responded to, a benevolent force, and man had the capacity to intuit this truth about nature and to order his life in accord with this insight. The thematic confusion attributed to Norris in *The Octopus* was, I argued, the product both of a critical disposition to seek out only "naturalistic" themes in the novel and thus to view any productive or benevolent role of nature and any affirmative view of man's capacities as anomalies, and of a failure to grant Norris, because he was a naturalist, any technical sophistication. Thus, for example, almost all readings of the novel had failed to recognize that Norris's dramatic rendering of the principal reflector in the novel, Presley, permitted Presley the integrity of his own beliefs and therefore did not at all times represent Norris's ideas. It was Presley who was fumbling his way toward insight rather than Norris who was confused.

In this reading of *The Octopus* I had, in a sense, found a critical mission, though it was to be a decade or so before I began to pursue it fully. Norris's themes in the novel, I had discovered, were far more affirmative than any attempt to interpret them in conventional naturalistic terms could hope to understand, and his means of rendering his themes were far more complicated than could be accommodated within a conventional notion of the heavy-handedness of the naturalistic novelist. When looked at closely as a fictional representation of beliefs about human nature and experience, the naturalistic novel, in short, was far more complex than it was believed to be within any traditional definition of the form and the movement.

I was not, however, at this time interested in developing the underlying method and thesis of my essay on *The Octopus* into a full-blown reexamination of the theory and practice of literary naturalism in America. Rather, for the next decade or so I engaged in the close study of the work of specific late nineteenth-century authors, with little discussion of naturalism in general, as in my books on Hamlin Garland in 1960 and Frank Norris in 1966. But I was nevertheless also building toward a more theoretical criticism of the fiction of the period in several ways. One was in my interest in making sense of Norris's literary criticism—another aspect of his work which was thought to be hopelessly confused—much of which bore on the issue of what was naturalism in America. (This concern led to my 1964 edition of Norris's criticism.) Another was in my increasing involvement in the work of the other important late nineteenth-century American natualists, Crane and Dreiser. By the mid-1960s I had given enough thought to all the major naturalistic fiction of the period to come to two related decisions. I would devote a great deal of specific attention to Dreiser because his work, more than any other writer's, characterized and defined naturalism in America, and I would also seek in a series of essays to describe and thus to redefine American naturalism as a whole during the late nineteenth century. Both of these efforts were pursued simultaneously over the next ten years. The first resulted in several books and editions of Dreiser, culminating in *The Novels of Theodore Dreiser: A Critical Study* (1975). The second was expressed in a number of articles, perhaps the most central of which were "Nineteenth-Century American Naturalism: An Essay in Definition" (1965) and "Nineteenth-Century American Naturalism: An Approach Through Form" (1976). Both concerns—my interest in Dreiser and my interest in naturalism as a whole—joined in "American Literary Naturalism: The Example of Dreiser" (1977).

Several common themes run through these essays of the late 1960s and 1970s in which I attempted to describe the general character of late nineteenth-century American naturalism. One was my desire to wipe the slate clean for a fresh look at the fiction of the period by analyzing the reasons—most of them extraneous to the fiction itself—for the critical disfavor of naturalism. The various "cases" against naturalism, I argued, derived largely from religious, philosophical, and political issues of the critic's moment, from the 1890s to the present, rather than from a close examination of the fiction itself. And the fiction itself, I then sought to demonstrate, was not antithetical to traditional humanistic and tragic values. (This, indeed, was the principal thrust of my 1978 Mellon Lecture, "American Literary Naturalism and the Humanistic Tradition.") These writers, I believed, were expressing a sense of the worth of the human enterprise whatever the limitations placed on human volition by the immediacies of social reality. Rather than a mindless adoption and crude dramatization of deterministic formulas, I found in their fiction instance after instance of an author's struggle to confront the conflict between old values and new experience in his time, a struggle which usually resulted in a vital thematic ambivalence. And, I concluded, it was this very ambivalence, rather than the certainties of the convinced determinist, which was the source of the fictional strength of the naturalistic novel of the period.

My attempts to describe the general characteristics of American naturalism by an examination of specific novels of Norris, Crane, and Dreiser resulted in my recognition not only of large-scale similarities in this fiction but also of major differences in each writer's response to the central drift of ideas in his time. There was indeed a drift, one derived from the inevitable awareness pressed upon writers coming of age in post-Civil War America that the conditions of urban and industrial life as well as the new understanding of man's animal origin seemed irreconcilable to the concepts of human dignity and freedom inherent in traditional religious, philosophical, and political belief. But each writer, I also discovered, was responding in his own distinctive way—in subject matter, in theme, and in form—to this large undercurrent of his age. Indeed, as a kind of key to this variability, I had noted as early as 1962, in "Frank Norris's Definition of Naturalism," the remarkable absence of a philosophical center in Norris's concept of naturalism, despite his debt to Zola, who had insisted on a materialistic and mechanistic foundation to his own conception of naturalism. This lacuna in Norris, I argued then and later found confirmed in my close reading of individual naturalists, characterized naturalism as a whole in America and was in part responsible for the great freedom of response (and hence variety) by writers to naturalistic tendencies. Naturalism in America, I was coming to see, was not a "school" and was perhaps not even a "movement." Rather—and I soon came to adopt these terms—it could best be described as an "impulse" to which there gradually accrued a "tradition."

Dreiser was of course the only major naturalist of his generation to have a career extending fully into the twentieth century, and my study of his work thus brought me into closer involvement with modern American writing. Indeed, from the mid-1970s to the present much of my work on naturalism has been devoted to the examination of its continuing presence in the twentieth century. As with my writing on naturalism in the 1890s, this criticism is of two kinds—book-length studies of individual authors, in which I seldom discuss their relationship with naturalism, as in my study of John Dos Passos's *U.S.A.* (1988), and essays on specific works or groups of works, in which I seek to raise issues about twentieth-century American naturalism in general, as in the introductions and essays of my *Twentieth-Century American Literary Naturalism: An Interpretation* (1982) (excerpted in this collection under the title "The Three Phases of American Literary Naturalism") and in such separately published articles as "Contemporary American Naturalism" (1985) and "American Naturalism in Its 'Perfected' State" (1991).

Much of this writing about twentieth-century naturalism has sought to establish the two interrelated points that naturalism, contrary to conventional critical belief, *did* continue as a significant and powerful tendency into modern and contemporary American expression, and that this continuity has taken the form of a variable impulse—that each new generation of writers attracted to naturalism has expressed itself in ways that both echo traditional naturalistic concerns and introduce the preoccupations and fictional methods of that generation. My discussions of twentieth-century American naturalism thus promote the idea of "phases" in the continuity of naturalism in America. Specific social conditions and intellectual movements, in other words, encourage the reemergence of naturalistic modes of expression, but this reemergence occurs not as a pastiche imitation but rather as a form in which the naturalistic impulse speaks to a historical moment in the voice of that moment. At first, in my *Twentieth-Century American Literary Naturalism*, I identified three such phases—the 1890s, the 1930s, and the late 1940s and early 1950s—but in my "Contemporary American Naturalism" I attempt to describe yet a fourth phase beginning in the late 1960s.

In addition to stressing the idea of variable phases, much of my writing about modern American literary naturalism has sought to demonstrate the related premise that naturalism has matured in the course of its presence in American expression. I had initially claimed, in my discussions of naturalism of the 1890s, that this fiction was more sophisticated in theme and technique than was commonly believed, but this claim was of course made in relation to the common belief. There were, however, notable weaknesses in this fiction, just as there were—I later argued—in the opening stages of any new form of expression. But in its later phases, I came to believe—and stated in my "American Naturalism in Its 'Perfected' State" and "Dreiser and the Naturalistic Drama of Consciousness" (1991)—naturalistic writers joined in the post-Jamesian drift toward greater complexity and indirection in the expression of theme. In particular, naturalistic writers from the 1930s onward rendered the interaction between social reality and the felt inner life with far greater subtlety and depth than had been true of earlier naturalists.

Both my efforts to break the hold of the criterion of an absolute determinism in the definition of American naturalism and to claim the persistence of naturalistic strains into twentieth-century American writing have been criticized for resulting in a definition of naturalism so loose and flexible that it is no longer a useful critical and historical construct. This criticism, it seems to me, returns the discussion of naturalism to an earlier phase of critical examination, when works in the movement were examined principally in relation to their adherence to Zolaesque beliefs. There always has been, and, it appears, there always will be, a desire to attach naturalism to a fully deterministic and thus a pessimistic core of belief. To be naturalistic, a novel must adhere to this core, otherwise it either is not naturalism or is confused naturalism. A flexible concept of naturalism as a tendency or impulse reflecting the various ways in which human freedom is limited or circumscribed and the various ways in which this truth is made palatable by combining it with traditional notions of human worth therefore won't do. But it will have to do, I believe, and can also serve an important critical and historical purpose, if the conflict between new truths and old beliefs, and the inevitable lack of a clear philosophical and tonal center which is the product of this conflict, are indeed the essential characteristics of the naturalistic impulse and tradition in American writing.

As is suggested by the presence in this collection of four reviews of full-scale studies of American naturalism that have been published during the last decade, there has been much recent interest in the movement. (A number of other important recent studies, such as those by Amy Kaplan, Daniel H. Borus, and Robert Shulman, contain large sections devoted to naturalism.) This is all to the good, as I note on several occasions. But my reviews, as well as my essay on recent tendencies in the editing of naturalistic texts ("Self-Censorship and the Editing of Late Nineteenth-Century Naturalistic Texts" [1985]), also reveal my concern that the study of naturalism often is still bedeviled by the incubus of determinism. Thus, the effort to return the texts of *The Red Badge of Courage* and *Sister Carrie* to discarded early states is posited in part on the critical preconception that an absolute determinism is central to naturalistic fiction. In addition, some recent criticism, such as Harold Kaplan's *Power and Order* and John J. Conder's *Naturalism in American Fiction*, continues to overstress, as in much criticism of the 1930s and 1940, either the baleful political consequences of deterministic belief or the pseudo-philosophical character of the naturalistic novel. And in other critical studies, such as Walter Benn Michaels's *The Gold Standard and the Logic of Naturalism* and Lee Clark Mitchell's *Determined Fictions*, recent theoretical approaches to literary study—a tendency toward revisionist deconstructive analysis in Mitchell, a reliance on New Historicist assumptions about an author's vulnerability to contemporary ideology in Michaels—result in a confirmation yet again of the deterministic center of American naturalism. A major and common difficulty with these various readings, I believe, is that they tend to delimit strictly and thus to diminish both the individual work of naturalistic fiction and the American naturalistic tradition as a whole and thus fail to account for the vitality and continuity of that tradition. I note at several points in this collection of essays Willard Thorp's comment in 1960 that naturalism somehow refuses to die in America. Thorp was in part bemused by this insight because the long and seemingly indestructible life of American naturalism owed little to critical understanding or support. Yet, it seems, as long as American writers respond deeply to the disparity between the ideal and the actual in our national experience, naturalism will remain one of the major means for the registering of this shock of discovery.

General Essays

ONE

The Three Phases of American Literary Naturalism

An important paradox characterizes the history of American literary naturalism. Although the movement has been attacked by literary journalists and academic critics since its origin in the 1890s, it has been one of the most persistent and vital strains in American fiction. As Willard Thorp noted in 1960, naturalism "refuses to die" in America despite the deep antagonism it usually inspires.[1] Few of our major twentieth-century novelists have escaped its "taint," and it is perhaps the only modern literary form in America that has been both popular and significant.

There are a number of reasons for the opposition to naturalism.[2] Because much naturalism is sordid and sensational in subject matter, it is often dismissed out of hand by moralists and religionists. The early naturalists were particularly vulnerable in this regard. A more meaningful antagonism arises from the feeling of many readers of naturalistic fiction that their basic assumptions about human nature and experience are being challenged. Man's faith in his innate moral sense and thus his responsibility for his actions, and his belief in the semidivine nature of the American experience and in the healing and preserving roles of family and love—these and many other traditional values appear to be under attack in the naturalistic novel. Many readers have also objected to the fullness of social documentation in most naturalistic fiction. From the early attack on naturalism as "mere photography" to the recent call for a fiction of "fabulation," the aesthetic validity of the naturalistic novel has often been questioned.

These traditional objections to naturalism arise for the most part from a priori beliefs about man and fiction. The most probing critics of naturalism have attacked it not on these grounds but on those implied by the ideological origins of the movement. They have argued that a fiction as ideological as naturalism should have a unified and coherent philosophical base and a distinctive form and style consistent with that base. This position has its origin, whether acknowledged or not, in the preeminence of Zola's theory of literary naturalism, and in particular in Zola's belief that the naturalist is a scientist manqué who describes human behavior as closely related to the demonstrable material factors that have conditioned it. Naturalism, in this still wide-spread view is above all social realism laced with the idea of determinism.[3] We live in a biologically and socially conditioned world, and it is the function of the novelist to demonstrate this truth. An entire generation of critics has argued, however, that naturalists have been hopelessly confused because they introduce elements of free will and moral responsibility into accounts of a supposedly necessitarian world.[4] Even Charles Walcutt, who avoids the trap of condemning naturalists for their allegiance to two seemingly irreconcilable systems of value (the "two streams" of his major study of naturalism in America),[5] nevertheless slips into the related position of faulting the movement for not produc-ing distinctive literary forms consistent with its deterministic philosophy. No wonder, then, that naturalism in America has always been in ill repute. Whether damned for degrading man beyond recognition by depicting him as a creature at the mercy of "forces" ("Not Men," in Malcolm Cowley's well-known phrase)[6] or attacked for inconsistency because of the presence of characteristics that fail to debase him, the naturalist has seldom lacked detractors.

Yet despite this unceasing and almost unanimous assault on almost every aspect of American naturalism, the movement, unlike its European counterpart, has continued to flourish. A number of reasons have been advanced to explain the hold of naturalism upon both our writers and our readers. Because of its documentary method, the naturalistic novel, it is argued, has a concreteness and circumstantiality particularly congenial to the American temperament. Alfred Kazin sums up this notion when he writes that "with us naturalism has been not so much a school as a climate of feeling, almost in the very air of our modern American life, with its mass patterns, its rapid social changes, its idolatry of the mechanical and of 'facts.'"[7] Naturalistic fiction is not only "familiar" in its solidity but is also, unlike much modern fiction, fully and strongly plotted. From *McTeague* to *Lie Down in Darkness*, the narrative as "story" is a powerful characteristic of the naturalistic novel even when it contains various experimental techniques. Naturalistic fiction also attracts many readers (while repelling others) because of its sensationalism. "Terrible things must happen to the characters of the naturalistic tale," Frank Norris wrote in 1896,[8] and so it has been ever since. The sensationalism of naturalistic fiction, however—its violence and sexuality, for example—has an appeal that strikes deeper than the popular taste for the prurient and titillating. The extraordinariness of character and event in the naturalistic novel creates a potential for symbolism and allegory, since the combination of the concrete and the exceptional immediately implies meanings beyond the surface. Naturalism is thus closely related to the romance in its reliance on a sensationalistic symbolism and allegory. And if, as Richard Chase and others have argued,[9] the romance—as in the fiction of Hawthorne and Melville—is the form most native to the distinctive American experience, then naturalism is a form that continues to fulfill this need in American life.

These explanations of the sources of appeal of naturalism in America—its closeness to many of the requirements of popular taste yet the implication of a deeper level of attraction as well—have prompted my own method in this study. My approach has not been the conventional one of beginning with a definition of naturalism derived from late nineteenth-century ideas and conditions and then judging writers in accordance with their degree of conformity to the definition. It is this critical procedure, as I have suggested, which has contributed to the misunderstanding of and hostility toward the movement. Because I have sought rather to write an empirical account of naturalism in America, I have begun with a loose sense or impression of what constitutes a naturalistic novel, an impression gathered largely from my earlier examination of American naturalistic fiction of the 1890s. After selecting a number of major novels that appear to bear a resemblance to this impression, I have attempted out of a close reading of these novels to derive a number of general ideas about naturalism in America without a commitment to the discovery of a single, static definition. I have, in brief, written a book about naturalism in which a detailed study of potentially naturalistic novels suggests that there is no neat definition applicable to the movement in America but rather a variable and changing and complex set of assumptions about man and fiction that can be called a naturalistic tradition.

The working hypothesis which guided my selection of novels for further consideration is that naturalistic fiction usually unites detailed documentation of the more sensationalistic aspects of experience with heavily ideological (often allegorical) themes, the burden of these themes being the demonstration that man is more circumscribed than ordinarily assumed. The two large ideas which emerged out of my examination of American novels of this kind since the early 1890s are that these works frequently contain significant tragic themes (I discuss my notion of naturalistic tragedy in my introduction and return to it often elsewhere), and that they fall into three distinct groups—the three waves of major novels by major new novelists in the 1890s, the 1930s, and the late 1940s and early 1950s. (It was this realization that helped determine the organization of my study.)

The reappearance of naturalism at several points in our literary history suggests that it has survived as a significant yet popular literary movement in America because it has responded to the preoccupations of particular moments of modern American life and has discovered appropriate forms for doing so. My task as an interpreter of this phenomenon was therefore threefold. I had to seek to identify the characteristics of naturalistic fiction at the particular moments during which the movement flourished in order to distinguish the distinctive qualities which crested during that decade. I had to confirm and identify more clearly than in my working hypothesis those characteristics that appear in naturalistic fiction from decade to decade and which thus represent the sustaining base of the movement. And I had to attempt to establish the relation between the naturalism of specific works and the permanent fictional worth of these works.

There is no need to discuss in detail the conditions and ideas that contributed to the development of a new literary sensibility in the 1890s.[10] Most students of American life are familiar with the premise that the 1890s were in fact distinguished less by major social and intellectual changes than by a full realization of changes that had occurred during the previous two decades—in particular, the rapid shift from a predominantly rural, agrarian civilization to an urban, industrial society, and the transition from traditional religious faith and moral belief to skepticism and uncertainty.

The realization by the generation coming of age in the 1890s that American life had changed radically since the Civil War helped compromise a key aspect of the American Dream—the faith that America guaranteed all men the free and just pursuit of self-fulfillment and of the good life. William Dean Howells's *The Rise of Silas Lapham*, published in 1885, is perhaps the last major endorsement of the operative truth of this faith. Howells's story of a Vermont farmer who discovers a paint mine on his property and who builds a successful business in the city without losing his moral honesty and courage affirms the unity of the ethical and material life in America. Silas, however, must eventually sacrifice his wealth and position to maintain his honesty, a sacrifice which reflects Howells' recognition of the increasingly destructive strength of the new urban business civilization in which his Vermont farmer finds himself.

Howells and his generation—the generation as well of Mark Twain and Henry James, all of whom were born in the late 1830s or early 1840s—maintained in varying degrees the ethical idealism of the preindustrial, pre-Darwinian America of their youth. A career such as Silas's reflects the hope that the average American can still "rise" to ethical courage despite the largely corrupt world in which he lives. But the generation of Stephen Crane, Frank Norris, and Theodore Dreiser (the generation of the early 1870s) found a hope of this kind not so much invalid as extraneous. City-wise (if not entirely city-bred), they believed that contemporary America was a closed rather than an open society and that life in this society was characterized by a struggle to survive materially rather than to prevail morally. Great industrial and financial combinations and self-serving national political parties appeared to control the fate of the nation as a whole, while the destiny of the common man of city and town—a destiny powerfully influenced by his personal and social background—appeared to be equally beyond individual control. The feeling was that man was limited, shaped, conditioned—determined, if you will—and the search was for appropriate symbolic constructs to express this sense. A half-understood Darwinism and a too-readily absorbed Spencerianism supplied one core of metaphor and symbol, and a crudely applied machine analogy the other. "Environment is a tremendous thing in the world and frequently shapes lives regardless,"[11] Stephen Crane wrote in 1893 in explanation of his theme in *Maggie*, a work in which he offered an animalistic slum as a controlling symbol, while in *The Red Badge of Courage* he was to speak of man trapped in the "moving box" of "iron laws of tradition and law."[12] Theodore Dreiser caught the drift of this view of man's condition in a characteristic blending of the cosmic and bathetic. "Among the forces which sweep and play throughout the universe," he wrote in *Sister Carrie*, "untutored man is but a wisp in the wind."[13]

Of course, young writers of the 1890s were aided in their understanding of "forces" by the work of Emile Zola and other late nineteenth-century European realists and naturalists. By the 1890s, Zola had wide currency in America, whether one read him avidly in the original French, as did Norris, or came to his ideas and interests indirectly, as did Crane and Dreiser.[14] Zola's revolt against romantic idealism, his acceptance of the grandiose claims of mid-nineteenth-century scientism, and his dismay over the social and political corruption of Second Empire France were responses to conditions of his day (conditions paralleled in 1890s America), which helped shape a view of literature in which man's pride in his distinctiveness had little place. Fiction, Zola believed, should above all be truthful rather than polite, amusing, or ennobling, and truth was achieved by depicting life in accord with scientific laws and methods—a goal that to Zola in the 1870s had about it the aura of a postmortem dissection of a diseased corpse. But present as well in this attitude, and feeding its intensity, were Zola's powerful anticlerical and antiestablishment beliefs. His scientism, in short, had at its roots a deep Enlightenment distrust of the supernatural and of the ways in which religious belief in particular often buttressed corrupt and weak social structures. Science, to Zola, was thus a form of faith, since he believed he was using its ideals and methods to achieve a more truthful account of the human condition.

The fiction of the first generation of American naturalists suggests the ways in which Zola and the naturalistic movement were absorbed and maintained in American literary expression. The work of Crane, Norris, and Dreiser in the 1890s has many of the obvious characteristics of Zoalesque naturalism. These writers also depict contemporary middle- and lower-class life free from superficial notions of the ideal and supernatural as controlling forces in experience, and they too find man limited by the violent and irrational within himself and by the oppressive restrictions within society. But aside from these overarching similarities to Zola and to each other, each writer is very much his own man. Each explores a different aspect of American life through his own imaginative response to his world rather than in accord with a pattern and philosophy established by Zola. Each responds, in other words, to the contemporary belief that the novel was the literary form especially capable of exploring neglected areas of the interaction between social reality and the inner life and that Zola was not the model for this effort but rather the leading wedge in a progressive literary movement.

The genius of American naturalism thus lies in the looseness and freedom with which American writers dealt with the gospel according to a European prophet. It was Zola's broad impulse toward depicting truthfully all ranges of life rather than his distinctive philosophy or literary method that was the source of the strength and persistence of the movement in America. American writers were moved by an excitement born of discovering meaning and form for themselves when they began, in the 1890s, to write of the twisted and meager lives of immigrant slum dwellers, of the easy slide into the illicit by young country girls in the city and by middle-aged bar managers desiring young country girls, and of the daily grind yet sporadic violent upheavals of lower-middle-class existence. Above all, these writers no longer accepted the "great lie" of nineteenth-century fiction—the convention that insofar as literary art is concerned relations between the sexes consist either of high romantic love or the minor rituals of middle-class courtship and marriage. Sex begins in their fiction to emerge as the great theme of modern art—the dynamic center of man's tragic nature as well as the subterranean living stream of his daily life.

The ideological core of American naturalism—a sense of man more circumscribed than conventionally acknowledged—does not precede this exploration of the "low" and "irrational" but rather derives from it. Naturalistic writers found that the poor—in education, intellect, and worldly goods—are indeed pushed and forced, that the powerful do control the weak, that few men can overcome the handicaps imposed upon them by inadequacies of body and mind, and that many men have instinctive needs that are not amenable to moral suasion or rational argument. But this observation of life as it is among the lowly—because it is not abstractly derived—does not produce a simple and single deterministic creed. Compassion for the fallen, hope of betterment for the lot of the oppressed, bitterness toward the remediable which lies unremedied—all the emotions which derive from a writer's sense that he is not a dispassionate observer of a scientific process but instead an imaginative presence infusing meaning and dignity and a sense of tragic potential into what he observes—create a living engagement between artist and subject matter that results in a fullness and complexity of expression rather than an emotionally sterile portrait of "forces at work."

This fullness and complexity characterize the tragic themes that are at the heart of American naturalism—both the naturalism of the 1890s and of later generations. One such theme is that of the waste of individual potential because of the conditioning forces of life. The notion that waste constitutes a tragic condition differs markedly from the Aristotelian belief that tragedy encompasses the fall of a noble man. The Aristotelian tragic hero has already reached full stature; his fall moves us because he is a man of worth who nevertheless is brought low. The naturalistic tragic hero is a figure whose potential for growth is evident but who fails to develop because of the circumstances of life. Stephen Crane, the 1890s writer perhaps most sensitive to the fundamental beliefs of his period, begins to explore this theme in *Maggie* (in the capacity of Maggie and Jimmie to respond to beauty),[15] and it receives major statement in the two great American naturalistic tragedies of the unfulfilled common man, *An American Tragedy* and *Studs Lonigan.*

Another important tragic theme within naturalism arises out of the failure of comparatively "successful" but essentially undistinguished figures to maintain in a shifting, uncertain world the order and stability they require to survive. The tragic effect here is again not Aristotelian; such characters as McTeague, Hurstwood, and the Joads do not fall from high place. Rather, they are wrenched by their desires or by other uncontrollable circumstances from their grooved but satisfying paths into the chaos of life "outside." They fall from midway—midway both in mind and status—rather than from a height.

A third tragic naturalistic theme concerns the problem of knowledge. The Aristotelian tragic hero may fail to understand himself or his condition during his descent, but he does in the end "discover" who he is and what has caused his fall. In the 1890s the weakening of a supernaturally sanctioned faith and the decline as well of belief in other transcendentally derived truths cast doubt on the ability of man to have a clear sense of himself in a complex and constantly shifting world. The allegorical setting of *The Red Badge of Courage* provides a powerful image of this condition. Man is alone and doubtful in an unknown world of struggle, yet he still searches in himself and in experience for confirmation of a traditional value—courage in this instance. In the end, he may believe he has discovered truth but neither Crane nor we are sure. Knowledge is now elusive, shifting, and perhaps even nonexistent except for solipsistic "certainties," but man's tragic fate is still to yearn for it, as Sergeant Croft and Augie March will also yearn in later years.

These important attempts in the 1890s to redefine the tragic experience help explain the paradox I noted earlier—the apparent contradiction between critical hostility to naturalism and the permanence and hold of the movement. On the one hand, the man of letters is troubled by the failure of naturalistic tragedy (that is, a fiction depicting the fall of man) to conform to an Aristotelian notion of the nature of tragedy, and he is also affronted by the apparent demeaning of man in naturalistic fiction.

On the other hand, several generations of readers of naturalistic fiction have grasped the validity and centrality of the naturalistic effort to adapt the theme of man's sense of his own importance yet of his propensity to fall (the essence of the tragic vision of life) to the conditions of modern American life. The American naturalistic tragic hero is not a noble figure who falls from high place and then discovers the reason for his fall. Because we are a society still committed to the dream of full development of each man's potential for the good life, we find it more moving to dramatize the crushing or blocking of the potential for fineness of mind and spirit than the loss of qualities already achieved. Because we are a nation that has celebrated fraternity as a democratic ideal, we are moved more by the destruction of one of our fellows than by the fall of the great of our society. And because we have believed that certain truths are universal, permanent, and comprehensible, we are moved by the realization that we can seldom know anything other than our own desires. No wonder that naturalism "refuses to die."

The form of the naturalistic novel in the 1890s as well as in later generations also reveals the capacity of naturalism to adapt a European source—in this instance the Zolaesque formula of massive documentation and a sensationalistic plot—to the specific needs of American life. In the America of the 1890s the need was above all for a device that would permit the full recording of new ranges of American experience and reveal as well the underlying nature of this experience. The need, in short, was for the symbolic and allegorical to reemerge as major forms of expression. Not that these are lacking in Zola; both the repetitive concrete detail and the sensationalism of Zola's novels contribute to a tendency toward symbolic expression in his fiction.[16] In American naturalism this tendency flowered into a powerful and all-pervasive tool that frequently pushes the American naturalistic novel into allegory. From *The Octopus* to *U.S.A.* and from *The Grapes of Wrath* to *The Naked and the Dead* and *The Adventures of Augie March*, American naturalists have sought to depict American life with a grandiosity of sweep and a largeness of meaning that has made the modern American naturalistic novel our epic literature.

Since the underlying theme of much American naturalistic fiction is the tragic incompleteness of life—how little we are or know, despite our capacity to be and our desire to know—it is not surprising that the shape of the allegorical representation of man's fate in the naturalistic novel of the 1890s is often of the circular journey, of the return to our starting point, with little gained or understood despite our movement through space and time. The effect of this symbolic structure is to suggest that not only are human beings flawed and unfulfilled but that experience itself does not guide, instruct, or judge human nature. One of the principal corollaries of a progressive view of time is the belief that man has the ability to interact meaningfully with his world and to benefit from this interaction. But the effect of the naturalistic novel is to reverse or heavily qualify this expectation. McTeague, Sister Carrie, and Henry Fleming are in a sense, motionless in time. They have moved through experience but still only dimly comprehend it and themselves, and thus their journeys through time are essentially circular journeys that return them to where they began. McTeague returns to the mountains of his youth and responds brutishly to their primeval enmity; Carrie still rocks and dreams of a happiness she is never to gain; and Fleming is again poised between gratuitous self-assurance and self-concealed doubt.

The form of the naturalistic novel of the 1890s thus engages us in a somewhat different aesthetic experience than does the form of a typical eighteenth- or nineteenth-century novel. Whatever the great range of theme and effect of earlier novels, we are more or less elevated by our experience of their imagined worlds. That deeply gratifying sense of knowing so well the characters of a novel that we are unwilling to part from them at the close of the book is one of the principal effects of a fiction in which the confident moral vision of the writer has encouraged him to depict life with richness and direction—with a sense, in short, that experience has a kind of describable weight and value. But the form of the naturalistic novel begins to create an effect of uncertainty, of doubt and perplexity, about whether anything can be gained or learned from experience—indeed, of doubt whether experience has any meaning aside from the existential value of a collision with phenomena.

If the form of the naturalistic novel of the 1890s is to be properly understood, however, it is necessary to qualify a view which maintains that its major impact is that of the inefficacy of time. For while the naturalistic novel does reflect a vast skepticism about the conventional attributes of experience, it also affirms the significance and worth of the seeking temperament, of the character who continues to look for meaning in experience even though there probably is no meaning. This quality appears most clearly in Dreiser's portrayal of Carrie, as it does later in Bellow's characterization of Augie. Carrie, whatever the triviality of her earlier quest or the fatuousness of her final vision, still continues to seek the meaning she calls happiness. It is present in a more tenuous form in the fact that Henry has survived his first battle—that is, his first encounter with life in all its awesome complexity—and is undismayed by the experience. And it exists faintly in the recollection we bring to McTeague's fate of his earlier responsiveness to the promise of Trina's sensuality and to the minor pleasures of middle-class domesticity. So the Carrie who rocks, the Fleming who is proud of his red badge, and the McTeague who stands clutching his gold in the empty desert represent both the inability of experience to supply a meaningful answer to the question that is human need and the tragic worth of the seeking, feeling mind.

Naturalism as it emerges in the 1890s thus takes on a configuration central to the movement as a whole in America. The naturalistic novelist is willing to concede that there are fundamental limitations to man's freedom but he is unwilling to concede that man is thereby stripped of all value. In particular, he finds significant the human drive to understand if not to control and he finds tragic the human capacity, whatever one's class or station, to suffer pain and defeat. In the 1890s the expression of these themes in naturalistic fiction is often fuzzy, as is frequently true of the early stages of any new literary movement, when strength of rebellion rather than clarity of affirmation is the principal goal. During the next two major phases of the movement in America—the 1930s and the late 1940s and early 1950s—the naturalistic novel assumes in each decade both a more clearly focused depiction of the tragic nature of experience and a depiction closely attuned to the distinctive concerns of that decade.

Naturalistic fiction of the 1930s has its roots in the social conditions of the decade and in the intellectual and literary currents of the previous decade.[17] James T. Farrell, John Dos Passos, and John Steinbeck did not look to the naturalists of the 1890s for their inspiration but rather found it in ideas of the 1920s about life and literature, ideas which helped them to explain and to express the seemingly imminent collapse of the American system in the 1930s. As early as the boom of the late 1920s many writers were beginning to feel that the average American was excessively shaped in belief and action by American economic values and practices even when he profited from this control. The Depression clarified and intensified this conviction. (It is useful to recall that two of the most powerful indictments of American middle class life and its capitalistic foundation, *U.S.A.* and *Studs Lonigan*, were begun in the late twenties, before the crash.) The reappearance of naturalistic themes in the fiction of the 1930s is conventionally attributed to the heavy freight of Marxist and Freudian ideas that writers of the age carried. Marxism, like Spencerianism in the 1890s, revealed the insignificance of the individual in the process (then evolutionary, now economic) of which he was a part; Freudianism, like atavism in the 1890s, stressed the presence in man's unconscious of a controlling past. But in fact the basic beliefs of Farrell, Dos Passos, and Steinbeck were affected less by these abstract deterministic ideas than by their oblique expression in such fiction of the 1920s as James Joyce's *Ulysses*, Sherwood Anderson's *Winesburg, Ohio*, and Theodore Dreiser's *An American Tragedy*. It was in these works that the novelist of the thirties found a moving representation of the theme inherent in Marxism and Freudianism that life placed tragic limitations on individual freedom, growth, and happiness. Many of the novelists of the twenties appeared to be saying that we live in a trivial, banal, and tawdry world that nevertheless encloses us and shapes our destinies. We seek to escape from this world into the inner life because only there do we seem to find the richness of feeling denied us in experience. But in fact we do not really escape. The retreat into the inner life transforms us into grotesque exaggerations of what we wish to be, or causes us (with fatal consequences) to seek the translation of fantasy into reality, or engages us in an endless search for the understanding and love denied us in life.

Some of these moving accounts of anomie in the modern world had a direct influence on the naturalists of the 1930s. More often, however, the great fiction of the 1920s transmitted indirectly but powerfully to the next generation of writers its pervasive theme of the beleaguered but feeling consciousness in an inhospitable world. It was the fate of the writers of the 1930s to come to this theme when it seemed to be not merely one of the truths of experience but the only truth. The crisis in American social life in the 1930s thus joined with the naturalistic tendencies in much of the fiction of the previous decade to help form a new flowering of the naturalistic novel.

"New flowering" implies not only repetition but a degree of innovation. One important area of innovation was the form of the naturalistic novel in the 1930s. The age was affected by a desire to believe in the unity of the national experience because of the commonality of the national disaster. We are made one by our tragic condition and we must therefore find ways to dramatize this awful unity. Writers struggled to create forms that would express this sense of oneness. Dos Passos sought to emulate in *U.S.A.* the formal conventions of the epic in range and in the representation of a national ethos. Farrell in *Studs Lonigan* worked in detail with a narrow segment of life with a conscious effort to achieve the effect of a microcosm in which the minutely observed would suggest the whole of which it was a reflection. And Steinbeck in *The Grapes of Wrath* combined these two devices. The biblical exodus overstructure of the Joads' journey implied a universality to their plight, while the interlacing of detailed accounts of their movements with the impersonal "inter-chapters" established a macrocosm-microcosm effect.

This desire to render through form a belief in the universality of the American dilemma is closely related to the heavy ideological burden of the naturalistic novel of the 1930s. The writer wished to communicate something important about all of American life, and this intent pushed him toward allegory as a means of achieving thematic clarity and strength. Yet he also wished to probe inwardly, to tell us about the individual consciousness within the "system" as a way of informing us about the system. This, too, had been Crane's intent in *The Red Badge of Courage*, a novel in which Henry's consciousness is the focus within an allegorically shaded action. But whereas Crane's allegory is fuzzy and ambivalent and his depiction of Henry's mind often fumbling, the typical naturalistic novelist of the 1930s presents both a more tightly structured and more apparent allegory and a more sophisticated rendering of a psychological reality. Dos Passos's Camera Eye and Farrell's indirect discourse technique draw upon some thirty years of experimentation by twentieth-century novelists with devices for the dramatization of the inner life.

The emphasis of naturalistic tragedy in the 1930s on the waste of the individual capacity for the good life emerges out of the naturalist's depiction of the interaction between an operative social morality and the thwarted self. Crudely stated, Studs, the Joads, and Charley Anderson fail because they live in a society in which mass values—principally those of a competitive and exploitative capitalism but also of other kinds—shape their lives. The theme of the destruction of the individual by a group value contains, however, the countertheme of the potential for growth by those who realize that there is a beneficial strength in a mass ethos when it is used to protect and nurture rather than control the individual. This interplay between a destructive possessiveness and a beneficial sharing is central to *The Grapes of Wrath*, in which the Joads move from the mass ethic of familial and personal self-centeredness (the "I") to an acceptance of responsibility for the well-being of all men (the "We"). It is also a major element in several strands of *U.S.A.* (a number of the biographies and all of the Camera Eye) that attempt to revivify the dream of an ideal democracy in which each man's freedom depends on his willingness to defend the freedom of all. And it is present in *Studs Lonigan* in that the self-destructive narrowness of Studs derives from his failure to experience a wider world.

The insight that in the group or society as a whole there is not only confinement but the possible release from confinement is acquired by a character of sensibility and feeling in the course of the novel. In the naturalistic novel of the 1930s, unlike that of the 1890s, knowledge is difficult but achievable. The greater difficulty now is doing. Characters such as the Camera Eye persona, Tom and Ma Joad, and even Studs come at last to know themselves and their worlds, but knowledge is not power but rather the tragic accompaniment of weakness. Nevertheless, the basic cast of the naturalistic novel of the 1930s—the diagnosis of an illness and the suggestion of a remedy—creates an effect different from that of the naturalistic novel of the 1890s. The concluding impression is not now one of circularity, of blankness and puzzlement as McTeague returns to the mountains or Fleming reckons up his growth. It is rather an effect of understanding and therefore of an element of hope as the Camera Eye realizes we are two nations, as Tom undertakes his discipleship of activism, and as Danny O'Neill emerges with a clear vision out of the same world that produced Studs. A permanent naturalistic theme—the capacity of men of all stations to feel deeply—is now expanded into an ability to understand as well, and in understanding there is promise for the future.

In its theme of hope from out of the ruins, the naturalistic novel of the 1930s evokes one of the principal attitudes of the decade, just as naturalistic fiction of the 1890s reflects the confusion and ambivalence of that moment. For as Richard Pells, among others, has noted, the chaos and turmoil of the social collapse of the 1930s did not cause despair among writers and intellectuals but rather the vitalizing expectation that out of the rubble of the old system and its values would emerge a society more capable of fulfilling the American dream.[18] As Farrell succinctly put it, he wrote *Studs Lonigan* as "an oblique expression of the fact that I have faith in man and I have faith in the future.[19]

In a series of influential essays written during the early and mid-1940s, a number of major critics announced the death of American naturalism. Philip Rahv noted its "utter debility,"[20] while Lionel Trilling and Malcolm Cowley located its fatal weakness in its metaphysical and fictional simplicity.[21] One reason for this assault, as Willard Thorp pointed out, was that the literary gods of the period were Kafka, Dostoevsky, and James, writers whose complex themes and symbolic forms appeared to be the antithesis of naturalism.[22] Another and less frequently acknowledged reason was political in origin. American naturalism of the 1890s was largely apolitical, but in the 1930s the movement was aligned with the left in American politics and often specifically with the Communist party. In the revulsion against the party that swept the literary community following the Soviet purges of the late 1930s and the Russian-German pact of 1939, it was inevitable that naturalistic fiction would be found wanting because the naturalists of that decade, it was now seen, had so naïvely embraced some form of communist belief. The critics who most vigorously attacked the naturalism of the 1930s in the decades which followed were usually those—like Rahv, Trilling, and Cowley—who themselves had held radical beliefs in the 1930s. What better way to cleanse their own ideological consciences, as well as to purge America of an infatuation with an alien and destructive political ideal, than to attack the fallen god of naturalism.

Yet at this very moment of critical rejection of naturalism and of the complementary New Criticism enthusiasm for lyric forms and orthodox belief, American literary naturalism, in the form of the early novels of Norman Mailer, William Styron, and Saul Bellow, once more came upon the scene. From the perspective of our own time, we can see that these and other new writers felt more continuity between their own literary ideals and those of the naturalists of the 1930s than did the critics of their day. Mailer, Styron, and Bellow were too young in the early 1930s to be "tainted" by communism, but they were not too young, by the late 1930s and early 1940s, to be responsive to the work of Farrell, Dos Passos, and Steinbeck.[23] Mailer later acknowledged the powerful impact upon him of *Studs Lonigan*, *U.S.A.*, and *The Grapes of Wrath* when he discovered them as a college freshman,[24] and both Mailer and Bellow viewed their early work as in the tradition of social realism pioneered by Dreiser.[25] Styron, of course, responded most of all to Faulkner, but the Faulkner of the 1930s can be plausibly viewed as a Southern exponent of several major naturalistic qualities in the fiction of the decade.

These new writers of the late 1940s and early 1950s identified with a frame of mind of the 1930s because they felt that their own age was also threatened by a loss of freedom. But now the sense of a tragic failure in American life was not triggered by the "mere" collapse of the economic system. The extermination camps, the atom bomb, the cold war in Europe and hot war in Korea, the McCarthy witch hunts—all contributed to a sense of malaise, of individual values and freedoms under immense pressure, which appeared similar to but far greater than the pressure of the Depression on traditional beliefs about the nature and destiny of the individual in America. The American economic system contributed to the tragic fates of Studs, Charley Anderson, and the Joads, but one of the impulses behind the depiction of their lives was the conviction that corrupt and destructive systems could be changed—that men of greater awareness and strength (a Danny O'Neill, a Thorstein Veblen, or a converted Tom Joad) could work for a better life for themselves and for others. But these events of the war years and postwar period offered massive evidence of the impotence of the informed will when confronted by the atavistic destructiveness of human nature and the vast, uncontrollable power of the social and political institutions of modern life. The distinctive note of the age was not the hope implicit in tragedy but the chaos present in the struggle for survival and power.

It has been conventional to identify the absorption by the writers of the time in the beleaguered individual attempting to survive in a world devoid of traditional meaning with the impact of French existentialism in America. By the late 1940s Sartre and Camus were being widely read and discussed in America, and there is little doubt that young writers of the period were as alive to their ideas as the young writers of the 1930s had been to Marxism. But in fact, as the best critics of the relationship between existentialism and American postwar writing have noted, the resemblances between the two movements are principally the result of an "affinity of mind" and a "shared consciousness" and are thus best studied as "mutually illuminating" rather than as the effect of the influence of one literature upon another.[26] French existentialism had its roots in the appeal to the contemporary French mind of specific late nineteenth-century philosophical ideas as aids in the explanation of twentieth-century European life. American thought of the late 1940s and early 1950s had an analogous nature and origin. The felt sense of many American intellectuals of the postwar period that communal life and belief were chaotic and irrational and that the only valid source of value lay in individual experience echoed both American naturalism of the 1890s and contemporary French existentialism. For these postwar American writers, the supernatural support of ethical systems was not only unproven but patently untrue; there remained only the individual seeking meaning in his own immediate experience. Thus there occurs a retreat both in existentialism and in the American naturalistic novel of the late 1940s and early 1950s from systems, codes, and structures in any form—from the army and its hierarchy of power, from the family, and from the "adoptive" mechanisms of society. And thus there is the centering of an oblique value on the seeker of the unknown in himself and life.

The deep roots in American life of the romantic individualism underlying this belief are readily apparent. What distinguishes this belief from that of an Emerson and therefore turns it in the direction of naturalism are both its tragic cast and its social emphasis. Defeat is now the natural condition of man, and defeat often means either the failure of life to answer the questions put to it or the answer by life with the resounding "Nothing" that Milton and Helen Loftis believe they hear. But those who nevertheless continue to seek answers in the face of evident defeat do so, as Henry Fleming and Carrie did and as Augie March does now, not in the context of nature or of the "natural" in man but in interaction with their fellow men and often in the city or the group. Meaning must be discovered, if it can be discovered, for oneself and is thus often solipsistically destructive, but it nevertheless is a meaning that has its origin in the collision between self and a particularized social reality.

The naturalistic novel of the late 1940s and early 1950s thus has its origin in traditional themes of the naturalistic novel, which are lent even greater authority and resonance by their resemblance to themes in the principal intellectual movement of the postwar period. *The Naked and the Dead, Lie Down in Darkness*, and *The Adventures of Augie March* are in part "debate" novels. Each in its own way undertakes to represent the opposing claims made upon the individual by the determining factors in his experience and by his quests for a distinctive meaning for himself and for a distinctive fate. Each novel fails to resolve this conflict or debate except for the depiction of the tragic fate of most men who seek. The conflict is discussed openly by the characters or by the narrative voice in *Lie Down in Darkness* and *Augie March* and is expressed allegorically in *The Naked and the Dead*. But whatever the mode of expression, the three novels share the naturalistic emphasis on identifying the forces that make for restriction of freedom while not rejecting the search for alternative values. Freedom in this debate is not categorically denied but is rather submitted to a close scrutiny of its nature and efficacy in a world consisting largely of conditions that limit and qualify it.

The form of the naturalistic novel of this period also has its own distinctive emphasis while maintaining the naturalistic commitment to the full portrayal of contemporary life. In the 1930s, naturalists sought to invent forms that would help express beliefs about man in relation to specific kinds of social experience and value; thus the panoramic or collectivistic characteristics of the naturalism of that period. In the late 1940s and early 1950s, writers pushed this experimental tendency in naturalism in the direction of forms that would represent their interest in fundamental philosophical questions about the nature and condition of man. The social base of naturalistic fiction is still apparent—we are accompanying a platoon on a specific mission or are in a middle class suburb or a Chicago neighborhood—but this material often takes on a nonrepresentational character as the author's interest in ideas impels him toward surreal and expressionistic symbolism. Cummings and the artillery piece and Croft and the mountain, or Peyton Loftis's bird and clock symbolism, or Thea and her eagle—all move naturalism toward Kafkaesque and Dostoevskean modes of expression, modes which most critics of the day failed to recognize because of the naturalistic context in which they occurred.

Naturalistic fiction of the late 1940s and early 1950s has led a precarious and ambivalent existence in recent literary history. When clearly apparent as naturalism because of its sensationalism and because of its author's public statements, as in the instance of *The Naked and the Dead*, it is denigrated for this quality. When its naturalism is obscured by more obvious characteristics, such as the Southern gothicism of *Lie Down in Darkness* or the picaresque form of *Augie March*, it is praised for these qualities. But these novels can best be viewed as the third major expression of the American attempt to explore at moments of national stress through highly structured dramatizations of particular social moments the problem of man's belief in his freedom in an increasingly restrictive world.

A major flaw in most discussions of naturalism is the belief that the movement is something new in Western history. Never before, it seems, had man's irrationality and bestiality, his circumscribed will, and his limited understanding been the subject of a serious and major literature. Prostitutes and depraved workmen, animalistic farmers and crazed artists (to note but a few of Zola's major characters) had no doubt appeared in literature before, but they had never been the principal figures of a significant literary movement. Surely, therefore, there was something new under the sun, and this something new undoubtedly derived from and was similar to the materialistic bias of modern science and contemporary society. But to view naturalism in this way is to mistake the surface for the essential. For if one adopts a broad and expansive view of man's conception of himself from the beginning to the present, one realizes that there have always been periods when theologians, philosophers, statesmen, and artists—that is, men attempting to interpret life—have had a bleak estimate of human nature and experience. Often belief during a period of this kind— the belief, say, of a St. Augustine, a Calvin, or a Hobbes—derives from a reaction against an exalted notion of man held during a previous period and a responsiveness to the oppressive conditions of contemporary life. Often this belief thus stressed that man's ability to choose, to express his will consciously and freely, is limited both by his own nature and by the world in which he lives. But this stress, which in every age in which it occurs takes on the distinctive texture and color of that age's social life and intellectual preoccupations, does not preclude the presence of a strain of humanistic value, a strain that also assumes a shape related to the interests and nature of the period. I am, of course, simplifying one of the most profound and complex rhythms in Western thought. But I nevertheless think that it can be granted that man has wavered between extremes of belief throughout history and that these extremes are therefore less absolute commentaries upon human nature and experience than metaphors in a huge and endless historical poem in which the poetic mood wavers continually from doubt and skepticism to celebration and faith.

Naturalism, as a worldwide late nineteenth- and early twentieth-century movement, is one such moment in this poem. And

American naturalism, as a specific phase of this worldwide movement, has had its own internal rhythm. The naturalism in America has largely been the product of the response of writers during specific historical moments to the pull both of permanent features of naturalistic expression and of particular naturalistic absorptions of the period. The presence of an internal rhythm in the history of American naturalism is confirmed by the principal biographical fact of the movement—that young men of great talent at three specific moments in American literary history have written long naturalistic novels but have gone on, at the end of these periods, to widely different individual interests. (Among major naturalists, perhaps only Dreiser violates this rule.)

American naturalists of the 1890s explored in a frequently muddled yet fundamental way the two interrelated concerns of American naturalism: the tragic nature of life because of the determining forces of experience, and the extent to which affirmative humanistic value and meaning could still be found despite man's conditioned life. These two concerns, the first more social, the second more abstractly philosophical, reappear in the decades of the 1930s and of the late 1940s and early 1950s. In particular, the naturalists of the late 1940s and early 1950s made even more explicit and clear the underlying dualism of the naturalism of the 1890s, a dualism in which the writer does not merely accept the reality of the conditioning forces of life but actively seeks belief and value within this reality.

The American naturalistic novel has not had a single dominant form or shape but rather several recurring forms among novels of different periods, a characteristic which suggests the existence of certain fundamental fictional responses to the naturalistic impulse. One such recurring form is the novel of group defeat, in which a powerful social or economic force causes the fall of a particular class or group of men, even though some individuals in this group are able to push through to a semimystical insight. In such novels as *The Octopus*, *The Grapes of Wrath*, and *The Naked and the Dead*, this is naturalism at its most epic and allegorical. Another continuing naturalistic form is the novel of questing, as in *The Red Badge of Courage*, *Sister Carrie* (for Carrie), and *The Adventures of Augie March*, in which the protagonist seeks inconclusively in a shifting, ambivalent, and often destructive world some form of certainty about himself. A third kind of naturalistic novel records the fall and death of figures completely overwhelmed by the conditions of their lives, as in *Maggie, McTeague,* and *Lie Down in Darkness.* In these works a compensating factor is the element of tragic pathos in the undoing of weak figures who nevertheless, aside from the specific circumstances of their existence, have the capacity for some satisfaction in their experience. And a final form of naturalism dramatizes in massive detail the failure of American society to offer an adequate context for the development of the felt life, as in *An American Tragedy, Studs Lonigan,* and *U.S.A.*

It would be futile to attempt to predict the future of naturalism in America, or even if it has a future. One can perhaps point, as recent harbingers, to the fiction of Joyce Carol Oates and to the transfer of some of the interests and techniques of literary naturalism to such forms as the film (for example, *The Deer Hunter*) and documentary narrative (for example, *In Cold Blood*). But we must wait to see.

1982

TWO

⊣American Literary Naturalism and the Humanistic Tradition⊢

My title announces a paradox. In the demonology of modern literary history, naturalism is usually the anti-Christ. Zola unleashed upon the world, so the conventional argument goes, a literature characterized by the squalid and degrading in human nature and by a deterministic philosophy that denied man moral responsibility for his actions. Zola and his European and American followers depicted man as an animal and civilization as a polite metaphor for the jungle. Thus it is implied that Zola's controlling vision of man was both retrogressive and antihumanist: the human animal was still principally bestial, and the passage of time created only the illusion rather than the reality of the progress of the human spirit. My effort, as suggested by my title, will be to work counter to this still widely held belief and to claim that naturalism, at its best and most permanent, maintains a humanistic tradition of literary expression in which a primary goal is the dramatization of the value and uniqueness of man's felt inner life. I will attempt to demonstrate this aspect of naturalism by saying something briefly about naturalism as a worldwide late nineteenth-century literary movement and by discussing more fully some characteristic examples of literary naturalism in America from the 1890s to the early 1950s.

A major flaw in most discussions of naturalism is the belief that the movement was something new in Western history. Never before, it seems, had man's irrationality and bestiality, his circumscribed will, and his limited understanding been the subject of a serious and major literature. Prostitutes and depraved workmen, animalistic farmers and crazed artists (to note but a few of Zola's major characters) had no doubt appeared in literature before, but they had never been the principal focus of a significant literary movement. Surely, therefore, there was something new under the sun, and this something new undoubtedly derived from and was similar to the materialistic bias of modern science and contemporary society. But to view naturalism in this way is to mistake the surface for the essential. For if one adopts a broad and expansive view of man's conception of himself from the beginning to the present, one realizes that there have always been periods when theologians, philosophers, statesmen, or artists—that is, men attempting to interpret life—have had a bleak estimate of human nature and experience. Often belief during a period of this kind— the belief, let's say, of a St. Augustine, a Calvin, or a Hobbes— derives from a reaction against an overexalted notion of man held during a previous period and a responsiveness to the oppressive conditions of contemporary life. Often this belief thus stresses that man's freedom to choose, to express his will consciously and freely, is limited both by his own nature and by the world in which he lives. But this stress, which in every age in which it occurs takes on the distinctive texture and color of that age's social life and intellectual preoccupations, does not preclude the presence of a strain of humanistic value, a strain that also assumes a shape related to the interests and nature of the period. I am, of course, grotesquely simplifying one of the most profound and complex rhythms in Western thought. But I nevertheless hope that we can agree that man has wavered between extremes of belief throughout history and that these extremes are therefore less absolute commentaries upon human nature and experience than metaphors in a huge and endless historical poem in which the poetic mood wavers continually from doubt and skepticism to celebration and faith.

Naturalism, as a worldwide late nineteenth- and early twentieth-century movement, is one such moment in this poem. Zola's revolt against romantic idealism, his acceptance of the grandiose claims of mid-nineteenth-century scientism, and his dismay over the social and political conditions of Second Empire France—all of these helped shape a view of literature in which man's pride in his distinctiveness had little place. Fiction, Zola believed, should above all be truthful rather than polite, amusing, or ennobling, and truth was achieved by depicting life in accord with scientific laws and methods—a goal which to Zola in the 1870s had about it the aura of a postmortem dissection of a diseased corpse. But present as well in this attitude, and feeding its intensity, were Zola's powerful anticlerical and antiestablishment beliefs. His scientism, in short, had at its roots a deep Enlightenment distrust of the supernatural and of the ways in which religious belief in particular often buttressed corrupt and weak social structures. Science, to Zola, was thus a form of faith, since he believed that he was using its ideals and methods to achieve a more truthful account of the human condition. And the belief that men can benefit from the truth—that the truth is worth pursuing for this reason—is a cornerstone of the humanistic tradition.

What, therefore, is the role and significance of Zola in the naturalistic tradition? On the one hand, there are the two mythic Zolas—the first, as viewed by his contemporaries, is a befouler of the human spirit; the second, as viewed by himself, is a scientific observer of the truths of experience that others have agreed neither to see nor to record. On the other hand, there is the Zola who represents the character of the naturalistic movement that I would like to stress—the Zola who in response to the social and intellectual currents of his time fashions literary works in which there is a complex joining of that which represents the limiting and inadequate in life and that which affirms a humanistic center to experience.

———

The fiction of the first generation of American naturalists suggests the ways in which Zola and the naturalist movement were absorbed and maintained in American literary expression. The work of Stephen Crane, Frank Norris, and Theodore Dreiser in the 1890s had many of the obvious characteristics of Zolaesque naturalism. These writers also depict contemporary middle- and lower-class life free from superficial notions of the ideal and supernatural as controlling forces in experience, and they too find man limited by the violent and irrational within himself and by the oppressively restrictive within society. But aside from these overarching similarities to Zola and to each other, each writer is very much his own man. Each explores a different aspect of American life out of his own imaginative response to his world rather than in accord with a pattern and philosophy established by Zola. Each responds, in other words, not to the mythic Zola I have described but rather to the broad-based contemporary belief that the novel was the literary form especially capable of exploring neglected areas of the interaction between social reality and the inner life and that Zola was not the model for this effort but rather merely the leading wedge in a progressive literary movement.

The genius of American naturalism, as in many other aspects of American life, thus lies in the looseness and freedom with which American writers dealt with the gospel according to a European prophet. It was Zola's broad impulse toward depicting truthfully all ranges of life rather than his distinctive philosophy or literary method that was the source of the strength and permanence of the movement in America. American writers were moved by an excitement born of discovering meaning and form for themselves when they began, in the 1890s, to write of the twisted and meager lives of immigrant slum dwellers, of the easy slide into the illicit by young country girls in the city and by middle-aged bar managers desiring young country girls, and of the daily grind yet potentially violent upheavals of lower middle-class existence. Above all, these writers no longer accepted the "great lie" of nineteenth-century fiction—the convention that insofar as literary art is concerned relations between the sexes consist either of high romantic love or the minor rituals of middle-class courtship and marriage. Sex begins, in their fiction, to emerge as the great theme of modern art—the dynamic center of man's tragic nature as well as the subterranean living stream of his daily life.

The ideological center of American naturalism—a sense of man more circumscribed than conventionally acknowledged—is not prior to this exploration of the "low" and "irrational" but rather derives from it. Naturalist writers found that the poor in education, intellect, and worldly goods are indeed pushed and forced, that the powerful do control the weak, that few men can overcome the handicaps imposed upon them by inadequacies of body and mind, and that many men have desires that are not amenable to moral suasion or rational argument. But this observation of life as it is among the lowly—because it is not abstractly derived—does not produce a simple and single deterministic creed. Elements of compassion for the fallen, of hope of betterment for the lot of the oppressed, of bitterness toward the remediable that lies unremedied—all the emotions that derive from the writer's felt sense that he is not a dispassionate observer of a scientific process but instead an imaginative presence infusing meaning and dignity and a sense of tragic potential into what he observes—this living engagement between artist and subject matter results in a fulness and complexity of expression rather than an emotionally sterile portrait of "forces at work."

The common impression that the naturalistic novel is a simplistic documentation of a thesis derives as well from the form of naturalistic fiction. The naturalistic novel appears to take a shape conditioned by the principle of documentation, since fulness and exactness of detail seem to be inevitable consequences of a desire to render the truth of a neglected phase of social experience. But in fact American naturalists shape this impulse toward the documentary into strikingly different forms, forms that are more indicative of contemporary experimental tendencies in fiction and of their own distinctive artistic motives than of a universal model of the naturalistic novel.

I hope by this point that I have made apparent the major characteristics of my belief that American naturalism can be considered part of a humanistic tradition. In brief, I hold that the responsiveness of American naturalists to the pulls of change and temperament and the commitment of most naturalists to a tragic view of man's condition represent the link between the movement and humanism. I cannot on this occasion expect to demonstrate this position fully. But by discussing in detail three naturalist novels from three different historical phases of the movement in America I can perhaps encourage a preliminary acceptance of the argument. Each of the three works—Stephen Crane's *Maggie: A Girl of the Streets* (1893), James T. Farrell's *Gas-House McGinty* (1933), and Norman Mailer's *The Naked and the Dead* (1948)—

portrays the lives of most men as enclosed and unfulfilled. Yet each writer depicts as well the unrealized life, and particularly the unrealized inner life, as a tragic condition. And, finally, each writer engages in this effort in a significantly different way, both in his conception of the theme and in his rendering of it.

Stephen Crane's *Maggie* is a naturalistic novel of the 1890s in a number of obvious ways. Crane had read his Zola—particularly *L'Assommoir*, Zola's novel of alcoholic and sexual degradation among lower-class Parisians—and had himself studied the Bowery slums. Moreover, he was aware, through his middle-class clerical family, of the convention both within sentimental fiction and tract moralizing in which a young girl's sexual fall in the city is used to mirror corruption in a society as a whole. Crane's plot of the seduction, of the fall into prostitution, and of the early death of a girl of the slums is thus archetypal in the cultural imagination of the 1890s, as are the alcoholism, the violence, and the mission religion of the slums as a setting. This is the "plot" and "setting" of the slum as imaginative reality during the decade, whether that reality appears in Zola, in social criticism, or in fictional and religious moralism.

Crane saw within this familiar material the opportunity to exploit metaphors of battle and imprisonment as striking expressions of his conception of the underlying truth of slum life. The opening chapters of *Maggie* present us with a day in the life of the Johnson family. (The family consists of Mr. and Mrs. Johnson, Jimmie, Maggie, and the babe Tommie.) The novel opens with Jimmie fighting the children of Devil's Row. He then fights one of his own gang. His father separates them with a blow. Maggie mistreats Tommie; Jimmie strikes Maggie; Mrs. Johnson beats Jimmie for fighting. Mr. and Mrs. Johnson quarrel. Mrs. Johnson beats Maggie for breaking a plate; Mr. Johnson strikes Jimmie with an empty beer pail. Mr. Johnson comes home drunk and he and Mrs. Johnson fight—all this in three rather short chapters.

The Johnsons' tenement is in a "dark region," and their apartment, "up dark stairways and along cold, gloomy halls," is like a cave. Crane's description of the Johnson children eating combines the warfare and cave images into a single metaphor of primitive competition for food: "The babe sat with his feet dangling high from a precarious infant chair and gorged his small stomach. Jimmie forced, with feverish rapidity, the grease-enveloped pieces between his wounded lips. Maggie, with side glances of fear of interruption, ate like a small pursued tigress."

Time passes. Mr. Johnson and the babe Tommie die; Mrs. Johnson becomes a habitual drunkard; and Maggie and Jimmie slip into permanent states of mind closely related to their condition of life. Jimmie becomes a Bowery tough whose "occupation for a long time was to stand on streetcorners and watch the world go by, dreaming blood-red dreams at the passing of pretty women. He menaced mankind at the intersections of streets." Jimmie is satisfied in his job as a teamster. Perched high on his large wagon, he can safely and openly express belligerency and arrogance toward pedestrians, policemen, and street car drivers. His only fear is the fire engine. "They had been known to overturn street cars. Those leaping horses, striking sparks from the cobbles in their forward lunge, were creatures to be ineffably admired." Knowing life only as a survival through strength, Jimmie admires and assigns value only to power.

Maggie is as limited in experience, awareness, and values as Jimmie. She gets a job in a clothing factory where she has "a stool and a machine in a room where sat twenty girls in various shades of yellow discontent." Her life alternates between the factory—"a dreary place of endless grinding"—and a home made a shambles by her drunken mother. Her only hope is to be rescued by a suitor, as she has seen maidens in distress rescued by handsome young men in Bowery melodramas. She endows the elegant bartender Pete with this role. He of course seduces and then deserts her. Mrs. Johnson casts her from the home, and Maggie drifts into prostitution and finally plunges to her death in the East River.

Several major characteristics of Crane's depiction of Jimmie and Maggie should now be apparent. Neither figure has any understanding of the world of ideas and experience outside the Bowery, and neither has the will or intelligence to make any sense of his life beyond a response to the immediacies of Bowery conditions. Jimmie survives because his ignorant contempt of the world lends him a certain strength; Maggie fails to survive because her ignorance is allied with desires that make her vulnerable. Given the importance of the Bowery in the fate of each figure, it is no wonder that Crane wrote on several occasions that the book "tries to show that environment is a tremendous thing in the world and frequently shapes lives regardless."

Yet this powerful deterministic theme in *Maggie* is not Crane's only comment in the novel on the origin and nature of human awareness. Jimmie and Maggie are also characterized, in two significant passages, in ways that suggest qualities of emotional and aesthetic sensibility that cannot be attributed to the environment, which far transcend the values of the battlefield and the needs of escape. In the chapter in which Crane details Jimmie's amoral career as a Bowery tough, he devotes a paragraph to Jimmie's most recent exploits:

> He developed too great a tendency to climb down
> from his truck and fight with other drivers. He had
> been in quite a number of miscellaneous fights, and in
> some general barroom rows that had become known
> to the police. Once he had been arrested for assaulting
> a Chinaman. Two women in different parts of the
> city, and entirely unknown to each other, caused him
> considerable annoyance by breaking forth,
> simultaneously, at fateful intervals, into wailings
> about marriage and support and infants.

But this passage is followed by:

> Nevertheless, he had, on a certain star-lit evening, said
> wonderingly and quite reverently: "Deh moon looks
> like hell, don't it?"

Maggie is depicted in a similar fashion. Pete has called on her for the first time, and she hopes he will call again soon.

> She spent some of her week's pay in the purchase of
> flowered cretonne for a lambrequin. She made it with
> infinite care and hung it to the slightly-careening

mantel. . . . She studied it with painful anxiety from different points in the room. She wanted it to look well on Sunday night when, perhaps, Jimmie's friend would come.

These moments are fleeting and have little or no effect upon the characters. Jimmie never again refers to a natural object; Pete ignores the lambrequin and Mrs. Johnson soon destroys it. Nevertheless, Crane has made his point: even a Jimmie or a Maggie has an inherent core of sensibility. Jimmie's reverence and awe in the face of natural beauty, and Maggie's sense that love is beauty and that beauty must therefore be made manifest if love is to be known, are among the most profound and permanent human emotions. Of course, Crane as an ironist is suspicious of profound emotions; he therefore seeks to distance himself from any hint of sentimentality by the lugubriousness of Jimmie's exclamation of awe and by the tawdriness of Maggie's expression of beauty. But he also wishes in these instances of inadequate expression of emotional truth to imply that in the Bowery the sensibility is betrayed and made ineffectual by the very act of translation from the unconscious and inarticulate to the expressive. The lives of Jimmie and Maggie have not supplied them with the means to give adequate expressive shape to their deepest feelings.

Nevertheless, the feelings are there. Maggie and Jimmie are not animals in a cage, despite the power and pervasiveness of the Darwinian metaphor in the novel, but are rather human spirits imprisoned in ignorance, fear, and despair. The tragedy of their lives is not only the ostensible one of having been beaten down by slum conditions but is also the less apparent but more poignant one of never having known either the depths of their own natures or the wondrous shapes that man can give the expression of his deepest sentiments.

Few writers of importance have been so neatly and destructively pigeonholed as has been James T. Farrell. To the general public, Farrell is a Marxist writer of the 1930s whose major work, the

Studs Lonigan trilogy, is a literal depiction of the Chicago slums of the period. There is little public awareness, however, that Farrell read widely and deeply in modern philosophy and literature during his four years at the University of Chicago in the late 1920s; that *Studs Lonigan*, though set in a first-generation Chicago Irish neighborhood, deals largely with lower middle-class families (Studs' father is a painting contractor and a landlord); and that Farrell was an active anti-Communist when it was far more common and fashionable for writers to be members of the party. I introduce these differences between legend and reality in Farrell's life and work in order to suggest that his best fiction—that is, his fiction of the 1930s—will reveal to the careful reader more than an endorsement of the clichés of literary history.

Farrell's short novel *Gas-House McGinty* is an excellent example of his fiction of this period at its most interesting. He had begun his first novel, *Studs Lonigan*, in 1929; by mid-1931 the book had expanded into two novels and was about to expand into yet a third. At this point, in the summer of 1931, while living in Paris, Farrell put *Studs* aside for several months in order to write *Gas-House McGinty*. His intent was not only to gain some relief from the effort required to complete his massive trilogy; he also wished to experiment in a shorter novel with the stream of consciousness form that he expected to exploit fully in the third volume of *Studs* when recounting Studs' deathbed delirium.

The principle setting of *Gas-House McGinty* is the dispatcher's office of a large Chicago express company in the late summer of 1920. McGinty, as chief dispatcher, is an important figure in this setting as well as elsewhere, and there are several coherent threads of action involving McGinty and other characters. But individual character and specific line of action are blurred in comparison with the overwhelming impact of the office itself. Farrell's intent is to portray with an almost expressionistic boldness and emphasis a pervasive aspect of the American experience—the mindless noise, crass horseplay, bigoted narrowness, and cut-throat infighting of day-to-day working-class life. The major reality of the office is its din—the endless racket of men shouting vacuous business details into telephones and obscenities at each other. This chaos of sound reflects the ignorance and darkness in which the men live. Their exchanges on sex, politics, and religion touch every base of popular prejudice and misinformation. Indeed, the dispatcher's office of the Continental Express Company has some of the same characteristics as Stephen Crane's East Side. Here, too, all is struggle as the men express their fears, frustrations, and envies in belligerency, in cringing obsequiousness, and in underhandedness. Struggle, however, is less for survival (as in the slums) than for the preservation of status—a theme which Joseph Heller was to explore more fully, though not more pointedly, in his recent *Something Happened*. *Gas-House McGinty* thus appears to be an excellent example of what in the 1930s was called a slice-of-life novel. Relatively plotless, with no heroes, it seeks to portray graphically a particular phase of American social life.

But the mind-numbing emptiness of McGinty's daily life—noise and backbiting at the office, a nagging wife at home—constitutes only one of the two major areas of his experience. Farrell in the 1920s had been influenced by the fiction of James Joyce and Sherwood Anderson and by the theories of Sigmund Freud. Beneath the conscious awareness of most men, Farrell had come to believe, lay emotions, desires, and perceptions that, though seldom understood by the individual, nevertheless powerfully affected his life. Freud offered Farrell a sexual explanation for the nature of much of this hidden life, and Joyce a striking means of representing it. But it was Anderson, as was so often true for American writers in the 1920s, who moved Farrell most deeply with his depiction of the commingled farce and pathos of the grotesque shapes we give our lives because of the suppression of our emotional natures.

Farrell introduces the theme of a center of unexpressed feeling in McGinty early in the novel, when McGinty escapes the vulgarity of the express office during his lunch hour and notices an amateur painter at work near the Chicago River.

> [McGinty] looked at the trestled Washington-Street
> bridge. He heard a fog horn, and through the trestles,
> toward the bend in the river, he saw a lake freighter,
> slowly growing forward. Bridge bells jingled, and the
> Randolph-Street bridge opened, and the boat came
> through. Nearer bells jangled. The jackknife
> Washington-Street bridge slowly split, its twin steel

arms drawing steadily apart and lifting with even,
precise strength, like the opening of some enormous
fan. He leaned against the rail, his perspiring hands
clasping it, his body a casing of tightly strung nerves.
Slowly, exactly, the bridge arms lifted, till its span
pointed to the sky, and the approaching boat came
between them.

The freighter, with another whine of its fog horn,
plowed onward and the bells behind Mac beat out
warnings.

And there was that damn fool picture painter down
there, painting as if there was no boat coming, and
nothing was happening. Why, that damned fool. He
couldn't even tell something when he saw it,
something prettier than painting a river so that
nobody would ever recognize it, something pretty,
perfect . . . *something*. . . . Why, that bridge opening
that way was like a miracle, like God doing it. It was
figures worked out, that's what it was, figures like the
figures he liked to work out at night. That bridge
pointing to the sky was figures worked out neat, on
clean white sheets of paper, with no mistakes, and no
erasures. That damn fool down there! To hell with his
picture! Let him paint them figures!

Farrell is here seeking, as Crane had done, to suggest a core of
sensibility in a character whose life is otherwise one of crudity
and crassness. In McGinty, this core is McGinty's sense of the
beauty of applied mathematics—the miracle of figures worked
out.

Farrell's fullest account of McGinty's interior life occurs in
a long chapter devoted to a modified stream of consciousness
representation of McGinty asleep and dreaming. Farrell had already established that McGinty can understand and feel; he now
goes on to depict the inevitable frustrations of a man of feeling
whose sensibility is imprisoned in a fat middle-aged body that

spends its life in a chaotic express office and a henpecked home. McGinty's dream thus expresses principally the frustrations of his life—sexual frustrations at home, frustration in the recognition of his worth at the office. His dream takes the form of a quest for satisfaction, and as is appropriate in dreams, his quest combines surrealistic farce and poetic symbol. It begins:

> Naked girls, with rubber-tired crowns set over flowing tresses, did the highland fling in a dimly orange field. McGinty, wearing a brown derby, a jock strap, and jingling ankle bracelets, tripped bumpkinishly into their midst. They circled around him, spraying onions at his feet, as he nature-danced, lifting himself from the ground and floating with each step. He suddenly halted, and stood watching the girls as they passed until his eyes became fastened upon one blond, whose left breast tip shone and sparkled like broken glass upon reflecting sunlight.
>
> Come and join us, join us, join us now! the girls sang, as they swept into twisting belly wiggles.
>
> McGinty took a hop, skip, and jump after the blond with the sparkling breast tip, and the girl vanished, leaving him to his sad self in the dimly orange field that darkened as tragic shadows lengthened over it. He retreated, with the darkness following him like a fierce pursuer.
>
> I am alone, alone, and there is a door. I will go through it. I like going through doors, and other doors are inside this door, and I will go through the door and all my life I will go through doors, McGinty singsonged with feeling.

The quest for fulfillment is difficult; McGinty makes his way through dream settings of hell, of an insane asylum, and of a ruined cityscape, and he feels fear, anxiety, and guilt in the course of his journey. But at last he is close to satisfaction. The Pope crowns him McGinty first King of All Ireland, and he is about to win his childhood sweetheart, Ellen May Mahoney. At this moment, a sharp elbow in his ear by his wife ends his dream.

There is of course much comic intent in Farrell's notion of McGinty's dream life, just as there is in Joyce's rendering of the unconscious experience of Leopold Bloom. Man as pure desire, man stripped clean of polite indirection, is often farcical. Yet desire is also pathetic, because it so often is both suppressed and doomed to frustration. Out of Farrell's complex rendering of a complex emotional reality there emerges a sense of McGinty not as a dissected specimen in a slice of life but as an intensely alive and distinctive human being.

The Naked and the Dead has a number of apparent naturalistic characteristics, as critics were quick to point out soon after the publication of the novel in 1948. Mailer's story of the American recapture of a small Japanese-held island is dominated by events in which man is depicted at his least heroic or ennobled, from the early incident of a soldier defecating in his trousers during the invasion to the climactic rout of a reconnaissance platoon when attacked by a nest of hornets. This aspect of the novel is aptly summed up by a soldier as he surveys a group of enemy corpses: "There damn sure ain't anything special about a man if he can smell as bad as he does when he's dead." *The Naked and the Dead* also owed an obvious debt to the naturalistic fiction of the 1930s in its Time Machine sections. Like the Biography portions of John Dos Passos's *U.S.A.*, these sections often exhibit a crude social determinism. We learn in brief impressionistic biographies of the major characters how they have been shaped and conditioned by their backgrounds. So we are presented with an archetypal Boston slum Irishman, a Brooklyn Jew, a Southern hillbilly, an Ivy-League liberal, and so on. Mailer's tendency toward viewing character in relation to ideas—an allegorical predilection that was to dominate his later work—is reflected as well in the overall shape and direction of *The Naked and the Dead*. The novel is structured upon two abstract naturalistic preoccupations—power and chance. Because experience teaches that life is conflict, men seek power, as do General Cummings and Sergeant Croft, each of whom in his own way wishes absolute control over the men under him. Cummings and Croft are opposed by conventionally more attractive figures—the liberal intellectual Lieutenant Hearn and the working-class Red Valsen. In the struggle between those desiring power and those questioning the nature and purpose of power, the victory is to the men of strength rather than to the men of ideas. Victory is more apparent than real, however, because in the end circumstances cannot be absolutely controlled; the inscrutable and untoward in life intervene, and Cummings and Croft find that they have achieved far less than they believed they had.

These various naturalistic qualities mesh into a novel whose themes and form appear to be both powerful and self-evident. Yet *The Naked and the Dead* also contains elements that are awkwardly unabsorbable into a simple naturalistic reading of the novel. In particular, the character of Sergeant Croft is more complex than a single-dimensional stereotype, and the second half of the novel—in which a reconnaissance platoon is forced to climb a mountain during a patrol behind enemy lines—contains a number of ambivalent qualities. Mailer himself, in several interviews after the publication of *The Naked and the Dead*, encouraged a closer look at the novel by a series of titillating statements about his intent in the work. Soon after the early reviews appeared, he said, "In the author's eyes, *The Naked and the Dead* is not a realistic documentary; it is, rather, a 'symbolic' book, of which the basic theme is the conflict between the beast and the seer in man." In 1951, Mailer dealt at greater length both with the limitations of a narrow naturalistic reading of the novel, despite its acknowledged naturalistic characteristics, and with the symbolic import of a major thread in the novel—the relationship of Sergeant Croft to the mountain. He began: "That terrible word 'naturalism.' It was my literary heritage—the things I learned from Dos Passos and Farrell. I took naturally to it, that's the way one wrote a book." Nevertheless, Mailer went on to say, "I really was off on a mystic kick. Actually—a funny thing—the biggest influence on *Naked* was *Moby Dick*. . . . I was sure everyone would know. I had Ahab in it, and I suppose the mountain was Moby Dick."

At first glance, Croft is an unlikely candidate for the role of a visionary pursuer of his own tragic fate. As dramatized in the first portion of the novel, Croft is a sadistic killer who seeks to compensate for his sexual and social inadequacies by dominance over men and events. Raised without love or understanding on the hard and bare west Texas plains of the 1930s, Croft develops early in life a need to have absolute control over his world, even if the fulfillment of this need requires the cultivation of hate and insensitivity as his principal code of life. Mailer's initial description of Croft in the Time Machine section devoted to him captures the potential machine-like destructiveness of the man:

> A lean man of medium height but he held himself so erectly he appeared tall. His narrow triangular face was utterly without expression. There seemed nothing wasted in his hard small jaw, gaunt firm cheeks and straight short nose. His gelid eyes were very blue . . . he was efficient and strong and usually empty and his main cast of mind was a superior contempt toward nearly all other men. He hated weakness and he loved practically nothing.

Yet Mailer ends this description with the cryptic comment: "There was a crude unformed vision in his soul but he was rarely conscious of it." It is this unconscious, inarticulate, undefinable "vision" that comes alive in Croft's response to Mount Anaka. When the patrol first glimpses the mountain, Croft above all is moved: "The mountain attracted him, taunted and inflamed him with its size. . . . He stared at it now, examined its ridges, feeling an instinctive desire to climb the mountain and stand at its peak. . . . His emotions were intense; he knew awe and hunger and [a] peculiar unique ecstasy. . . ." Later, closer to the mountain, Croft refines this response: "Again, he felt a crude ecstasy. He could not have given the reason, but the mountain tormented him, beckoned him, held an answer to something he wanted. It was so pure, so austere." Mount Anaka holds "the answer" to something Croft wants, and for the first time in his life his desire for control—unlike as in his relations with his father, his wife, and his weak-willed enlisted men and fuzzy-minded officers—is matched by a force "pure" and "austere" in its unconquerable aloofness. For the mountain remains inviolable; the patrol, despite Croft's extraordinary efforts, is routed in its attempt to climb the mountain. Afterwards, again viewing its height from a distance, "Deep inside himself, Croft was relieved that he had not been able to climb the mountain." Yet the following day, seeing it for the last time before the patrol returned to its own lines,

> The old torment burned in him again. A stream of wordless impulses beat in his throat and he had again the familiar and inexplicable tension the mountain always furnished him. . . .
> Croft kept looking at the mountain. He had lost it, had missed some tantalizing revelation of himself.
> Of himself and much more. Of life.
> Everything.

Like Ahab, Croft has found a compelling concrete objectification of his otherwise unformed and generalized quest for knowledge and power. Mailer himself, in one of his interviews, sought to describe the indefinable nature of this quest for Croft. The mountain, Mailer said, meant "death and man's creative urge, fate, man's desire to conquer the elements—all kinds of things that you never dream of separating and stating so baldly." The mountain is indeed all of these things to Croft, though our knowledge of Mailer's later work suggests that its beauty and desirability lie perhaps most of all in the opportunity it offers for man to face immediately and concretely his ultimate destiny— that is, his death and annihilation.

It is now time to note several major similarities among the various naturalistic characters I have been describing. Maggie, Jimmie, McGinty, and Croft are all less than admirable figures whose lives and minds have been forced into unlovely shapes by their worlds. That is their naturalistic condition. Yet they are also figures who have not lost the human capacity to feel awe and wonder. True, they fail to understand the nature of their feelings, and they also fail to hold the particular form or object that represents their feelings. But they have felt deeply and powerfully and significantly. And that is their naturalistic condition in a tragic humanistic context.

As I suggested at the opening of my paper, this broad similarity in the depiction of the inner life of characters otherwise cut into cardboard shapes by the circumstances of their lives takes on resonance and permanence within the naturalistic tradition from the individuality of each writer's rendering of the theme. Each writer is responsive to personal and contemporary preoccupations that lend distinctiveness to his depiction of the subject. Crane involves us in a *fin-de-siècle* joining of fine writing and abject subject matter, and he seeks to portray a particularly aesthetic notion of the inarticulate felt life. Farrell has a modernist interest in capturing both the deadening repetitive circumstantiality of everyday experience and the wild fantasizing of the inner life, and his idea of the inner life relies heavily on Freud. And Mailer moves us toward the writer's absorption in the ideologically abstract and physically repellent in experience that characterizes much recent fiction. Each writer, in short, has made a central humanistic concern integral to his naturalism in ways that suggest the dynamic responsiveness of naturalism to the changing nature of the American experience. Each writer has thus gathered strength from the naturalist tradition as well as contributed to its permanence within the modern American imagination.

1978

THREE

⌐American Literary Naturalism⊢

The Example of Dreiser

American literary naturalism has almost always been viewed with hostility. During its early years the movement was associated with Continental licentiousness and impiety and was regarded as a literature foreign to American values and interests. "We must stamp out this breed of Norrises," a reviewer of *McTeague* cried in 1899.[1] In our own time, though antagonism to naturalism is expressed more obliquely, it is as deeply rooted. A typical discussion of the movement is frequently along the following lines.[2] The critic will examine the sources of naturalism in late nineteenth-century scientism, in Zola, and in post-Civil War industrial expansion. He will note that to a generation of American writers coming of age in the 1890s the mechanistic and materialistic foundations of contemporary science appeared to be confirmed by American social conditions and to have been successfully applied to the writing of fiction by Zola. But he will also note that Stephen Crane, Frank Norris, and Theodore Dreiser were often muddled in their thinking and inept in their fiction, and he will attribute these failures to their unfortunate absorption of naturalistic attitudes and beliefs. Our typical critic will then discover a second major flowering of naturalism in the fiction of James T. Farrell, John Steinbeck, and John Dos Passos in the 1930s. He will remark that scientism has been replaced by Marxism and that the thinking of this generation of naturalists is not so much confused as doctrinaire, but his account of their work will still be governed by the assumption that naturalism is a regrettable strain in modern American literary history.

Indeed, the underlying metaphor in most accounts of American fiction is that naturalism is a kind of taint or discoloration, without which the writer would be more of an artist and through which the critic must penetrate if he is to discover the essential nature and worth of the writer. So those writers who most clearly appear to be naturalists, such as Dreiser and Farrell, are almost always praised for qualities that are distinct from their naturalism. We are thus told that Dreiser's greatness is not in his naturalism[3] and that he is most of all an artist when not a philosopher.[4] And so the obvious and powerful thread of naturalism in such major figures as Hemingway, Faulkner, and (closer to our own time) Saul Bellow is almost always dismissed as an irrelevant and distracting characteristic of their work.

This continuing antagonism to naturalism has several root causes. One of the clearest is that many critics find naturalistic belief morally repugnant. But whereas earlier critics stated openly their view that naturalism was invalid because man was as much a creature of divine spirit as animal substance, the more recent critic is apt to express his hostility indirectly by claiming that naturalistic novelists frequently violate the deterministic creed that supposedly informs their work and are therefore inconsistent or incoherent naturalists. On one hand, this concern with philosophical consistency derives from the naturalist writer's interest in ideas and is therefore a justifiable critical interest. On the other, there seems little doubt that many critics delight in seeking out the philosophically inadequate in naturalistic fiction because man is frequently portrayed in this fiction as irredeemably weak and deluded and yet as not responsible for his condition. It is the rare work of fiction of any time in which threads of free will and determinism do not interweave in a complex pattern that can be called incoherent or inconsistent; on strictly logical grounds man either has free will or he does not. Yet it is principally the naturalistic novel that is damned for this quality, which suggests that it is the weighting of this inconsistency toward an amoral determinism—not its mere presence—that is at stake.[5]

Another source of the hostility of modern critics to the naturalistic novel lies in recent American political history. American naturalism of the 1890s was largely apolitical, but in the 1930s the movement was aligned with the left wing in American politics and often specifically with the Communist party. In the revulsion against the party that swept the literary community during the 1940s and 1950s, it was inevitable that naturalistic fiction of the 1930s would be found wanting because the naturalists of that decade, it was now seen, had so naïvely embraced some form of communist belief. The most influential critical discussions of American naturalism during the 1940s and 1950s—Philip Rahv's "Notes on the Decline of Naturalism," Malcolm Cowley's "'Not Men': A Natural History of American Naturalism," and Lionel Trilling's "Reality in America"[6]—have as an underlying motive a desire to purge American literature and its historiography of an infatuation with an alien and destructive political ideal.

A final reason for the antagonism toward naturalistic fiction is that several generations of academic critics have been attracted by an increasingly refined view of the aesthetic complexity of fiction. They have believed that a novel must above all be organic—that is, be the product of a romantic imagination—and they have found principally in the work of Hawthorne, Melville, Faulkner, and to a lesser extent James, that enlargement of metaphor into symbol and that interplay of irony and ambivalence that bring fiction close to the complex indirection of a metaphysical lyric. Stephen Crane is the only naturalistic writer whose fiction satisfies these expectations, and his work is generally held to be uncharacteristic of the nonartistry of a movement more adequately represented by Dreiser.[7]

I do not wish to suggest by this brief survey of the critical biases that have led to the inadequate examination of American naturalism that there are not naturalistic novels muddled in conception and inept in execution. But just as we have long known that the mind-set of an early nineteenth-century critic would little prepare him to come to grips with the essential nature and form of a romantic poem, so we are coming to realize that a generation of American critics has approached American literary naturalism with beliefs about man and art that have frequently distorted rather than cast light upon the object before them.

Theodore Dreiser is the author whose work and career most fulfill the received notion of American naturalism; indeed, it is often difficult to determine the demarcation between literary history and critical biography in general discussions of American naturalism, so completely is Dreiser as thinker and writer identified with the movement in America. It would be instructive, therefore, to test the example of Dreiser—to note, initially and briefly, those characteristics of his career and work that lead us to describe him as a naturalist; and then, more fully, to examine some of the naturalistic elements in his fiction. But unlike so much of the criticism of naturalism I have been describing, I do not wish to undertake this test with the assumption that Dreiser's fiction is confused in theme and form because he is not a consistent naturalist or that his work is best when he is least naturalistic. In short, I do not wish to consider his naturalism as an unfortunate excrescence. Rather, I want to see how his naturalistic predispositions work in his fiction and whether or not they work successfully.

Dreiser was born an outsider. His parents were of Catholic, German-speaking immigrant stock and throughout Dreiser's youth the large family was agonizingly poor. As a young man Dreiser sought the success and position that his parents had lacked and also shed the religious and moral beliefs which, he believed, had appeared to shackle them. While a young reporter in Pittsburgh in the early 1890s, he found his deepest responses to life confirmed by his reading of Herbert Spencer and Balzac. There were, he believed, no discernible supernatural agencies in life, and man was not the favored creature of divine guidance but an insignificant unit in a universe of natural forces. Although these forces, whether biological or social, were the source of racial progress, they often crushed the individual within their mechanistic processes. Like many of his generation, Dreiser found that the observed realities of American society supported this theory of existence. The mills and libraries of Pittsburgh were evidence of progress, but the lives of the immigrant foundry workers—to say nothing of the lives of Dreiser's own errant sisters and brothers—appeared dwarfed and ephemeral compared with the grinding and impersonal power of a vast economic system and a great city. Yet the city itself, as Balzac had amply demonstrated, was exciting and alluring, and not all were crushed who sought to gain its wonders. In *Sister Carrie* Dreiser was to write, "Among the forces which sweep and play throughout the universe, untutored man is but a wisp in the wind."[8] But though Hurstwood is swept away by these forces, and though Carrie's career is that of a storm-tossed ship, Carrie survives and indeed grows in understanding by the close of the novel. So accompanying Dreiser's endorsement of an amoral determinism there exists a disconcerting affirmation of the traditionally elevating in life—of Carrie, for example, as a figure of "emotional greatness," that is, of imaginative power. Forty-five years after *Sister Carrie* Dreiser joined the Communist party while celebrating in his last two novels the intuitive mysticism at the heart of Quaker and Hindu belief. Here, in brief, at the two poles of his career and work is the infamous intellectual muddle of Dreiser and, by extension, of naturalism itself. And this muddle appears to be matched by a corresponding lack of control and firmness in fictional technique. Dreiser documents his social scene with a pseudoscientific detachment yet overindulges in personal philosophical disquisitions; he attempts to write a "fine" style but produces journalistic cliché and awkwardness.

So in most important ways Dreiser fulfills the conventional definition of the American naturalist. All the major paradoxes are present: his identification with the "outsider," which was to lead to a contemptuous view of the mainstream of middle-class American life, yet his lifelong worship of "success"; his acceptance of a "scientific" mechanistic theory of natural law as a substitute for traditional views of individual insight and moral responsibility, yet his affirmation of many of these traditional views; and his deep response to a major European novelist, including the form of his fiction, yet his seeming neglect of style and form. I cannot hope to discuss these major characteristics of Dreiser as a naturalist as each appears in his eight novels. But I can pursue the vital naturalistic theme of mechanistic determinism in two of his principal novels, *Jennie Gerhardt* and *An American Tragedy*, and thereby reach toward at least a modest understanding of the example of Dreiser.[9]

Dreiser began *Jennie Gerhardt* in early 1901, soon after the publication of *Sister Carrie*. He wrote most of the novel during the next two years, though he did not complete it until late 1910. Like *Sister Carrie*, *Jennie Gerhardt* is about a girl from a poor family who has several sexual affairs with men of higher station but who emerges from her adventures not only unsullied but also elevated in character and insight. The novel differs from *Sister Carrie* primarily in Dreiser's characterization of Jennie and of Lester Kane, the principal man in Jennie's life. Kane, at least on the surface, is a more powerful, successful, and contemplative figure than Hurstwood, and Jennie differs from Carrie in that she is a warm and generous giver rather than a taker.

In the course of the novel, Jennie is seduced first by Senator Brander, by whom she has a child, Vesta, and then by Lester Kane. She and Kane are attracted to each other by a powerful natural "affinity" and they live together contentedly for several years. But because Lester is gradually forced to accept that a permanent union with Jennie would adversely affect his business career and the comfortable certainties of his social and family life, they do not marry. Eventually they part, Lester marries Letty Gerald, a woman of his own class, and Jennie suffers the death of both her father and Vesta.

One of the major scenes in *Jennie Gerhardt* is Lester's visit to Jennie after the death of Vesta. Deeply depressed by Vesta's death and by his realization that he erred in leaving Jennie, Lester tells her "it isn't myself that's important in this transaction [that is, life itself] apparently; the individual doesn't count much in the situation. I don't know whether you see what I'm driving at, but all of us are more or less pawns. We're moved about like chessmen by circumstances over which we have no control."[10] This famous pronouncement, which has supplied several generations of literary historians with a ubiquitous image for the philosophical center of American naturalism, requires careful analysis both in its immediate context and in relation to the novel as a whole if it is to be properly understood.

Whatever the general truth of Lester's words, they represent a personal truth. His pawn image expresses both his sense of ineffectuality in the face of the central dilemma of his life and a covert supernaturalism that has characterized his thought throughout the novel despite his overt freethinking. Earlier he had attributed his difficulties merely to bad luck. But by the time he and Jennie separate, he has elevated and generalized "fate" into a specific force that is at once social, supernatural, and (as far as he is concerned) malevolent:

> It was only when the storms set in and the winds of adversity blew and he found himself facing the armed forces of convention that he realized he might be mistaken as to the value of his personality, that his private desires and opinions were as nothing in the face of a public conviction; that he was wrong. The race spirit, or social avatar, the "Zeitgeist" as the Germans term it, manifested itself as something having a system in charge, and the organization of society began to show itself to him as something based on possibly a spiritual, or, at least, supernatural counterpart. (373–74)

Lester's speculative statement that men are but pawns in the control of circumstances is thus in part an explanation and a defense of his own conduct. In particular, it is a disguised apology to Jennie for his failure to marry her when he could have done so. But it is also a powerful means of characterizing Lester. Throughout his life he had lived for the moment and had postponed making decisions about the direction of his life. But the decisionless flow of time contained an impetus of events that constituted an implicit and irreversible decision, and when Lester at last awoke to the fact that his life had been decided for him, he bitterly and angrily blamed fate.

Because Lester is a perceptive and on the whole an honest figure, his belief that men are pawns involves more than a rationalization of his own indecisiveness and ineffectuality. His belief also aptly characterizes social reality as that reality has been dramatized in the novel. The pressure of circumstances on Lester in his relationship with Jennie has indeed been intense, from their initial meeting within the convention of a seduction—a convention that appeared to preclude marriage—to the later opposition of Lester's personal, business, and social worlds to the continuation of the relationship. In a passage cut from Chapter XL of the final holograph of the novel, Dreiser himself, as narrator, echoed Lester's attribution of superhuman powers to social force. "The conventions in their way," he wrote, "appear to be as inexorable in their workings as the laws of gravitation and expansion. There is a drift to society as a whole which pushes us on in a certain direction, careless of the individual, concerned only with the general result."[11]

In his final position as one deeply puzzled by the insignificance of the individual, Lester therefore reflects a persistent strain in Dreiser's thought. Before making his pawn speech to Jennie, Lester had "looked down into Dearborn Street, the world of traffic below holding his attention. The great mass of trucks and vehicles, the counter streams of hurrying pedestrians, seemed like a puzzle. So shadows march in a dream" (400). The scene effectively images both Lester's and Dreiser's belief that life is a helter-skelter of activity without meaning either for its observers or for the "shadows" who give it motion. As a man aware of the direction of modern thought, Lester is able to give this view of life an appropriate philosophical framework. In the years that pass after Vesta's death, his response to life, Dreiser tells us, becomes "decidedly critical":

> He could not make out what it was all about. In
> distant ages a queer thing had come to pass. There
> had started on its way in the form of evolution a
> minute cellular organism which had apparently
> reproduced itself by division, had early learned to
> combine itself with others, to organize itself into
> bodies, strange forms of fish, animals, and birds, and
> had finally learned to organize itself into man. Man,
> on his part, composed as he was of self-organizing
> cells, was pushing himself forward into comfort and
> different aspects of existence by means of union and
> organization with other men. Why? Heaven only
> knew. . . . Why should he complain, why worry, why
> speculate?—the world was going steadily forward of

> its own volition, whether he would or no. Truly it
> was. (404–5)

It must not be assumed, however, that Lester's pessimistic response to the "puzzle" of man's role in a mechanistic world is Dreiser's principal and only philosophical theme in *Jennie Gerhardt*. For Jennie, though not Lester's equal in formal knowledge or in experience, is his equal in the "bigness" of her responsiveness to the underlying reality of life, and she discovers not only puzzlement and frustration in life but also an ineradicable beauty. Dreiser therefore follows his comments on Lester's critical outlook with an account of Jennie's final evaluation of life. This evaluation, because of its source and its strategic location, has significance equal to Lester's beliefs. Jennie, Dreiser writes,

> had never grasped the nature and character of
> specialized knowledge. History, physics, chemistry,
> botany, geology, and sociology were not fixed
> departments in her brain as they were in Lester's and
> Letty's. Instead there was the feeling that the world
> moved in some strange, unstable way. Apparently no
> one knew clearly what it was all about. People were
> born and died. Some believed that the world had been
> made six thousand years before; some that it was
> millions of years old. Was it all blind chance or was
> there some guiding intelligence—a God? Almost in
> spite of herself she felt that there must be something—
> a higher power which produced all the beautiful
> things—the flowers, the stars, the trees, the grass.
> Nature was so beautiful! If at times life seemed cruel,
> yet this beauty still persisted. The thought comforted
> her; she fed upon it in her hours of secret loneliness
> (405).

Jennie and Lester's complementary views of life represent Dreiser's own permanent unresolved conception of the paradox of existence. To both figures the world "was going steadily forward of its own volition," apparently guided by some unknowable power. Individuals counted for little in this process, but individuals of different temperaments might respond to the mechanism of life in different ways. One kind of temperament might be bitter and despairing, another might affirm the beauty that was inseparable from the inexplicable mystery of life. It has frequently been noted that Dreiser himself held both views at different stages of his career—that he stressed a cruelly indifferent mechanistic universe in *Hey Rub-a-Dub-Dub* (1920) and a mechanistic world of beauty in *The Bulwark* (1946). It has not been as fully realized that he held the two positions simultaneously as well as consecutively and that he gave each position equal weight and dramatic expression in *Jennie Gerhardt* without resolving their "discrepancy." For to Dreiser there was no true discrepancy; there was only the reality of distinctive temperaments that might find truth in each position or, as in his own case, of a temperament that might find an element of truth in both. Dreiser's infamous philosophical inconsistency is thus frequently a product of his belief that life is a "puzzle" to which one can respond in different ways, depending on one's makeup and experience.

The naturalistic "philosophy" of deterministic mechanism in Dreiser's novels is therefore usually secondary, within the fictional dynamics of each novel, to the role of the concept as a metaphor of life against which various temperaments can define themselves. Or, to put the matter another way, Lester's belief in one kind of mechanistic philosophy and Jennie's in another are less significant fictionally than the depiction of Jennie as a woman of feeling and of Lester as a man of speculative indecision. But it should also be clear that in attributing a secondary fictional role to the mechanistic center of *Jennie Gerhardt* I am not saying that the philosophy muddles the novel or that the novel is successful for reasons other than the philosophy. I am rather saying that the philosophy and the fiction are one and inseparable. As a late nineteenth-century novelist, Dreiser absorbed and used naturalistic ideas. But he did not do so, at his best, in a way that can be distinguished from his absorption of an understanding of character and of experience in general. It is this unity of understanding and of purpose that gives Dreiser's novels their power. At his most successful, Dreiser embodies in his novels the permanent in life not despite the ideas of his own time but because, like most major artists, he uses the ideas of his own time as living vehicles to express the permanent in man's character and in man's vision of his condition and fate.

Most students of American literature are aware that Dreiser derived the central plot and much of the detail of *An American Tragedy* from the Chester Gillette-Grace Brown murder case of 1906. Less commonly known is that although Dreiser's principal source—the reports of Gillette's trial in the *New York World*—presented him with a wealth of detail about Gillette's life in Cortland (the Lycurgus of the novel) leading up to the murder of Grace Brown, it offered only a few hints about Gillette's experiences before his arrival in that city. Thus, Book One of *An American Tragedy*, which deals with Clyde's early life in Kansas City, is in a sense "invented." Such major events of this portion of the novel as Clyde's sister's pregnancy, his job at the Green-Davidson Hotel, his longing for Hortense, and the automobile accident that concludes the book have no source in Gillette's life.

Because Dreiser in Book One is "inventing" a background for Clyde it is possible to view this section of the novel as the application to fiction of a simplistic deterministic ethic in which the author crudely manufactures hereditary and environmental conditions that will irrevocably propel the protagonist toward his fate. So, in Book One, we are offered Clyde's weak and fuzzy-minded father and coldly moralistic mother. We discover that Clyde is a sensitive youth who longs for the material and sensual pleasures of life but lacks the training, strength, and guile necessary to gain them. Ergo: weakness and desire on the one hand and irresistible attraction yet insurmountable barriers on the other will resolve themselves into an American tragedy.

Dreiser in this opening section of the novel is indeed seeking to introduce the deterministic theme that a young man's nature and early experience can solidify into an inflexible quality of mind that will lead to his destruction. Yet once said, this observation is as useless to criticism as the equally true statement that *King Lear* is about the failure and triumph of love. For Dreiser in Book

One of *An American Tragedy* is not a simple and simpleminded naturalist applying a philosophical theory to documentary material but rather a subtle fictional craftsman creating out of the imagined concrete details of a life an evocative image of the complex texture of that life.

Clyde's desire for "beauty and pleasure"[12] in Book One is in direct conflict with his parents' religious beliefs and activities, and thus Clyde's dominant impulse from early boyhood is to escape. At fifteen he makes his first major break from his parents' inhospitable mission existence and toward the life he desires when he gets a job as assistant clerk at a drugstore soda fountain. This position, with its accompanying "marvels" of girls, lively talk, and "snappy" dressing, offers a deeply satisfying alternative to the drab religiosity of Clyde's boyhood. He recognizes the appeal of this new world "in a revealing flash": "You bet he would get out of that now. He would work and save his money and be somebody. Decidedly this simple and yet idyllic compound of the commonplace had all the luster and wonder of a spiritual transfiguration, the true mirage of the lost and thirsting and seeking victim of the desert" (I, 26).

Dreiser's summary of Clyde's response to the lively worldliness of the soda fountain introduces a theme, and its imagery and tone, that pervades the entire novel. Clyde's need—his thirst—has the power to transform "spiritually" the tawdry and superficial world of the drugstore into the wondrous and exalted. So frequent and compelling is Dreiser's use of "dream" in connection with Clyde's longing that we sometimes fail to realize that his desires also have a basically religious context in which his "dream" is for a "paradise" of wealth and position ruled by a "goddess" of love. Clyde at this moment of insight at the soda fountain is truly converted. He has rejected the religion of his parents only to find a different kind of heaven to which he pledges his soul with all the fervor and completeness of his parents' belief. Yet like their "cloudy romance" of a heaven above, Clyde's vision of a "paradise" below is a "true mirage." He has thus not really escaped from his parents, and his initiation into life at the soda fountain and later at the Green-Davidson is no true initiation, for he has merely shifted the nebulous and misdirected longings of his family from the unworldly to the worldly. He still has the naïveté, blindness, and absolute faith of his parents' enthusiasm and belief. And because he is, like them, a true believer, he does not learn from experience and he does not change.

Clyde's job as a bellhop at the Green-Davidson is both an extension and an intensification of his conversion experience at the soda fountain. To Clyde, the hotel is "so glorious an institution" (I, 33), a response which at once reflects the religiosity of its sexual attractions and their embodiment in a powerful social form. The Green-Davidson has both an intrinsic and an extrinsic sexuality. So deep and powerful is Clyde's reaction to its beauty and pleasure—to its moral freedom, material splendor, and shower of tips—that he conceives of the hotel as a youth does his first love. The Green-Davidson to Clyde is softness, warmth, and richness; it has a luxuriousness that he associates with sensuality and position—that is, with all that is desirable in life: "The soft brown carpet under his feet; the soft, cream-tinted walls; the snow-white bowl lights set in the ceiling—all seemed to him parts of a perfection and a social superiority which was almost unbelievable" (I, 42). "And there was music always—from somewhere" (I, 33). Clyde thus views the hotel both as "a realization of paradise" and as a miraculous gift from Aladdin's lamp, two images of fulfillment that, in their "spiritualizing" of his desires, appropriately constitute the center of his dream life.

But the hotel has a harsh and cruel sexuality in addition to its soft, warm, and "romantic" sensuality. Older women and homosexuals prey on the bellhops, who themselves frequent whores, and the hotel offers many instances of lascivious parties on the one hand and young girls deserted by their seducers on the other. Clyde, because of his repressed sexuality, cannot help responding to this aspect of sex with "fascination" despite his fears and anxieties. The sexual reality of the hotel is thus profoundly ambivalent. Clyde longs above all for the "romance" of sex and for warmth and a sense of union, but the overt sexuality that he in fact encounters is that of hardness, trickery, and deceit—of use and discarding. Both Clyde's unconscious need and his overt mode of fulfillment join in his response to Hortense. "Your eyes are just like soft, black velvet," he tells her. "'They're wonderful.' He was thinking of an alcove in the Green-Davidson hung with black velvet" (I, 112). Clyde unconsciously desires "softness" and later finds it in Roberta, but he is also powerfully drawn by the "hardness" of wealth and sexual power that he is to find in Sondra and that he first encounters at the Green-Davidson. Thus he endows Hortense with an image of warm softness that reflects his muddled awareness of his needs. For though Hortense is properly associated in his mind with the Green-Davidson because of their similar sexual "hardness," she is incorrectly associated with an image of softness and warmth.

Clyde's belief that the Green-Davidson is a "glorious . . . institution" also represents his acceptance of the hotel as a microcosm of social reality. So he quickly learns that to get ahead in the world—that is, to ingratiate himself with his superiors and to earn large tips—he must adopt various roles. So he accepts the hierarchy of power present in the elaborate system of sharing tips that functions in the hotel. So he realizes that he must deceive his parents about his earnings if he is to have free use of the large sums available to him as an eager novice in this institution. And because the world of the Green-Davidson—both within the hotel and as hotel life extends out into Clyde's relations with the other bellhops and with Hortense—also contains Clyde's introduction into sexual desire and sexual warfare, he assumes that the ethics of social advance and monetary gain are also those of love. Thus, when in Lycurgus he aspires to the grandeur of Sondra and her set, his actions are conditioned by an ethic derived from the Green-Davidson—that hypocrisy, dishonesty, role-playing, and sexual deceit and cruelty are the ways in which one gains what one desires and that these can and should be applied to his relationship with Roberta.

The major point to be made about Dreiser's rendering of the Green-Davidson Hotel as an important experience in Clyde's life is that we respond to his account not as an exercise in determinism but as a subtle dramatization of the ways in which a distinctive temperament—eager, sensitive, emotional, yet weak and directionless—interacts with a distinctive social setting that supplies that temperament with both its specific goals and its operative ethic. Again, as in *Jennie Gerhardt*, there is a naturalistic center to this fictional excellence. It is correct to say that Clyde's life is determined by his heredity and environment. But, once more, as in *Jennie Gerhardt*, the naturalism and the fictional strength are inseparable. The naturalism is not an obstacle to the excellence but the motive thrust and center of the bedrock fictional portrayal of how people interact with their worlds and why they are what they are.

To sum up. One of the major conventions in the study of American naturalism is that naturalistic belief is both objectionable in its own right and incompatible with fictional quality. But the example of Dreiser reveals that the strength often found in a naturalistic novel rests in the writer's commitment to the distinctive form of his naturalistic beliefs and in his ability to transform these beliefs into acceptable character and event. We are moved by the story of Jennie and Lester and by the account of Clyde's career not because they are independent of Dreiser's deepest beliefs but rather because they are successful narratives of man's impotence in the face of circumstances by a writer whose creative imagination was all of a piece. Until we are willing to accept that the power of a naturalistic writer resides in his naturalism, we will not profit from the example of Dreiser.

1977

FOUR

Dreiser and the
Naturalistic Drama
of Consciousness

*A*merican naturalistic fiction has generally been judged to be either inadequate or inept in its portrayal of the inner life. The strengths of the movement, we are told, lie elsewhere—in the dramatization of the vast forces that control man and in the massing of the specifics of everyday life. A Maggie or McTeague is too occupied by the struggle to survive in a hostile universe to reflect on his or her condition. And a Henry Fleming, who does use the occasional pauses in the battle of life to make this effort, is severely limited by his defective mental equipment. There are, in short, no long night vigils of concentrated and productive thought for naturalistic protagonists; their difficult journeys through the slums, deserts, and battlefields of life are far too immediately pressing.

This generalization about American naturalism has had a long history. Initially, it contributed to the dismissal of naturalism on moral grounds. The thinness of representation of the inner life in a naturalistic novel was held to reveal its author's belief in the animal basis of human behavior. Later, as in Lionel Trilling's well-known attack on Dreiser in his essay "Reality in America," it often disguised a political animus.[1] Dreiser's inability to deal adequately with ideas in his fiction, including the mental life of his protagonists, was inseparable from the inadequacy of his political beliefs. More recently, the position has received several kinds of more extended discussion. Warren French, for example, in an effort to explain the stages of Steinbeck's career, adopts Henry James's term "drama of consciousness" to describe a fiction antithetical to that of naturalism. The "striking distinction" between Dreiser's characters and those of James, French believes, is that Dreiser's "are not represented as conscious of what they are doing or as capable of any self-analysis of their motivations, while the James characters are. . . ." Thus, French continues, "a useful distinction may be made . . . between fictions that deal essentially with characters whose creators represent them as aware of what they are doing and of the potential consequences of these actions, and those fictions that deal essentially with characters envisioned by their creators as at the mercy of such forces as 'environment, heredity, instinct, and chance'. . . ."[2] A rather different but still basically dismissive attitude toward the naturalistic portrayal of consciousness occurs in Sandy Petrey's essay "The Language of Realism, The Language of False Consciousness: A Reading of *Sister Carrie*." Petrey's position is not that Dreiser fails to render the inner life of his characters but that he does it so badly. Whenever Dreiser shifts, Petrey argues, from external objects and events to the inner life, his language goes mushy and bathetic and thus falsifies that life. Petrey offers the infamous epilogue on Carrie as an obvious example.[3] A final and most recent variation on the traditional belief that naturalistic fiction is antithetical to the dramatization of consciousness is that found in some Marxist and New Historicist criticism. Here, the issue of the naturalist's ability to render a character's complexity of mind is resolved by assuming that characters in fiction are principally vehicles for the expression of social and economic values. A figure such as Trina or Carrie, therefore, in an almost parodic endorsement of presumed naturalistic beliefs, is largely the product of the environment of belief of her day and thus lacks a distinctive temperament and inner life.[4]

My principal observation about these more recent critical attitudes is that, as often occurs in literary criticism, an unsympathetic critic will invariably not find what he is not expecting to find. If a reader of a naturalistic novel does not find in it dramas of consciousness in the form of Jamesian analysis, in which the narrative voice shares with us a character's extended musings, he will of course assume that naturalistic fiction lacks dramas of consciousness. And when he does find lachrymose patches of purple prose devoted to a character's state of mind, as in *Sister Carrie* or *The Octopus*, he will assume that these are the author's only means of rendering interior states. And, of course, if he regards fiction principally as a form of obliquely represented social history, he will not find the rendering of distinctive states of mind of much interest even if he does recognize their presence. My own sense of naturalistic fiction, on the other hand, is that the naturalistic novelist does indeed often seek to write a drama of consciousness. He will, however, make this attempt on his own terms, and though these terms may vary in nature, depth, and success from novelist to novelist and from novel to novel, they nevertheless constitute a significant phase of naturalistic fiction.

The writer whom I will examine to illustrate the dramatization of consciousness in naturalistic fiction is Theodore Dreiser, the figure who is indeed most often singled out to demonstrate the inadequacy of psychological representation in naturalism. In each of three novels I will discuss—*Sister Carrie*, *Jennie Gerhardt*, and *An American Tragedy*—the male protagonist faces a major crisis. Hurstwood must decide if he will steal the money he has discovered in his employers' safe and elope with Carrie. Lester Kane must decide whether to continue living with Jennie and thereby sacrifice the secure and comfortable world afforded him through his family's wealth and position. And Clyde Griffiths must decide if he will go through with his plan to murder the pregnant Roberta and thus be free to marry Sondra. The three crises are similar in that none of the figures facing these decisions conceives of them in moral terms despite the obvious ethical dimensions of theft, desertion, and murder. Rather, each character is tormented by various desires or fears that are in conflict with each other. We are still primarily creatures of instinctive emotional responses, Dreiser reminds us several times in *Sister Carrie* and dramatizes throughout his fiction, even though social and moral convention may impose sanctions and penalties on these responses and their consequent actions in the belief that they are the result of rational choice. The function of the naturalistic novelist, therefore, is to dramatize as convincingly and as powerfully as possible the struggle between conflicting emotions in the consciousness of his characters.

In addition, the naturalistic novelist will seek to render consciousness as concretely as possible—that is, to find physical equivalents for states of mind. Taine's famous dictum that "vice and virtue are only products like vitriol and sugar" reflects the widely shared naturalistic assumption that all dimensions of life, including those which had been previously held to be "spiritual" rather than "material" aspects of experience, not only have describable concrete sources but can best be understood in terms of the concrete. What is especially distinctive in Dreiser's representation of consciousness as comprising a struggle between conflicting emotions that can best be depicted by means of physical analogues is that he refines this belief and method in the course of his career from their direct and obvious representation in *Sister Carrie* to an oblique and complex rendering in *An American Tragedy*.

In Chapter XXVII of *Sister Carrie*, George Hurstwood faces a crisis in his effort to win Carrie.[5] His wife, strongly suspecting an infidelity, has locked him out and is threatening him with divorce and bankruptcy. And Carrie herself, now aware that Hurstwood is married, is refusing to see him. Deeply troubled by these seemingly insoluble difficulties, Hurstwood, rather "roseate" with wine, prepares to close down Fitzgerald and Moy's for the night. As usual, he tries the door of the safe in his small office to ensure that it is locked. When to his surprise the door opens, he looks in the money drawers of the safe and finds that they contain both the day's receipts and an additional bundle of cash in bills. "'Count them,' said a voice in his ear." He does so, and discovers that the safe contains over $10,000 in cash.

> "Why don't I shut the safe?" his mind said to itself, lingering. "What makes me pause here?"
> For answer came the strangest words:

"Did you ever have ten thousand dollars in
ready money?"[6]

Dreiser is here dramatizing Hurstwood's conflicting impulses with a traditional yet powerful device. That part of him
desiring Carrie creates a spokesman for this desire, a voice, which
itself suggests an act that is a possible first step in the fulfillment of
desire—count the money. Hurstwood's consciousness, however,
also contains another voice—that of conformity to the regular
and normal course of action in order to avoid the consequences
of the irregular and abnormal—and this voice suggests, in the
form of a question, an act contrary to that of the first voice:
"Why don't I shut the safe?"

For a moment, Hurstwood's sense of order overcomes desire, and he returns the money to the safe. But instead of going
on to lock the safe, he pulls down the office window curtains and
tries the office door to make sure that it is locked. After a moment's thought, however, he unlocks the office door and turns
up the light. These two sets of actions are of course also specific
physical equivalents, in exact parallel to his interior voices, of his
divided state of mind.

Hurstwood, however, despite having unlocked the office
door, still does not lock the safe. Instead, he thinks of the possible
solution offered by the money and so again opens the safe and
takes out the cash. But then, "Lord! what was that? For the first
time he was tense, as if a stern hand had been laid upon his
shoulder." There is in fact no cause for alarm, but Hurstwood
nevertheless, for a second time, replaces the money in the safe
and partly closes the door. Dreiser now pauses in the action to
discourse at some length on the struggle between desire and fear
in Hurstwood, in which "The clock of thought ticks out its wish
and its denial." As Hurstwood reflects on his dilemma, "He went
over his situation once again, his eye always seeing the money in
a lump, his mind seeing what he would do." The two images of
a "firm hand on his shoulder" and "the money in a lump" are
yet another rendering in physical terms of Hurstwood's psychic
state.

Overcome for the moment by the attraction of "what [the
money] would do," Hurstwood again opens the safe and for the
third time removes the money. The bills, as he holds them in his

hand, "were so smooth, so compact, so portable." With the money in his hand, however, he thinks of the scandal and of the police. "They would be after him." He therefore once again returns the money to the safe. He almost immediately realizes, however, that he has placed the money in the wrong drawers (there are two money drawers, one containing the day's receipts, the other the large sum), and he therefore takes out both the money and the drawers to correct the error. At this moment, the safe door clicks shut. Hurstwood "looked about him and decided instantly. There was no delaying now. . . . At once he became the man of action." But even as he is leaving the saloon with the money in a satchel, he realizes "That was a mistake."

The scene has usually been discussed and praised for its thematic significance. Hurstwood, we now realize fully, is indecisive and bumbling despite his appearance to Carrie and Drouet of a man of strength and control. And the final moment of the scene, of Hurstwood fleeing with the money only after a decision has been made for him and despite his awareness of the potentially doleful consequences of his action, is Dreiser's commentary on the basic human condition in which desire lacks the resources of mind and will to translate itself into successful fulfillment. But though the scene may lend itself on analysis to a discussion of the abstract "forces" governing human affairs—desire, fate, and will, for example—it is on its primary level of fictional discourse principally a dramatization of Hurstwood's consciousness in operation, with concrete analogues serving as the vehicle for this dramatization. As in a dream allegory, inner voices articulate specific options for action; as in a play, "stage action" dramatizes specific states of mind; and as in a poem, concrete images express underlying emotions.

These repetitive devices—to say nothing of the constant repetition of the acts of removing and replacing the money—reveal clearly the central truth of Hurstwood's consciousness at this moment—his indecisive wavering between fear and desire. Their repetitiveness, clarity, and concreteness, as well as Dreiser's compression of the subject matter of theft and adultery into one scene, push the moment toward the melodrama often associated with naturalism. But it is effective melodrama. Here, Dreiser appears to be saying, is a weak mind in turmoil. And in Hurstwood's voices of temptation and retribution, in his pulling curtains down and turning lights up, and in his thoughts of a hand on his shoulder and of a pile of greenbacks we have a rendering of that consciousness that holds and persuades.

Lester Kane, in *Jennie Gerhardt*, faces at several key points during the novel a difficult decision about Jennie. Although he loves Jennie and is content when with her, he is also, despite his pose as a modern man of independent views, troubled by the potential loss of his standing in his family and in his business and social worlds because of his irregular union with Jennie. His response to this conflict is to postpone making a decision until forced to. Midway through the novel, for example, Lester is provided with an opportunity to break off their relationship when, while living with Jennie in a small house in a Chicago suburb, he discovers that she some years earlier had had a child by Senator Brander, a fact which she had hidden from him. Lester is angry with Jennie over her lack of "confidence" in him, as he puts it. "You and I had that, I thought," he tells her. In the absence of that quality, he continues, "I don't see my way clear to ever hold more than a tentative relationship with you. . . . The thing is too tangled." At that moment, Lester "went to the window and stared out. There were some trees in the yard, where the darkness was settling. He wondered how this would really come out, for he liked a home atmosphere. . . . "[7]

This passage is a minor though suggestive example of Dreiser's more complex and probing means for the rendering of consciousness in *Jennie Gerhardt* than that which I have described as present in *Sister Carrie*. Lester's pride has been hurt by what he considers to be Jennie's defection, and he wishes to express his irritation and authority. Yet he is not willing to give Jennie up. His state of mind, in other words, is confused and ambivalent, and he himself is not fully aware of his deepest emotions. He knows principally that he is troubled. When Lester looks out the window into the yard and sees trees in the approaching darkness he is therefore viewing both a physical phenomenon and a metaphor for an internal state of mind. He is looking, in short, both outwardly and inwardly. As a material phenomenon, the trees in the gloom are precise; as a metaphor for a psychic reality, they are suggestive and connotative. And it is at this point of conjunction that there occurs a distinctive moment in the naturalistic drama of consciousness. The external world is specific and concrete; the trees and the darkness are real for Lester and for anyone else viewing them. But the perception of this reality, by Lester or anyone, is individual and relative. The viewer perceives in the trees and the darkness an image of experience that corresponds vaguely and roughly to a personally meaningful but otherwise indescribable state of consciousness. Unlike *Sister Carrie*, in which Dreiser used physical constructs as exact reflections of specific states of mind, in *Jennie Gerhardt* these constructs suggestively rather than precisely render in symbolic form the emotional complexities of man's deepest nature.

A parallel incident to the one I have been discussing occurs not long after. Lester and Jennie's relationship has been discovered by Lester's family, and Lester's brother Robert has come to Lester's Chicago office to attempt to persuade Lester to leave Jennie. Lester still does not wish to make a decision about Jennie, though he now accepts that he will soon have to do so. After Robert leaves, "Lester sat down in his easy-chair by the window . . . and gazed ruminatively out over the flourishing city. Yonder was spread out before him life with its concomitant phases of energy, hope, prosperity, and pleasure . . . " (239). The external image in this instance is more precise in its rendering of Lester's state of mind because he himself has begun to see more clearly the implications of remaining with Jennie. To do so, he now realizes, means the loss of that side of his life represented by the richly vibrant experience of the "flourishing city." But even in this precision there is a powerful suggestiveness to the metaphor. For Lester's life with Jennie has been that of secret nooks and crannies—of upstairs rooms at her parents' home, from which he seldom emerges, or of obscure houses far out in the suburbs. This narrow and hidden world of secret pleasure is now contrasted to an open and expansive cityscape. We thus now realize that it is Lester's fear of the enclosed and entrapped, a fear buried deep in his consciousness, which has stimulated his responsiveness to the open and free world outside his window, and that the two images—of entrapment and of freedom—constitute in their complex interaction his drama of consciousness at this moment in his psychic history.

The climactic scene in *Jennie Gerhardt*, as well as the fullest and most intense moment in Dreiser's dramatization of Lester's consciousness, occurs toward the end of the novel. Lester and Jennie have long since parted; Lester has married Letty; and Jennie's daughter Vesta has recently died. Lester, who has always harbored doubts about his treatment of Jennie, visits her in a downtown Chicago hotel and attempts to comfort her. Jennie is pleased by this attention, but

> all the while [Lester] was thinking he had treated her badly. He went to the window and looked down into Dearborn street, the world of traffic below holding his attention. The great mass of trucks and vehicles, the counter streams of hurrying pedestrians, seemed like a puzzle. So shadows march in a dream. (400)

On the one hand, Lester seems in this passage to be reaching toward a philosophical insight into the ironic discrepancy that exists between the self-preoccupied scrambling and scurrying of quotidian life and the recognition, available only to those who distance themselves from the hurly-burly, of the ineluctable meaninglessness of it all. But to emphasize the philosophical dimension of the passage is to neglect Dreiser's consistent use of such moments as metaphorical reflections of distinctive states of mind, as moments in the drama of a consciousness rather than as generalized philosophical observations. Thus, what is principally communicated in Lester's view from the hotel window is his desire to escape responsibility both for the pain he has caused Jennie and for his own unfulfilled emotional life. That this is his motive is made clear by what he then tells Jennie, in an often quoted passage that immediately follows his view from the window. "It isn't myself that's important in this transaction apparently," he tells her; "the individual doesn't count much in the situation. I don't know whether you see what I'm driving at, but all of us are more or less pawns. We're moved about by circumstances over which we have no control" (401).

Well, yes and no. Certainly social convention of various kinds in Jennie's and Lester's lives has played a role in determining their fates, in shaping them into pawns. But in attributing powerlessness to himself, Lester is also conveniently ignoring the role played in his present condition by his own desire for a comfortable life and by his disinclination to make disturbing decisions. What is being represented to us at this moment in Lester's continuing drama of consciousness is his adoption of a philosophical position that can help explain and excuse what has happened to him and Jennie. Looking out of the window into Dearborn street, Lester perceives in the human condition what it is necessary for him to perceive.

Chapter XLVI of Book Two of *An American Tragedy* is devoted to the train journey by Clyde and Roberta from Fonda to Utica—the second leg in their trip to the North Woods that will culminate in Roberta's drowning. Clyde has reached Fonda from Lycurgus, while Roberta has made her way there from her parents' farm near Biltz. During their separation, the pregnant Roberta has, she believes, successfully pressured Clyde into a promise of marriage, and Clyde, desperate to escape any commitment to Roberta because of his far more rewarding relationship with Sondra, has concocted a scheme to kill Roberta in some remote mountain lake and to disguise the murder as an accidental drowning.

The trip to Utica thus rests on a series of ironies. The couple is on a prenuptial holiday, yet Clyde, thinking ahead to his eventual disappearance after Roberta's death, has insisted that they travel separately on the train. This charade, in which they pretend not to know each other, is of course their essential condition. Roberta has no awareness of Clyde's plan or of the extent of his hate and anger, and Clyde has lost touch with Roberta's capacity for love. Dreiser's effort in the chapter is to render dramatically the terrible distinction between appearance and reality in the lives of Clyde and Roberta at this moment—the distinction between the ostensible nature of the journey, a holiday in the country, and Clyde's true motives and feelings about the trip. His method is to combine the fullness and explicitness of the psychological representation he had used when describing Hurstwood before the safe and the far more economical but probing and suggestive form of representation that characterizes Lester's musings in front of windows.

Most of the chapter is in the form of psychological dramatization known as *style indirect libre* or free indirect discourse, a technique that indeed dominates this portion of the novel until Roberta's death. Dreiser had begun to experiment with this technique in a number of short stories of approximately 1915–22 and had developed it into a powerful device for the rendering of consciousness.[8] Thus, throughout the journey to Utica, as Clyde rides alone, with Roberta in another part of the train, Clyde's thoughts are presented to us in the third person but in a diction and syntax that imply that they are the unmediated expression of Clyde's thought processes. So, for example, Clyde thinks of what he must do in Utica:

> He was going to buy a straw hat in Utica to-day—he
> must remember that—a straw hat with a Utica label,
> which he would wear instead of the present one.
> Then, when she was not looking, he would put the
> old one in his bag with his other things. That was
> why he would have to leave her for a little while after
> they reached Utica—at the depot or library or
> somewhere—perhaps as was his first plan, take her to
> some small hotel somewhere and register as Mr. and
> Mrs. Carl Graham or Clifford Golden or Gehring
> (there was a girl in the factory by that name) so if
> they were ever traced in any way, it would be
> assumed that she had gone away with some man of
> that name.[9]

These reflections by Clyde are on the most conscious level of his mind, as is suggested by the full and correct sentence form and by the logical sequence of ideas in which they are expressed. Dreiser has thus reached a point in his depiction of consciousness when he does not have to rely on the melodramatic physicality on which he had depended for Hurstwood before the safe—of constant repetitive acts and images—because the device of free indirect discourse permitted him to render consciousness both fully and precisely while confining the area of dramatic action to the mind of the protagonist. Here are Clyde's thoughts themselves, Dreiser appears to be saying, and therefore no re-expression of these thoughts through acts or metaphors is necessary.[10]

But these thoughts are limited to Clyde's fully conscious reflections—the concerns of a man about to undertake a difficult enterprise that requires precision and refinement if it is to have a successful outcome. On a deeper level of consciousness, however, Clyde is functioning far more emotionally. At this level, a number of powerful feelings demand expression, and like Lester before a window, they achieve an oblique but compelling representation through the objects that Clyde sees from his train window. Dreiser seeks to make immediately evident the difference between Clyde's more conscious reflections and these more profound emotional qualms (which are also in a form of indirect discourse) by placing each object seen or responded to by Clyde within parentheses and in italics and by expressing each in a brief passage of often fragmentary sentences—as though each is a sudden stab of feeling interrupting Clyde's efforts to elaborate his plan.

Clyde's most pervasive underlying emotion is of course fear. Will he be caught. So, the first such passage in italics, which occurs while Clyde is awaiting the train at Fonda, combines what he sees and his response to what he sees into a single image of fear: "(*Why was that old man in that old brown winter suit and hat and carrying that bird cage in a brown paper bag looking at him so? Could he sense anything? Did he know him? Had he ever worked in Lycurgus or seen him before?*)" But once Clyde is on the train, these passages of external vision that interrupt Clyde's planning become—like Lester's observations from a window—more indirect and complex in their symbolism. Although some of the passages continue to express directly his fears— "(*Oh, the grimness and the terror of this plan! Could he really execute it?*)"—others appear on the surface to be merely neutral objects of his vision from the train window. For example, three such objects of sight (each separated from the other by an extended passage in which Clyde continues to refine his plan) are:

(*Those five birds winging toward that patch of trees over there—below that hill.*)

(*Those nine black and white cows on that green hillside.*)

(*Those three automobiles out there running almost as fast as this train.*)

These observations, each in parallel form to suggest that they comprise a unit, are in fact not neutral in the context of Clyde's plan. The birds swiftly flying to a grove of trees reflect the freedom and safety Clyde desires; the black and white cows on a hillside suggest the emotional ambiguity of the plan (freedom and happiness for him, death for Roberta) within an idyllic setting (Indeed, the last line of reflection before this passage reads, "The blackness of this plot of his!"); and the automobiles moving almost as fast as the train imply pursuit. In short, just as Clyde's more conscious rehearsal of his plan moves in logical order from the arrival at Utica to Roberta's death at Big Bittern, so in these images of physical reality that he observes from his window there is a logical progression of emotions from his desire to escape Roberta to the complex feelings attendant on the murder itself to fear of pursuit and capture.

The trip to Utica also contains, in direct counterpoint to Clyde's interlaced passages of reflection and of objects seen from the train window, several sections in which Roberta also thinks and sees. And the two consciousnesses in ironic juxtaposition, as I noted earlier, are, as they make their way toward a common tragic destiny, Dreiser's commentary on a central aspect of the human condition. But I have concentrated on Clyde in this discussion to make clear that Dreiser has come a considerable distance, both in his conception of consciousness and in the technical skill necessary to express this broadened conception, from the representation of a similar conflict between desire and fear in Hurstwood. This distance can be accounted for in several ways. It derives in part from the difference between an inexperienced writer of fiction attempting his first novel and the mature writer of some twenty-five years' experience. It also reveals the difference between the literary climate of the late 1890s, when despite some experimentation by a new generation of novelists, the methods of Victorian fiction were still dominant, and the climate of the

1920s, in which there was widespread endorsement of the belief that the dramatization of the inner life was the principal business of fiction. But for Dreiser in particular, and for American naturalism especially, these differences are less significant than the common and on the whole successful effort by Dreiser in all three of the novels I have been discussing to render consciousness—an effort and a success which thus constitute a refutation of the common assumption, which I examined at the opening of this paper, that both Dreiser and naturalism in general neglect or inadequately depict the drama of consciousness. I have sought, rather, to demonstrate that Dreiser attempted to represent the interior life from the very beginning of his career, and that he also did so with increasing control, depth, and suggestiveness. Man, to Dreiser, was not a creature whose conscious will and moral insight control his actions. But man's inner nature, in all its chaotic flux of varying emotions, was nevertheless one of Dreiser's principal fields of action, and he increasingly extended and refined his means of rendering this aspect of human experience.

1991

The Late
Nineteenth Century

FIVE

⊣Nineteenth-Century American Naturalism⊢

An Essay in Definition

Most literary critics and historians who attempt definitions are aware of the dangers and advantages inherent in this enterprise. But few, I believe, recognize that many literary genres and modes have their barriers of established terms and ideas to overcome or outflank. The writer who seeks to define tragedy usually finds that his definition takes shape around such traditional guideposts as the tragic hero, the tragic flaw, recognition and catharsis, and so on. American naturalism, as a concept, has two such channeled approaches to its definition. The first is that since naturalism comes after realism, and since it seems to take literature in the same direction as realism, it is primarily an "extension" or continuation of realism—only a little different. The second almost inevitable approach involves this difference. The major distinction between realism and naturalism, most critics agree, is the particular philosophical orientation of the naturalists. A traditional and widely accepted concept of American naturalism, therefore, is that it is essentially realism infused with a pessimistic determinism. Richard Chase argues that American naturalism is realism with a "necessitarian ideology," and George

J. Becker (defining all naturalism, including American) considers it as "no more than an emphatic and explicit philosophical position taken by some realists," the position being a "pessimistic materialistic determinism."[1] The common belief is that the naturalists were like the realists in their fidelity to the details of contemporary life, but that they depicted everyday life with a greater sense of the role of such causal forces as heredity and environment in determining behavior and belief.

This traditional approach to naturalism through realism and through philosophical determinism is historically justifiable and has served a useful purpose, but it has also handicapped thinking both about the movement as a whole and about individual works within the movement. It has resulted in much condescension toward those writers who are supposed to be naturalists yet whose fictional sensationalism (an aspect of romanticism) and moral ambiguity (a quality inconsistent with the absolutes of determinism) appear to make their work flawed specimens of the mode.

I would like, therefore, to propose a modified definition of late nineteenth-century American naturalism.[2] For the time being, let this be a working definition, to be amplified and made more concrete by the illustrations from which it has been drawn. I suggest that the naturalistic novel usually contains two tensions or contradictions, and that the two in conjunction comprise both an interpretation of experience and a particular aesthetic recreation of experience. In other words, the two constitute the theme and form of the naturalistic novel. The first tension is that between the subject matter of the naturalistic novel and the concept of man that emerges from this subject matter. The naturalist populates his novel primarily from the lower middle class or the lower class. His characters are the poor, the uneducated, the unsophisticated. His fictional world is that of the commonplace and unheroic in which life would seem to be chiefly the dull round of daily existence, as we ourselves usually conceive of our lives. But the naturalist discovers in this world those qualities of man usually associated with the heroic or adventurous, such as acts of violence and passion that involve sexual adventure or bodily strength and which culminate in desperate moments and violent death. A naturalistic novel is thus an extension of realism only in the sense that both modes often deal with the local and contemporary. The naturalist, however, discovers in this material the extraordinary and excessive in human nature.

The second tension involves the theme of the naturalistic novel. The naturalist often describes his characters as though they are conditioned and controlled by environment, heredity, instinct, or chance. But he also suggests a compensating humanistic value in his characters or their fates that affirms the significance of the individual and of his life. The tension here is that between the naturalist's desire to represent in fiction the new, discomforting truths that he has found in the ideas and life of his late nineteenth-century world, and also his desire to find some meaning in experience that reasserts the validity of the human enterprise. The naturalist appears to say that although the individual may be a cipher in a world made amoral by man's lack of responsibility for his fate, the imagination refuses to accept this formula as the total meaning of life and so seeks a new basis for man's sense of his own dignity and importance.

The naturalistic novel is therefore not so superficial or reductive as it implicitly appears to be in its conventional definition. It involves a belief that life on its lowest levels is not so simple as it seems to be from higher levels. It suggests that even the least significant human being can feel and strive powerfully and can suffer the extraordinary consequences of his emotions, and that no range of human experience is free of the moral complexities and ambiguities that Milton set his fallen angels to debating.[3] Naturalism reflects an affirmative ethical conception of life, for it asserts the value of all life by endowing the lowest character with emotion and defeat and with moral ambiguity, no matter how poor or ignoble he may seem. The naturalistic novel derives much of its aesthetic effect from these contrasts. It involves us in the experience of a life both commonplace and extraordinary, both familiar and strange, both simple and complex. It pleases us with its sensationalism without affronting our sense of probability. It discovers the "romance of the commonplace," as Frank Norris put it. Thus, the melodramatic sensationalism and moral "confusion" that are often attacked in the naturalistic novel should really be incorporated into a normative definition of the mode and be recognized as its essential constituents.

The three novels that I have chosen to illustrate this definition, and also to suggest the possible range of variation within it, are Frank Norris's *McTeague* (1899), Theodore Dreiser's *Sister Carrie* (1900), and Stephen Crane's *The Red Badge of Courage* (1895). These works are important novels by the three leading late nineteenth-century American naturalists, and each novel has frequently been read as a key example of its author's values and his fictional form. A definition drawn from these three novels will not be applicable to all late nineteenth-century naturalistic fiction. But, given the significance of these writers and of these novels, it would, I believe, be a useful introduction to this major movement in American literary history.

A good deal of *McTeague* is devoted to depicting the routine, ordered world of Polk Street, the lower middle class service street in San Francisco on which McTeague practices and lives. The life of Polk Street enters the novel in two ways—through set pieces describing street activities or the daily lives of the central characters in relation to the life of the street, and through constant incidental allusion to its activities and inhabitants. Norris dramatically establishes Polk Street as above all a life of the repetitious and constant. The street exists as a source of the ordered and the routine in McTeague's life, as a world where the harness shop, the grocery, and the car conductors' coffee joint are always available in their set roles, where the children go to school at the same time each day, followed by the shop clerks coming to work, and so on. McTeague is settled and content in this life, and we recognize that his inner needs and outer world are in harmony.

A central theme in Norris's work is that beneath the surface of our placid, everyday lives there is turbulence, that the romance of the extraordinary is not limited to the distant in time and place but can be found "in the brownstone house on the corner and in the office building downtown."[4] Norris therefore used the incident that had stimulated him to write the novel, a vicious murder in a San Francisco kindergarten, as a controlling paradox in *McTeague* as in scene after scene he introduces the sensational into the commonplace activities and setting of Polk Street. So we have such incidents as McTeague grossly kissing the anesthetized Trina in his dental parlor, or the nearly murderous fight between Marcus and McTeague at the picnic. Some of the best moments in the novel powerfully unite these two streams of the common-place and the extraordinary. In one such moment the frightened and incoherent Trina, having just found Maria's corpse with its cut throat and its blood-soaked clothes, rushes out into the everyday routine of Polk Street and has difficulty convincing the butcher's boy that something is wrong or even convincing herself that it is not improper "to make a disturbance and create a scene in the street."[5]

Norris believed that the source of this violence beneath the surface placidity of life is the presence in all men of animal qualities that have played a major role in man's evolutionary development but which are now frequently atavistic and destruc tive.[6] Norris's theme is that man's racial atavism (particularly his brute sexual desires) and man's individual family heritage (alcoholic degeneracy in McTeague's case) can combine as a force toward reversion, toward a return to the emotions and instincts of man's animal past. McTeague is in one sense a "special case" of reversion, since his atavistic brutality is in part caused by his degenerate parents. He is also, however, any man caught up in the net of sex, and in this second aspect of man's inherited animal nature Norris introduces a tragic element into McTeague's fall, an element that contributes to the novel's thematic tension.

In describing the courtship of Trina and McTeague, Norris is at pains to stress their overt sexual innocence yet intuitive sexuality. The woman in Trina "was not yet awakened; she was yet, as one might say, without sex" (14). For McTeague, Trina is his "first experience. With her the feminine element suddenly entered his little world. It was not only her that he saw and felt, it was the woman, the whole sex, an entire new humanity" (16). Despite their innocence and lack of experience, both react intuitively and atavistically—McTeague desiring to seize and pos-sess her, she instinctively withdrawing yet desiring to be con-quered.

The most important sexual encounter between McTeague and Trina occurs at the B Street Station where McTeague for a second time proposes. When Trina hesitates, he seizes her "in his enormous arms, crushing down her struggle with his immense strength. Then Trina gave up, all in an instant, turning her head to his. They kissed each other, grossly, full in the mouth" (48). Within the literary conventions of the day, this kiss symbolizes

Trina's sexual submission. At this moment the strands in the web of sexual determinism begin to pull taut, for "the instant she allowed him to kiss her, he thought less of her. She was not so desirable, after all" (48). McTeague senses this diminution along with a dim awareness "that this must be so, that it belonged to the changeless order of things—the man desiring the woman only for what she withholds; the woman worshipping the man for that which she yields up to him. With each concession gained the man's desire cools; with every surrender made the woman's adoration increases" (48). Norris is concerned in this second meeting not with a special flaw in McTeague or Trina but with a sexual determinism affecting all men. The possessive sexual desire of the man aroused by the first woman he experiences sensually, the instinctive desire of the woman for sexual submission responding to the first man who assaults her—these are the atavistic animal forces that bring Trina and McTeague together.

A major theme in *McTeague* is therefore that of the sexual tragedy of man and woman. Caught up by drives and instincts beyond their control or comprehension, they mate by chance. In *McTeague* sex is that which comes to all men and women, disrupting their lives and placing them in relationships that the sanctity of marriage cannot prevent from ending in chaos and destruction. Norris does not tell the old tale of the fallen fornicator, as he does in *Vandover and the Brute,* but rather reaches out toward the unexplored ground of the human dilemma of sexual attraction.

The tension between this deterministic aspect of *McTeague* and its humanistic element does not lie in McTeague as a fully developed tragic figure. Rather, it is contained in the theme that man can seldom escape the violence inherent in his own nature, that man's attempt to achieve an ordered world is constantly thwarted by man himself. Norris devotes much attention to the element of order in the details of McTeague's life not only because of his belief in the romance of the commonplace but because the destruction of that order is the source of the tragic quality in McTeague's fall and of our own compassionate involvement with him despite his grotesqueness. Norris carefully documents McTeague's life as a dentist and as an inhabitant of Polk Street because the habitual tasks and minor successes of this life represent the order and stability that McTeague requires. In the course of the novel we begin to feel compassion for him as he becomes a victim of Trina's avarice and as we recognize that his emerging brutality is at least partly the result of the destruction of his world. When McTeague learns that he can no longer practice dentistry, his reaction is that of a man whose life is emptied of all meaning. In a scene of considerable power Trina comes upon him sitting in his dental chair, "looking stupidly out of the windows, across the roofs opposite, with an unseeing gaze, his red hands lying idly in his lap" (51). We are never completely one with McTeague; his brute strength and dull mind put us off. But because he is trapped in the universal net of sex, and because we recognize the poignancy of the loss of his world, we respond to him ultimately as a human being in distress, as a figure of some significance despite his limitations—as a man, in short, whose fall contains elements of the tragic.

For *McTeague* is in part a tragic novel. True, McTeague neither bears full responsibility for his fate nor is he in any sense noble or profound. He is rather like Gervaise in *L'Assommoir*: they are both poor creatures who want above all a place to rest and be content, yet who are brought low by their needs and desires. There is a sense of common humanity in McTeague's fall, and that quality is perhaps the modern residue of the tragic theme, since we are no longer certain of man's transcendent nobility or of the reality of major responsibility for our fates. The theme of *McTeague* is not that drunkenness leads to a tragic fall, but that tragedy is inherent in the human situation given man's animal past and the possibility that he will be dominated by that past in particular circumstances. Norris does not deny the strength of man's past or present animality, but neither does he deny the poignancy of the fall of even such a gross symbol of this animality as McTeague. It is out of this tension that much of the meaning and power of the novel arises.

Even more than Norris, Theodore Dreiser creates a sense of the solidity of life. His early novels in particular affirm that we cannot escape the impact of physical reality and that this fact is one of the few that man may know with certainty. So the several worlds of Carrie—her sister's working class existence, her life with

Drouet in Chicago and with Hurstwood in New York—achieve a sense of massiveness both in their painstaking documentation and in their inescapable effect on Carrie. The effect on us, however, is not only to enforce a sense of the importance of clothes, of furniture, of how much one owes the grocer and of exactly how much one earns and spends—the impact, too, is of normalcy, of the steady pace of life, since life does indeed seem to be measured out in coffee spoons. Dreiser's ability to capture the tangible commonplace of everyday existence powerfully suggests that the commonplace and everyday are the essence of experience, particularly since he returns again and again to the unexciting details of the furnishings of an apartment or the contents of a meal. Moreover, Dreiser's dispassionate tone contributes to this effect. This is not to say that his fiction lacks an ironic dimension. He frequently sets events or beliefs in ironic juxtaposition, as when Carrie is worried that Hurstwood will discover that she and Drouet are unmarried though she herself is unaware that Hurstwood is married. But Dreiser's irony differs from Crane's intense and pervasive ironic vision of life, a vision that colors every incident or observation in Crane's work with the implication that things are not what they seem. Dreiser's plodding, graceless paragraphs imply the opposite—that the concrete world he so seriously details is real and discernible and that nothing can shake or undermine it.

Dreiser's central theme in *Sister Carrie*, however, sets forth the idea—Lionel Trilling to the contrary[7]—that the physically real is not the only reality and that men seek something in life beyond it. His theme is that those of a finer, more intense, more emotional nature who desire to break out of their normal solid world—whether it be a Carrie oppressed by the dull repetitiousness and crudity of her sister's home, or a Hurstwood jaded by the middle class trivialities of his family—that when such as these strive to discover a life approximate to their natures they introduce into their lives the violent and the extraordinary. Carrie leaves her sister's flat for two illicit alliances, attracted to each man principally by the opportunities he offers for a better life. Drouet and Hurstwood represent to her not so much wealth or sexual attraction as an appeal to something intangibly richer and fuller in herself. She is drawn to each in turn, and then finally to Ames, because each appeals to some quality in her temperament that she finds unfulfilled in her life of the moment. Dreiser's depiction of her almost asexual relations with all of these men represents less his capitulation to contemporary publishing restrictions (although some of this is present) than his desire that the three characters reflect the upward course of Carrie's discovery and realization of her inner nature. Finally, Carrie's career on the stage symbolizes both the emotional intensity she is capable of bringing to life and the fact that she requires the intrinsically extraordinary and exciting world of the theater to call forth and embody her emotional depth.

Hurstwood's suicide can be explored as a typical example of Dreiser's combination of the concretely commonplace and the sensational. It takes place in a cheap Bowery hotel. Hurstwood's method is to turn on the gas, not resolutely but hesitantly, and then to say weakly, "What's the use?" as he "stretched himself to rest."[8] Dreiser thus submerges an inherently sensational event in the trivial and unemotional. He not only "takes the edge off" the extraordinariness of the event by his full and detached elaboration of its commonplace setting but also casts it in the imagery of enervation and rest. This scene is in one sense a special instance, since Hurstwood seeks death as a refuge. But Dreiser's total effect as a novelist is often similar to the effect produced by this scene as he dramatizes throughout *Sister Carrie* the solidity and therefore seeming normalcy of experience and yet its underlying extraordinariness if man seeks beyond the routine. His principal aesthetic impact, however, is different from that of Norris, who appears to combine the sensational and commonplace much as Dreiser does. Norris's effect is basically that of dramatic sensationalism, of the excitement of violence and sudden death. Dreiser's effect is more thematic and less scenic because he colors the sensational with the same emotional stolidity with which he characterizes all experience. It is not only that the sensational and extraordinary exist in our commonplace lives, Dreiser appears to say, but that they are so pervasive and implicit in our experience that their very texture differs little from the ordinary course of events. Thus, such potentially exciting and dramatically sensational moments in Dreiser's fiction as the seduction of Jennie Gerhardt or the imprisonment of Frank Cowperwood have an almost listless dullness compared to Norris's treatment of parallel events in his fiction.

Carrie, like many of Dreiser's characters, has her life shaped by chance and need. Chance involves her with Drouet and later plays a large role in Hurstwood's theft and therefore in her own departure with him. Her needs are of two kinds—first to attain the tangible objects and social symbols of comfort and beauty that she sees all around her in Chicago and New York, and then to be loved. Of the major forces in her life, it is primarily her desire for objects that furnish a sense of physical and mental well-being—for fine clothing and furniture and attractive apartments and satisfactory food—which determines much of her life. As she gains more of these, her fear of returning to poverty and crudity—to her sister's condition—impels her to seek even more vigorously. Much of the concrete world that Dreiser fills in so exhaustively in *Sister Carrie* thus exists as a determining force in Carrie's life, first moving her to escape it, as in her encounters with working-class Chicago, and then to reach out for it, as when Drouet takes her to a good restaurant and buys her some fashionable clothes and so introduces into her imagination the possibility of making these a part of her life.

But Carrie's response to her needs is only one side of her nature. She also possesses a quality that is intrinsic to her being, though its external shape (a Drouet, a dress seen on the street) is determined by accidental circumstance. For in this his first novel Dreiser endows Carrie with the same capacity to wonder and to dream that he felt so strongly in himself. It is this ability to dream about the nature of oneself and one's fate and of where one is going and how one will get there and to wonder whether happiness is real and possible or only an illusion—it is this capacity which ultimately questions the reality and meaning of the seemingly solid and plain world in which we find ourselves.

This "dream" quality underlies the most striking symbol in the novel, the rocking chair. The rocking chair has correctly been interpreted as principally a symbol of circularity because Carrie rocks on her first night in Chicago and again at the novel's close in her New York apartment.[9] Dreiser seems to imply by the symbol that nothing really has happened to Carrie, that although her outer circumstances have changed, she is essentially the same both morally and spiritually. The symbol does indeed function in this way, but it also, in its persistence, reflects Carrie's continuing ability to wonder about herself and her future and this reveals that her imaginative response to life has not been dulled by experience. Although she had not achieved the happiness that she thought accompanied the life she desired and which she now has, she will continue to search. Perhaps Ames represents the next, higher step in this quest, Dreiser implies. But in any case, she possesses this inner force, a force which is essentially bold and free. Although it brings her worry and loneliness—the rocking chair symbolizes these as well—it is an element in her that Dreiser finds estimable and moving. She will always be the dreamer, Dreiser says, and though her dreams take an earthly shape controlled by her world, and though she is judged immoral by the world because she violates its conventions in pursuit of her dreams, she has for Dreiser—and for us, I believe—meaning and significance and stature because of her capacity to rock and dream, to question life and to pursue it. Thus Carrie seeks to fulfill each new venture and gain each new object as though these were the only realities of life, and yet by her very dissatisfaction and questioning of what she has gained to imply the greater reality of the mind and spirit that dreams and wonders. The rocking chair goes nowhere, but it moves, and in that paradox lies Dreiser's involvement with Carrie and his ability to communicate the intensity and nature of her quest. For in his mind, too, the world is both solid and unknowable, and man is ever pursuing and never finding.

The Red Badge of Courage also embodies a different combination of the sensational and commonplace than that found in *McTeague*. Whereas Norris demonstrates that the violent and the extraordinary are present in seemingly dull and commonplace lives, Crane, even more than Dreiser, is intent on revealing the commonplace nature of the seemingly exceptional. In *The Red Badge* Henry Fleming is a raw, untried country youth who seeks the romance and glory of war but who finds that his romantic, chivalric preconceptions of battle are false. Soldiers and generals do not strike heroic poses; the dead are not borne home triumphantly on their shields but fester where they have fallen; and courage is not a conscious striving for an ideal mode of behavior but a temporary delirium derived from animal fury and social pride or fear. A wounded officer worries about the cleanliness of his uniform; a soldier sweats and labors at his arms "like a laborer in a foundry";[10] and mere chance determines rewards and punishments—the death of a Conklin, the red badge of a Fleming. War to Crane is like life itself in its injustice, in its mixing of the ludicrous and the momentarily exhilarating, in its self-deceptions, and in its acceptance of appearances for realities. Much of Crane's imagery in the novel is therefore consciously and pointedly anti-heroic, not only in his obviously satirical use of conventional chivalric imagery in unheroic situations (a soldier bearing a rumor comes "waving his [shirt] bannerlike" and adopting "the important air of a herald in red and gold" [5]) but also more subtly in his use of machine and animal imagery to deflate potentially heroic moments.

Crane's desire to devalue the heroic in war stems in part from his stance as an ironist reacting against a literary and cultural tradition of idealized courage and chivalry. But another major element in his desire to reduce war to the commonplace arises from his casting of Fleming's experiences in the form of a "life" or initiation allegory. Henry Fleming is the universal youth who leaves home unaware of himself or the world. His participation in battle is his introduction to life as for the first time he tests himself and his preconceptions of experience against experience itself. He emerges at the end of the battle not entirely self-perceptive or firm-willed—Crane is too much the ironist for such a reversal—but rather as one who has encountered some of the strengths and some of the failings of himself and others. Crane implies that although Fleming may again run from battle and although he will no doubt always have the human capacity to rationalize his weaknesses, he is at least no longer the innocent.

If *The Red Badge* is viewed in this way—that is, as an antiheroic allegory of "life"—it becomes clear that Crane is representing in his own fashion the naturalistic belief in the interpenetration of the commonplace and the sensational. All life, Crane appears to be saying, is a struggle, a constant sea of violence in which we inevitably immerse ourselves and in which we test our beliefs and our values. War is an appropriate allegorical symbol of this test, for to Crane violence is the very essence of life, not in the broad Darwinian sense of a struggle for existence or the survival of the fittest, but rather in the sense that the proving and testing of oneself, conceived both realistically and symbolically, entails the violent and the deeply emotional, that the finding of oneself occurs best in moments of stress and is itself often an act of violence. To Crane, therefore, war as an allegorical setting for the emergence of youth into knowledge embodies both the violence of this birth and the commonplaces of life that the birth reveals—that men are controlled by the trivial, the accidental, the degradingly unheroic, despite the preservation of such accoutrements of the noble as a red badge or a captured flag. Crane shows us what Norris and Dreiser only suggest, that there is no separation between the sensational and the commonplace, that the two are coexistent in every aspect and range of life. He differs from Norris in kind and from Dreiser in degree in that his essentially ironic imagination leads him to reverse the expected and to find the commonplace in the violent rather than the sensational beneath the trivial. His image of life as an unheroic battle captures in one ironic symbol both his romanticism and his naturalism—or, in less literary terms, his belief that we reveal character in violence but that human character is predominantly fallible and self-deceptive.

Much of Crane's best fiction displays this technique of ironic deflation. In *Maggie*, a young urchin defends the honor of Rum Alley on a heap of gravel; in "The Blue Hotel," the death of the Swede is accompanied by a derisive sign on the cash register; and in "The Bride Comes to Yellow Sky," the long awaited "chivalric" encounter is thwarted by the bride's appearance. Each of these crucial or significant events has at its core Crane's desire to reduce the violent and extraordinary to the commonplace, a reduction that indicates both his ironic vision of man's romantic pretensions and his belief in the reality of the fusion of the violent and the commonplace in experience.

As was true of Norris and Dreiser, Crane's particular way of combining the sensational and the commonplace is closely related to the second major aspect of his naturalism, the thematic tension or complexity he embodies in his work. *The Red Badge* presents a vision of a man as a creature capable of advancing in some areas of knowledge and power but forever imprisoned within the walls of certain inescapable human and social imitations. Crane depicts the similarity between Henry Fleming's "will" and an animal's instinctive response to crisis or danger.

He also presents Fleming's discovery that he is enclosed in a "moving box" of "tradition and law" (21) even at those moments when he believes himself capable of rational decision and action—that the opinions and actions of other men control and direct him. Lastly, Crane dramatizes Fleming's realization that although he can project his emotions into natural phenomena and therefore derive comfort from a sense of nature's identification with his desires and needs, nature and man are really two, not one, and nature offers no reliable or useful guide to experience or to action. But, despite Crane's perception of these limitations and inadequacies, he does not paint a totally bleak picture of man in *The Red Badge*. True, Fleming's own sanguine view of himself at the close of the novel—that he is a man—cannot be taken at face value. Fleming's self-evaluations contrast ironically with his motives and actions throughout the novel, and his final estimation of himself represents primarily man's ability to be proud of his public deeds while rationalizing his private failings.

But something has happened to Fleming that Crane values and applauds. Early in the novel Fleming feels at odds with his comrades. He is separated from them by doubts about his behavior under fire and by fear of their knowledge of his doubts. These doubts and fears isolate him from his fellows, and his isolation is intensified by his growing awareness that the repressive power of the "moving box" of his regiment binds him to a group from which he now wishes to escape. Once in battle, however, Fleming becomes "not a man but a member" and he is "welded into a common personality which was dominated by a single desire" (30). The "subtle battle brotherhood" (31) replaces his earlier isolation, and in one sense the rest of the novel is devoted to Fleming's loss and recovery of his feeling of oneness with his fellows. After his initial success in battle, Henry loses this quality as he deserts his comrades and then wanders away from his regiment in actuality and in spirit. His extreme stage of isolation from the regiment and from mankind occurs when he abandons the tattered soldier. After gaining a "red badge" which symbolically reunites him with those soldiers who remained and fought, he returns to his regiment and participates successfully in the last stages of the battle. Here, as everywhere in Crane, there is a deflating irony, for Henry's "red badge" is not a true battle wound. But despite the tainted origin of this symbol of fraternity,

its effect on Henry and his fellows is real and significant. He is
accepted gladly when he returns, and in his renewed confidence
and pride he finds strength and a kind of joy. Crane believed that
this feeling of trust and mutual confidence among men is essential,
and it is one of the few values he confirms again and again in his
fiction. It is this quality that knits together the four men in the
open boat and lends them moral strength. And it is the absence
of this quality and its replacement by fear and distrust that characterizes the world of "The Blue Hotel" and causes the tragic
denouement in that story.

Crane thus points out that courage has primarily a social
reality, that it is a quality which exists not absolutely but by
virtue of other men's opinions, and that the social unity born of
a courageous fellowship may therefore be based on self-deception
or on deception of others. He also demonstrates that this bond
of fellowship may be destructive and oppressive when it restricts
or determines individual choice, as in the "moving box" of the
regiment. Fleming, after all, at first stands fast because he is afraid
of what his comrades will do or think, and then runs because he
feels that the rest of the regiment is deserting as well. But Crane
also maintains that in social cohesion man gains both what little
power of self-preservation he possesses and a gratifying and necessary sense of acceptance and acknowledgment difficult to attain
otherwise. Crane therefore establishes a vital organic relationship
between his deflation of the traditional idea of courage and his
assertion of the need for and the benefits of social unity. He
attacks the conventional heroic ideal by showing that a man's
actions in battle are usually determined by his imitation of the
actions of others—by the group as a whole. But this presentation
of the reality and power of the group also suggests the advantages
possible in group unity and group action.

There is, then, a moral ambiguity in Crane's conception of
man's relationship with his fellows, an ambiguity which permeates his entire vision of man. Henry Fleming falsely acquires a
symbol of group identity, yet this symbol aids him in recovering
his group identify and in benefiting the group. Man's involvement
with others forces him into psychic compulsion (Henry's running
away), yet this involvement is the source of his sense of psychic
oneness. Henry is still for the most part self-deceived at the close
of the novel, but if he is not the "man" he thinks he has become,

he has at least shed some of the innocence of the child. Crane's allegory of life as a battle is thus appropriate for another reason besides its relevance to the violence of discovery. Few battles are clearly or cleanly won or lost, and few soldiers are clearly God's chosen. But men struggle, and in their struggle they learn something about their limitations and capacities and something about the nature of their relations with their fellow men, and this knowledge is rewarding even though they never discover the full significance or direction of the campaign in which they are engaged.

The primary goal of the late nineteenth-century American naturalists was not to demonstrate the overwhelming and oppressive reality of the material forces present in our lives. Their attempt, rather, was to represent the intermingling in life of controlling force and individual worth. If they were not always clear in distinguishing between these two qualities in experience, it was partly because they were novelists responding to life's complexities and were not philosophers categorizing experience, and partly because they were sufficiently of our own time to doubt the validity of moral or any other absolutes. The naturalists do not dehumanize man. They rather suggest new or modified areas of value in man while engaged in destroying such old and to them unreal sources of human self-importance as romantic love or moral responsibility or heroism. They are some distance from traditional Christian humanism, but they have not yet reached the despairing emptiness of Joseph Wood Krutch's *The Modern Temper*. One should not deny the bleak view of man inherent in McTeague's or Hurstwood's decline or in Fleming's self-deceptions, but neither should one forget that to the naturalists man's weaknesses and limited knowledge and thwarted desires were still sources of compassion and worth as well as aspects of the human condition to be more forthrightly acknowledged than writers had done in the past.

Nor is naturalism simply a piling on of unselective blocks of documentation. A successful naturalistic novel is like any successful work of art in that it embodies a cogent relationship between its form (its particular combination of the commonplace and sensational) and its theme (its particular tension between the individually significant and the deterministic). There is a major difference, within general similarities, between Norris's discovery of the sensational in the commonplace and Crane's dramatization of the triviality of the sensational. This variation derives principally from the differing thematic tension in the two novels. Norris wishes to demonstrate the tragic destruction of McTeague's commonplace world by the violence inherent in all life, whereas Crane wishes to dramatize Fleming's violent initiation into the commonplace nature of the heroic. Norris and Crane occupy positions in American naturalism analogous to that of Wordsworth and Byron in English romanticism. Like the poetry of the two earlier figures, their fiction expresses strikingly individual and contrasting visions of experience, yet does so within a body of shared intellectual and literary assumptions belonging to their common historical and literary moment. The naturalistic novel is thus no different from any other major literary genre in its complex intermingling of form and theme, in its reflection of an author's individual temperament and experience within large generic similarities, and—at its best—in its thematic depth and importance. We have done a disservice to the late nineteenth-century American naturalists by our earlier simplistic conception of their art.

1965

SIX

⊣Nineteenth-Century American Naturalism⊢

An Approach Through Form

Most critics who discuss American literary naturalism do so both warily and wearily. What is one to say about this significant yet intellectually disreputable body of literature that ranges from the stylism of Crane to the antistylism of Dreiser, that is often characterized by a species of adolescent awe at the fact that the human will is circumscribed, and that, with the exception of Dreiser, continues into modern American literature more as a long shadow than as a living presence? After one has noted the foreign influences, the documentation of sensational lower class life, the too-ready absorption of contemporary scientism, and the intellectual confusion, there seems little to say, except perhaps to speculate on the twist of literary fortune that casts up this sport on the American scene while for the most part sparing our English cousins.

Edwin Cady's essay "Three Sensibilities: Romancer, Realist, Naturalist," in his *The Light of Common Day* (1971), is typical of much discussion of American naturalism. In order to distinguish among the major nineteenth-century American literary movements, Cady adopts the strategy of defining the literary sensibility or temperament that produced a characteristic work within each movement. He is remarkably perceptive and persuasive in describing the sensibilities of the romancer and the realist—the quality of mind which seeks to transcend the limitations of experience in the one and to affirm the moral and aesthetic value of our limited but shared perception and experience in the other—but his strategy fails him when he reaches naturalism. At this point he throws up his hands in despair at the incongruity between what naturalists appeared to believe about human nature and what such a belief implies about their sensibilities. He therefore concludes that in fact there is no such thing as a naturalist sensibility; there are only covert humanists and ameliorists playing with naturalistic ideas and subject matter. "Upon Norris and all the other artists of his richly endowed generation," Cady writes, "the sensibility of the naturalist exerted a magnetic pull. Nobody was a naturalist. There really are no naturalists in American literature. Everybody born after the Civil War felt and responded after his fashion to the terrible pull of sensibility in the grounds for which nobody finally believed."[1]

Cady's observation is of course true, but its truth is for the most part critically unproductive. Almost every major writer in any age is a humanist, and in more or less degree the distinctive shape he gives his qualified endorsement of the human condition is a literary mask—be it romanticist, realist, or naturalist—through which a gifted and feeling man speaks. To say that there are no true naturalists but only the "magnetic pull" of a contemporaneously compelling literary mask is to state an extreme instance of a general truth. Moreover, like so many critics of American naturalism, Cady begins with an ideal construct of the naturalistic ethos—principally that of a universe of forces in which man is an insignificant and even contemptible figure—and then finds that few naturalists coherently or consistently inform their work with this ethos. Thus, he approaches naturalism with the almost instinctive distaste of the intellectual toward writers who handle ideas sloppily.

What, then, are we to do with American naturalism, since it seems intractable to criticism and since we cannot erase it from out literary history? A possible way out of our dilemma is to seek critical approaches or strategies that bypass the hazards which result from considering naturalism primarily as a movement closely allied to its contemporary intellectual and social background. We might posit, for example, a critic of naturalism who has read a great many novels from Defoe to the recent past but little else. This reader would have a kind of sophisticated innocence. He would possess much awareness of how fiction works as an art form and of major changes in the form of the novel throughout its history, but he would be unaware of all matters involving the origins and the ideological and cultural context of particular moments in the history of the form. From the vantage point of this sophisticated innocence, our critic could look at some characteristic late nineteenth-century American novels to determine if they share, not traces of evolutionary thought or Zolaesque sensationalism, but rather a distinctive fictional style or shape that can be interpreted as a response of this generation of writers to their experience and which distinguishes this moment from other moments.

To begin, then. From the angle of vision of a sophisticated innocence, a work of fiction takes its form from its narrative of what happens to people when they interact with each other, or within themselves, or with their worlds, and thus create physical or psychological events. The major tradition in English and American fiction until the closing decades of the nineteenth century was to depict most sequences of events—that is, the physical, intellectual, or spiritual movement of characters through time— as progressive. Narratives were progressive not merely in the superficial sense of the moral romance, in which good characters were rewarded and evil ones punished, but also in the deeper sense of most great fiction from *Tom Jones* and *Pamela* to *The Scarlet Letter* and *Middlemarch*. Tom wins his Sophia and Pamela her Mr. B., the scarlet letter at last does its office, and Dorothea and Ladislaw though not as fresh as they once were are also not as illusioned. The world, in short, may be a difficult place, and man is imperfect, but the passage of time profits the bold and good-hearted and leavens life with judgment if not with wisdom. The major characteristic of the form of the naturalistic novel is that it no longer reflects this certainty about the value of experience but rather expresses a profound doubt or perplexity about what happens in the course of time.

When I say "the form of a naturalistic novel," I mean, of

course, not a single, describable entity but a complex of devices and techniques that differs in degree and kind from writer to writer and from novel to novel while still sharing certain general and therefore abstractable tendencies. In a book-length study, I would attempt to discuss all of the more prominent of these narrative tendencies. But on this occasion, I can examine only one—the naturalistic symbol—though I hope that it is a choice that usefully illustrates my principal observation about the form of the naturalistic novel.[2]

Here, then, are three late nineteenth-century narratives that a reader bred on earlier fiction would expect to end with an effect of progressive development or change: a story in which an honest working-class man begins to move into the lower middle class because of his occupation and because of an advantageous marriage; one in which a girl from the provinces survives the storms and hazards of the city and gains great success because of her natural abilities; and a third in which a raw country youth takes part in a great battle and proves his courage both to himself and to his comrades. In each of these novels—*McTeague, Sister Carrie*, and *The Red Badge of Courage*—there is a pervasive and striking symbol which, in a sense, accompanies the protagonist on his adventures. McTeague's is that of gold—the gold he works with as a dentist, the gold of Trina's hoard that he later covets, the gold mine that he discovers late in the novel, and in particular the gold-tooth advertising sign that to him means success and prominence in his profession and therefore a confirmation of his shaky sense of personal and social sufficiency. Carrie's symbol is that of the rocking chair in which she so often sits and muses about the happiness that she longs for, whether her anticipated happiness be that of pleasure, success, or beauty. And Henry Fleming's is a wound, a red badge of courage that testifies to his fellows that he is not the coward he fears he may be.

A major characteristic of each of these symbols is that it functions ironically within the structure of its novel. McTeague acquires more and more gold, from his initial small dental supply to the gold tooth to Trina's gold coins to an entire mine. Yet despite his gain of this symbol of wealth and therefore presumably of class and esteem, his movement from midway in the novel is downward both socially and personally until he reaches his final condition of a pursued animal. Carrie looks out over the teeming streets on her first night in Chicago and rocks and dreams of a happiness that consists of smart clothes, flashy men, and evenings at the vaudeville theatre. Eight years later, at the close of the novel, she is a famous New York musical comedy actress and has acquired all of these and more but she still rocks and dreams of a happiness that might be hers if only she could devote herself to the art of dramatic expression. And Fleming, having run from the battlefield in terror, acquires his red badge by a blow from one of his own retreating comrades. But when his red badge of ignominy is divorced from its source, it quickly begins to act upon others and eventually upon Henry as a sign of his honorable participation in battle.

I do not wish to suggest that these symbols and the narratives in which they occur are entirely similar. Obviously, there is much difference in tone, in depth of implication, and in literary success between Norris's arbitrary and often fulsome gold symbolism, Dreiser's skillful and evocative use of the rocking chair as a rhythmic symbol in several senses, and Crane's reliance on an intense verbal as well as structural irony when describing the effects of Henry's wound. Yet the symbols perform parallel roles in their respective narratives in that they structure and inform our sense not only that human beings are flawed and ineffectual but also that experience itself does not guide, instruct, or judge human nature. One of the principal corollaries of a progressive view of time is the belief that man has the capacity to interact meaningfully with his world and to benefit from this interaction. But the effect of the naturalistic novel, as is suggested by its symbolic structure, is to reverse or heavily qualify this expectation. McTeague, Carrie, and Fleming are in a sense motionless in time. They have moved through experience but still only dimly comprehend it and themselves, and thus their journeys through time are essentially circular journeys that return them to where they began. McTeague returns to the mountains of his youth and stands dumb and brutelike before their primeval enmity; Carrie still rocks and dreams of a happiness she is never to gain; and Fleming is again poised between gratuitous self-assurance and half-concealed doubt.

The form of the naturalistic novel therefore engages us in a somewhat different aesthetic experience than does the form of an archetypal eighteenth- or nineteenth-century novel. Whatever the great range of theme and effect of earlier novels, we are more or less instructed and elevated by our experience of their imagined worlds. That deeply gratifying sense of knowing so well the characters of a novel that we are unwilling to part from them at the close of the book is one of the principal effects of a fiction in which the confident moral vision of the writer has encouraged him to depict life with fullness, richness, and direction—with a sense, in short, that both internal and external experience have a kind of describable weight and value. But the form of the naturalistic novel begins to create an effect of uncertainty, of doubt and perplexity, about whether anything can be gained or learned from experience—indeed, of wonder if experience has any meaning aside from the existential value of a collision with phenomena. For what do the massively ironic symbols of McTeague's gold, Carrie's rocking chair, and Fleming's wound tell is but that life is sliding or drifting rather than a march and that the ultimate direction and possible worth of experience are unfathomable.

If the naturalistic novel is to be properly understood, however, it is necessary to qualify a view which maintains that its major impact is that of the inefficacy of time. For while the naturalistic novel does reflect a vast skepticism about the conventional attributes of experience, it also affirms the significance and worth of the skeptical or seeking temperament, of the character who continues to look for meaning in experience even though there probably is no meaning. This quality appears most clearly in Dreiser's portrayal of Carrie, who, whatever the triviality of her earlier quest or the fatuousness of her final vision, still continues to seek the meaning she calls happiness. It is present in a more tenuous form in the fact that Henry has survived his first battle—that is, his first encounter with life in all its awesome complexity—and is undismayed by the experience. And it exists faintly in the recollection we bring to McTeague's fate of his earlier responsiveness to the promise of Trina's sensuality and to the minor pleasures of middle class domesticity. So the Carrie who rocks, the Fleming who is proud of his red badge, and the McTeague who stands clutching his gold in the empty desert represent both the pathetic and perhaps tragic worth of the seeking, feeling mind and the inability of experience to supply a meaningful answer to the question that is human need. The naturalistic symbol thus accrues to the protagonist a vital ambivalence. It is both a sign of his identity, in that it represents the static reality of his goal or quest in an uncertain, shifting world, and it is a sign of the impossibility of fulfilling goals or of discovering meaning in a world of this kind.

Since I have been discussing the naturalistic novel in relation to some basic changes in the form of fiction, it would be useful to look forward to the modern novel in order to clarify the significant connection between the fumbling and tentative efforts of the naturalists to reflect through form a new vision of experience and the conscious and sophisticated formalistic experiments by many twentieth-century novelists that have been directed toward achieving a similar end. Obviously, some of the most distinctive qualities of the fiction of Norris, Dreiser, and Crane are in the mainstream of the nineteenth-century novel—the full documentation of Norris and Dreiser, for example, and the arch cleverness of Crane's narrative voice at its worst. Yet by again concentrating on the naturalistic symbol, we can see, I think, how the naturalistic novel stands on the threshold of the modern novel. First, as Richard Ellmann reminds us, one of the basic qualities of Joyce's fiction is his demonstration that "the ordinary is the extraordinary,"[3] that the movement of two men through a commonplace June day in Dublin contains a universe of emotional force and moral implication, though this universe may be expressed by such symbolic acts as those of masturbation and defecation. The gold tooth, rocking chair, and superficial head wound are also commonplace, even tawdry objects and events that symbolize complex and elemental emotions of pride, desire, and fear. Second, the ironic symbolic structure of the naturalistic novel anticipates the absence in much modern serial art of a progressive and developmental notion of time. Because Carrie is still rocking, because McTeague has returned to his original animal state (original both to him and to his species), and because Fleming, despite his wound, is still naively self-deceptive, we realize that time in the shape of experience has been less useful for these characters than it had been for a Dorothea Brooke or a Hester. Soon, indeed, novelists such as Joyce and Virginia Woolf and Faulkner were to discover even more innovative and radical ways to represent through form the insignificance of the forward movement of time in comparison to the timelessness that is the union of a character and his past.

I can perhaps now suggest, after having glanced both backwards and forwards, that the distinctiveness of the form of the naturalistic novel lies in the attempt of that form to persuade us, in the context of a fully depicted concrete world, that only the questioning, seeking, timeless self is real, that the temporal world outside the self is often treacherous and always apparent. The naturalistic novel thus reflects our doubts about conventional notions of character and experience while continuing to affirm through its symbolism both the sanctity of the self and the bedrock emotional reality of our basic physical nature and acts. Put in terms of the history of art, the late nineteenth-century naturalistic novel anticipates both the startling, convention-destroying concreteness and the profound solipsism of much modern art.

At this point we can usefully return to Cady and those other critics who have approached naturalism primarily in relation to its origin and ideas and can note the value of this approach once the stylistic distinctiveness and direction of the naturalistic novel have been established. The influence of Darwinism and French fiction, the notion that man is a brute and life a struggle, the belief that we are but ciphers in either a cosmic storm or a chemical process—this kind of awareness about what the naturalists absorbed and believed can help clarify our understanding of the themes that preoccupied individual naturalists in the muddy pool that is the coming together of a particular temperament and a historical moment. We need not ask which came first or which was predominant—the temperament, the overt beliefs and influences of the age, or the unconscious stumbling of a generation toward a different kind of fictional form. We need only realize that for this particular moment in literary history we have been neglecting the last as a way of controlling and shaping our awareness of the first two. We neglect at our peril the fact that *Moby Dick*, whatever else it may be, is a story of a whale hunt, and we are also in danger, critically speaking, when we neglect the equally simple observation that most late nineteenth-century naturalistic novels are about people who seem to be going nowhere.

1976

SEVEN

⊣The Problem of Philosophy in the Naturalistic Novel⊢

My starting point is the unalarming but often ignored premise that there is an important difference between studying a writer's philosophy as a system of ideas and examining a specific novel by him as a philosophical novel—that is, as a work in which an ideology explicitly expressed by the author within the novel serves as a means of explicating and evaluating the novel. This issue in the interpretation of fiction is especially pertinent to the criticism of the naturalistic novel, since naturalistic fiction— as in much of the work of Frank Norris and Theodore Dreiser— often contains quasi-philosophical discourse that is both blatantly intrusive and puerile in content. To properly criticize this kind of naturalistic fiction it is necessary, I would suggest, to recognize that ideas in fiction are not always what they seem to be.

The first point I would like to make about philosophical ideas in fiction is that they can serve as metaphors as well as discursive statements. Ideas of this kind are a special form of "objective correlative"—special because we usually associate that term with the concrete image. Their principal role in a novel is not to articulate a particular philosophy at a particular moment but rather to contribute to an emotional reality in the work as a whole. We have come to realize that ideas have played such metaphoric roles in other literary forms in earlier literary periods. We are no longer likely to discuss Alexander Pope primarily as a spokesman for specific eighteenth-century philosophical or literary beliefs, though these beliefs are expressed by Pope in his poems. Rather, we now recognize that Pope's beliefs represent metaphoric equivalents of certain perennial states of mind and that it is these equivalents that constitute the permanent poetic thrust of his work.

We have not, however, recognized that ideas in the modern philosophical novel can be interpreted as we have interpreted ideas in earlier and different literary forms. Indeed, the fact that there is a subgenre of modern fiction called "the novel of ideas" implies that ideas in fiction are a special literary phenomenon and that philosophical fiction is thus a special class of fiction. There are several reasons for this failure to recognize the similarity between the role of ideas in fiction and in other literary forms. The ability of the novelist to engage in lengthy philosophical discourse leads us initially to think of his ideas principally as ideas. In addition, the modern novel often expresses ideas that— unlike those of Pope—are either familiar or viable. Thus, when Thomas Mann or D. H. Lawrence voices an idea about politics or about love, his reader is apt to consider the statement as above all an idea about politics or love. He is less apt to realize that the idea might have the same relationship to the theme and form of the novel as a particular action, character, or setting.

These comments on ideas as metaphors are intended to introduce my first example of ideological expression in fiction, a passage from Frank Norris's *Vandover and the Brute*. The passage occurs at the close of chapter 14 of the novel. Vandover, a young middle-class artist, has been living a debauched life in San Francisco since his return from Harvard. At this point in the novel, he has just discovered that he can no longer draw. His sensual excesses have caused him to contract the disease of general paralysis of the insane (or paresis), an early symptom of which is the loss of finer muscular coordination. On the night that Vandover discovers his illness, he looks over the roofs of the sleeping city and hears a flood of sound, as though from an immense beast. Norris then comments in his own voice:

> It was Life, the murmur of the great, mysterious force
> that spun the wheels of Nature and that sent it
> onward like some enormous engine, resistless,
> relentless; an engine that sped straight forward,
> driving before it the infinite herd of humanity, driving
> it on at breathless speed through all eternity, driving it
> on no one knew whither, crushing out inexorably all
> those who lagged behind the herd and who fell from
> exhaustion, grinding them to dust beneath its myriad
> iron wheels, riding over them, still driving on the herd
> that yet remained, driving it recklessly, blindly on and
> on toward some far-distant goal, some vague
> unknown end, some mysterious, fearful bourne
> forever hidden in thick darkness.[1]

The passage is a statement of the idea that life is a struggle for existence. Life and its agent Nature are depicted mechanistically, as an engine that drives humanity forward, crushing the weak in the process. Although this process is ultimately beneficial, since it presses the race "forward," the primary emphasis in the passage is on the terror and awe-inspiring inexorableness of natural force. The meaning of the passage can be extracted from the novel to attribute a "hard" Darwinian philosophy to Norris, or it can be used as a commentary on the theme of the novel—that Vandover, a "laggard" in the herd of humanity because of his self-indulgence, has been caught up in the processes of nature (in this instance a debilitating disease) and will ultimately be destroyed, as indeed he is. In either instance, the passage is viewed principally as "philosophy"—that is, as an indication that Norris subscribes to a particular belief and that this belief is at the heart of *Vandover and the Brute*.

Vandover and the Brute, however, is only indirectly or

secondarily a novel about the struggle for existence. It is primarily a novel about the choices open to the artist in late nineteenth-century America. On the one hand, Norris associated art with man's "higher" self and with effort; it represents man's ability to pursue energetically the life of the spirit. On the other hand, he believed that the artist is often the victim of excessive sensibility and sensual self-indulgence. Norris's ideal artist is close to that depicted by Browning—a figure of robust spirituality who fronts life directly. But Norris's conception of the artist was also colored by the nineteenth-century myth of the demonic, self-destructive artist as that myth reaches from Byron and Poe to Oscar Wilde and the aesthetes of the 1890s. Both of these views are present in *Vandover and the Brute*, but the novel is informed principally by Norris's deep-seated belief that though the Browningesque ideal exists as ideal, most artists are incapable of reaching it and therefore succumb to their demonic tendencies.[2]

Norris's method of dramatizing this belief in *Vandover and the Brute* was to cast Vandover's decline in the form of a middle-class parable. After being introduced to the pleasures of the city, Vandover commits the heinous sin of seducing, getting pregnant, and not marrying a middle-class girl. He then loses the positive influences of Home and a Good Woman, and falls under the dominion of Drink, Gambling, and Disreputable Women until—a second heinous sin—he gambles and dissipates away his inheritance and is left ravaged by disease and poverty. *Vandover* is thus above all a parable of the Way to Hell available to the young American artist in a late nineteenth-century American city.

It is now clear, I trust, that Norris used the idea or philosophy of the struggle for existence in *Vandover and the Brute* primarily to make concrete the dangers inherent in the career of a self-indulgent, middle-class artist. The struggle-for-existence idea in *Vandover*, in other words, is principally an image of fear. Norris does indeed subscribe to the idea as idea, but the major function of this idea in the novel is not to state the idea but to dramatize the emotion. Its role is to make compelling an emotion that exists independent of the idea, an emotion that Norris might have expressed by some other means. His choice of this particular idea as a metaphor of fear was therefore primarily a product both of the contemporary pervasiveness and vitality of the idea and of its adaptability to his own ends.

Much of the critical attack on Norris in recent years has been concentrated on his simpleminded and overstated philosophical ideas. But ideas of this kind can contribute to a novel if they have principally a metaphoric function. Once it is recognized that fear permeates Norris's depiction of the artist, it is necessary to evaluate his philosophical passages dealing with the artist at least in part on the basis of the metaphoric impact of these passages rather than entirely on the basis of their intrinsic superficiality or melodramatic imagery. The philosophy of these passages may indeed be both superficial and overstated, but it can nevertheless successfully communicate the reality of fear. In all, the philosophy of the struggle for existence in *Vandover* should be viewed as a modern critic might view the pastoralism of a Renaissance poet. It should be considered primarily as a device by which the artist can transform a quasi-philosophical idea into evocative metaphor. The artist's success in this endeavor, whether he be Renaissance poet or naturalistic novelist, is more dependent upon his emotional resources and literary skill than on the permanent validity of the idea that serves as his controlling metaphor.

The second point that I intend to make about philosophical ideas in fiction is that such ideas are often inadequate guides to the interpretation of the novel in which they appear. Although the novelist seems to be supplying in a philosophical passage an interpretive key to the events he is portraying, he may have a false or superficial discursive grasp of the meaning of these events. Since an author's explicit commentary can run counter to the dramatic action of a novel, the function of the critic may be to apply yet another critical truism current in the criticism of other literary forms—that an artist is often an unsatisfactory commentator on the meaning of his own work. Again, it is more difficult to apply this dictum to the criticism of fiction than to the interpretation of other forms. An authorial comment within the work itself—as in a philosophical passage in a novel—appears to have more validity than an authorial comment in a letter or an essay. The first kind of comment seems weighty because of its immediacy; the second—removed from the work in time and place—can be viewed more objectively. But the history of literature abounds in examples of writers who are both great artists and inadequate critics of their own work, and we should not permit the presence of an author's philosophy in his novel to obscure the possibility of authorial myopia when we interpret that novel.

The philosophical passage from the work of Theodore Dreiser that I will examine occurs in *Sister Carrie* at the opening of chapter 8. At the close of the previous chapter, Carrie has left the Hansons' Chicago flat to move into a room that Drouet has taken for her. In nineteenth-century sentimental terms, she is soon to decide that a comfortable existence as a fallen woman is preferable to the hard life of a poor but honest working girl. Dreiser begins chapter 8 with a lengthy philosophical commentary on Carrie's action:

Among the forces which sweep and play throughout
the universe, untutored man is but a wisp in the wind.
Our civilization is still in a middle stage, scarcely
beast, in that it is no longer wholly guided by instinct;
scarcely human, in that it is not yet wholly guided by
reason. On the tiger no responsibility rests. We see
him aligned by nature with the forces of life—he is
born into their keeping and without thought he is
protected. We see man far removed from the lairs of
the jungles, his innate instincts dulled by too near an
approach to free-will, his free-will not sufficiently
developed to replace his instincts and afford him
perfect guidance. He is becoming too wise to hearken
always to instincts and desires; he is still too weak to
always prevail against them. As a beast, the forces of
life aligned him with them; as a man, he has not yet
wholly learned to align himself with the forces. In this
intermediate stage he wavers—neither drawn in
harmony with nature by his instincts nor yet wisely
putting himself into harmony by his own free-will. He
is even as a wisp in the wind, moved by every breath
of passion, acting now by his will and now by his

instincts, erring with one, only to retrieve by the other, falling by one, only to rise by the other—a creature of incalculable variability. We have the consolation of knowing that evolution is ever in action, that the ideal is a light that cannot fail. He will not forever balance thus between good and evil. When this jangle of free-will and instinct shall have been adjusted, when perfect understanding has given the former the power to replace the latter entirely, man will no longer vary. The needle of understanding will yet point steadfast and unwavering to the distant pole of truth.

In Carrie—as in how many of our worldlings do they not?—instinct and reason, desire and understanding, were at war for the mastery. She followed whither her craving led. She was as yet more drawn than she drew.[3]

The philosophy of the passage combines Spencerian evolutionary ideas and popular "ethical culture" thought, a combination much in vogue among liberal, nondenominational clergymen in the 1890s. Man is pictured as a dualistic creature. He still responds instinctively to life because of his animal heritage, yet he is also capable of rational choice. Nature ("the forces of life") is the absolute moral norm: if man were entirely instinctive in his actions, he would be in accord with that norm; if by free will he could choose the way of nature, he would also be acting correctly. Evolution is progressing in the direction of complete rational choice of nature's way. But at present man often finds himself divided and misled because of the conflicting demands of instinct and reason.

The passage, as becomes obvious in the concluding short paragraph, is an apology for Carrie's impending choice of an immoral life with Drouet. Carrie will sense the "wrongness" of the decision, Dreiser implies, because of the glimmerings of reason. But she is dominated by her instinctive needs—by the fact that Drouet represents at this point the full, rich life of Chicago that her imagination has pictured, and that he will supply shelter, warmth, clothing, and food (as well as appreciation and a kind of love) on a level far superior to that offered by the Hansons and on a level commensurate with her sensual nature, with her "craving for pleasure."[4] These instinctive needs associate Carrie with "the tiger [on whom] no responsibility rests"; but they do not disassociate her actions from moral judgment. Man's "reason" permits him to recognize that Drouet represents an inadequate—that is, immoral—fulfillment of Carrie's instinctive needs. Carrie herself, however, finds her instinctive needs too strong, her reason undeveloped and indecisive, and so she "followed whither her craving led. She was as yet more drawn than she drew."

Dreiser's attempt in the passage is to free Carrie from moral responsibility for her action—to suggest that not only Carrie but most men at this intermediate stage of evolutionary development are more led (and misled) than leading. But the passage also judges Carrie's action even though it does not judge Carrie herself. Going to live with Drouet—that is, sexual immorality— is not the "way of nature," Dreiser suggests. Some day, when evolution has progressed further, the "ideal" and the "distant pole of truth" will unwaveringly guide man, and the unmistakable implication is that they will not guide him toward sexual promiscuity.

The passage is readily understandable in the context of the late 1890s. Dreiser had just depicted his heroine as about to undertake a promiscuous life; his philosophical comments permitted him to placate the moral values of his age. Indeed, his comments also placated his own moral sense, for Dreiser in 1899 was in many ways still a conventional moralist when publicly judging the actions of others. A problem arises, however, if one attempts to apply the meaning of the passage to an interpretation of the dramatic action of the novel as a whole—that is, if one concludes that the reader is supposed to sympathize and identify with Carrie's instinctive drive towards "happiness" and "beauty" throughout the novel while simultaneously condemning the means she uses to achieve these goals. Such an interpretation of the novel as a whole is false. The three men in Carrie's life— Drouet, Hurstwood, and Ames—represent an upward movement on Carrie's part. Drouet introduces Carrie to a middle-class world of comfort, show, and finery; Hurstwood to a world of personal and social power; and Ames to that of the intellect. Each relationship serves to refine Carrie's response to life, to raise her above her previous values and desires to a higher stage of development and awareness. Happiness and beauty will never be hers, Dreiser tells us at the end of the novel, but it is clear that she is at least seeking them at a higher level with Ames than was possible with the Hansons. Within the dramatic context of the novel, therefore, Carrie's two illicit relationships are the opposite of what Dreiser has suggested about such relationships in his philosophical passage. They are moral rather than immoral, since they contribute to Carrie's "spiritual" development. In the course of the novel Dreiser has unconsciously changed his moral norm from one that explicitly condemns specific acts of immorality to one that implicitly renders these acts as moral if they contribute to a larger good.

Dreiser's philosophical comments in chapter 8 play a meaningful fictional role at that particular point of the novel. They contribute to the reader's compassion for Carrie ("a wisp in the wind") while disarming his possible moral judgment of her. The comments, in other words, are part of Dreiser's characterization of Carrie. But if we accept these comments as relevant to the themes of the novel as a whole, we will be interpreting and evaluating *Sister Carrie* on a level appropriate to the articulated conventional moral philosophy of Dreiser's day rather than on the level of Dreiser's inarticulate unconventional sense of the meaning of experience, a sense expressed by the dramatic action of the novel. And it is no doubt Dreiser's responses to life rather than his explicit comments on life that are the source of the "power" that many readers acknowledge in his fiction.

I have been attempting to suggest by means of two philosophical passages in American naturalistic novels that criticism of fiction must explicate such passages as complex fictional constructs rather than respond to them solely as ideas. The literal meaning of such passages may represent only a portion of their meaning (as in *Vandover*) or it may be an inadequate meaning (as in *Sister Carrie*). The presence in fiction of ideas of this kind is not, I believe, an immediate sign of aesthetic weakness. Rather, their presence suggests the rhetorical similarities between fiction and other literary forms in which ideas have always been more or less than ideas. All writers are "makers," and an idea in a novel is as much a "made" object as a character or an event. Our difficulty as critics of naturalistic novels that are also philosophical novels stems in part from our professional intellectuality, since we tend to assume that writers, as intellectuals, do not make ideas but think them. Our task as critics of philosophical fiction, however, requires that we not only understand an idea in a novel but, in a sense, that we refuse to understand it.

1970

EIGHT

Frank Norris's Definition of Naturalism

*F*rank Norris's definition of naturalism is important because an understanding of his use of the term may help to explain both his own practice of fiction and the more general American reaction to Zoalesque literary principles. My reason for reintroducing the much-debated question of Norris's definition is that I believe new light can be shed on the subject by the examination of not only his well-known "A Plea for Romantic Fiction," but also his less known "Zola as a Romantic Writer" and his relatively unknown "Weekly Letter" in the *Chicago American* of August 3, 1901.[1]

Norris placed realism, romanticism, and naturalism in a dialectic, in which realism and romanticism were opposing forces, and naturalism was transcending synthesis. Realism, to Norris, was the literature of the normal and representative, "the smaller details of every-day life, things that are likely to happen between lunch and supper."[2] Moreover, realism does not probe the inner reaches of life; it "notes only the surface of things."[3] Howells is Norris's archetype of the realistic writer. Romanticism differs from realism both in its concern for "variations from the type of normal life,"[4] and in its desire to penetrate beneath the surface of experience and derive large generalizations on the nature of life. Romanticism explores "the unplumbed depths of the human heart, and the mystery of sex, and the problems of life, and the black, unsearched penetralia of the soul of man."[5] To Norris "the greatest of all modern romanticists" is Hugo.[6]

Now what of naturalism? Although Norris at times called Zola a romanticist, it is clear that he intended in that designation to emphasize Zola's lack of affinity to Howellsian realism rather than to eliminate naturalism as a distinctive descriptive term.[7] Naturalism, as conceived by Norris, resolved the conflict between realism and romanticism by selecting the best from these two modes and by adding one constituent ignored by both. In his "Weekly Letter" to the *Chicago American* of August 3, 1901, he partially described this synthesis. He began with a distinction between Accuracy and Truth. Accuracy is fidelity to particular detail; Truth is fidelity to the generalization applicable to a large body of experience. Since a novel may therefore be accurate in its depiction of a segment of life and yet be untrue, Norris inquired what is the source of truth in fiction, if a literal transcription of life itself is inadequate. He began to find his way out of this dilemma when he asked:

It is permissible to say that Accuracy is realism and Truth romanticism? I am not so sure, but I feel that we come close to a solution here. The divisions seem natural and intended. It is not difficult to be accurate, but it is monstrously difficult to be True; at best the romanticists can only aim at it, while on the other hand, mere accuracy as an easily obtainable result is for that reason less worthy.[8]

Norris then asked:

Does Truth after all "lie in the middle?" And what school, then, is midway between the Realists and Romanticists, taking the best from each? It is not the school of Naturalism, which strives hard for accuracy and truth? The nigger is out of the fence at last, but must it not be admitted that the author of *La Débâcle* (not the author of *La Terre* and *Fécondité*)[9] is up to the present stage of literary development the most adequate, the most satisfactory, the most just of them all?[10]

Naturalism, in short, abstracts the best from realism and romanticism—detailed accuracy and philosophical depth. In addition, naturalism differs from both modes in one important characteristic of its subject matter. As Norris explained in his *Wave* essay on "Zola as a Romantic Writer":

That Zola's work is not purely romantic as was Hugo's lies chiefly in the choice of Milieu. These great, terrible dramas no longer happen among the personnel of a feudal and Renaissance nobility, those who are in the fore-front of the marching world, but among the lower—almost the lowest—classes; those who have been thrust or wrenched from the ranks, who are falling by the roadway. This is not romanticism—this drama of the people, working itself out in blood and ordure. It is not realism. It is a school by itself, unique, somber, powerful beyond words. It is naturalism.[11]

What is particularly absorbing in this definition is that it is limited entirely to subject matter and method. It does not mention materialistic determinism or any other philosophical idea, and thus differs from the philosophical orientation both of Zola's discussions of naturalism and of those by modern critics of the movement.[12] Norris conceived of naturalism as a fictional mode that illustrated some fundamental truth of life within a detailed presentation of the sensational and low. Unlike Zola, however, he did not specify the exact nature of the truth to be depicted, and it is clear that he believed Hugo's "truth" as naturalistic as Zola's. With Norris's definition in mind, then, we can perhaps understand his remark to Isaac Marcosson that *The Octopus* was going to be a return to the "style" of *McTeague*—"straight naturalism."[13] Although the early novel is consciously deterministic in its treatment of human action and the later one dramatizes a complex intermingling of free will and determinism, this contradiction is nonexistent within the philosophical vacuum of Norris's definition.

Norris's definition, however, is not only significant for his own fictional practice. It also clarifies some fundamental characteristics of the naturalistic movement in America. It suggests that for many Americans influenced by European naturalistic currents, the naturalistic mode involved primarily the contemporary, low, and sensational, which was elaborately documented within a large thematic framework. The writer might give his work a philosophical center—indeed, the naturalistic mode encouraged such a practice. But the core ideas or values present in particular works tended to be strikingly diverse from author to author, as each writer approached his material from an individual direction rather than from the direction of an ideological school. American naturalism, in other words, has been largely a movement characterized by similarities in material and method, not by philosophical coherence. And perhaps this very absence of a philosophical center to the movement has been one of the primary reasons for its continuing strength in this country, unlike its decline in Europe. For writers as different as Dreiser and Crane, or Farrell and Faulkner, have responded to the exciting possibilities of a combination of romantic grandioseness, detailed verisimilitude, and didactic sensationalism, and yet, like Norris, have been able to shape these possibilities into works expressing most of all their own distinctive temperaments.

1962–63

NINE

Stephen Crane's *Maggie* and American Naturalism

Stephen Crane's *Maggie: A Girl of the Streets* has often served as an example of naturalistic fiction in America. Crane's novel about a young girl's fall and death in the New York slums has many of the distinctive elements of naturalistic fiction, particularly a slum setting and the theme of the overpowering effect of environment. Crane himself appeared to supply a naturalistic gloss to the novel when he wrote to friends that *Maggie* was about the effect of environment on human lives. Yet the novel has characteristics that clash with its neat categorization as naturalistic fiction. For one thing, Crane's intense verbal irony is seldom found in naturalistic fiction; for another, Maggie herself, though she becomes a prostitute, is strangely untouched by her physical environment. She functions as an almost expressionistic symbol of inner purity uncorrupted by external foulness. There is nothing, of course, to prevent a naturalist from depending on irony and expressionistic symbolism, just as there is nothing to prevent him from introducing a deterministic theme into a Jamesian setting. But in practice the naturalist is usually direct. He is concerned with revealing the blunt edge of the powerful

124

forces that condition our lives, and his fictional technique is usually correspondingly blunt and massive. When Zola in *L'Assommoir* and *Nana* wished to show the fall into prostitution of a child of the slums, his theme emerged clearly and ponderously from his full description of the inner as well as outer corruption of Nana and from his "realistic" symbolism. Crane's method, on the other hand, is that of obliqueness and indirection. Irony and expressionistic symbolism ask the reader to look beyond literal meaning, to seek beyond the immediately discernible for the underlying reality. Both are striking techniques that by their compelling tone and their distortion of the expected attempt to shock us into recognition that a conventional belief or an obvious "truth" may be false and harmful. Perhaps, then, *Maggie* can best be discussed by assuming from the first that Crane's fictional techniques imply that the theme of the novel is somewhat more complex than the truism that young girls in the slums are more apt to go bad than young girls elsewhere.[1]

The opening sentence of *Maggie* is: "A very little boy stood upon a heap of gravel for the honor of Rum Alley."[2] The sentence introduces both Crane's theme and his ironic technique. By juxtaposing the value of honor and the reality of a very little boy, a heap of gravel, and Rum Alley, Crane suggests that the idea of honor is inappropriate to the reality, that it serves to disguise from the participants in the fight that they are engaged in a vicious and petty scuffle. Crane's irony emerges out of the difference between a value that one imposes on experience and the nature of experience itself. His ironic method is to project into the scene the values of its participants in order to underline the difference between their values and reality. So the scene has a basic chivalric cast. The very little boy is a knight fighting on his citadel of gravel for the honor of his chivalrous pledge to Rum Alley. Crane's opening sentence sets the theme for *Maggie* because the novel is essentially about man's use of conventional but inapplicable abstract values (such as justice, honor, duty, love, and respectability) as weapons or disguises. The novel is not so much about the slums as a physical reality as about what people believe in the slums and how their beliefs are both false to their experience and yet function as operative forces in their lives.

Let me explore this idea by examining first the lives of the novel's principal characters and then the moral values that control their thinking about their lives. Crane uses two basic images to depict the Bowery. It is a battlefield and it is prison. These images appear clearly in the novel's first three chapters, which describe an evening and night in the life of the Johnson family during Maggie's childhood. The life of the family is that of fierce battle with those around them and among themselves. The novel opens with Jimmie fighting the children of Devil's Row. He then fights one of his own gang. His father separates them with a blow. Maggie mistreats the babe Tommie; Jimmie strikes Maggie; Mrs. Johnson beats Jimmie for fighting. Mr. and Mrs. Johnson quarrel. Mrs. Johnson beats Maggie for breaking a plate; Mr. Johnson strikes Jimmie with an empty beer pail. Mr. Johnson comes home drunk and he and Mrs. Johnson fight—all this in three rather short chapters. Crane's fundamental point in these chapters is that the home is not a sanctuary from the struggle and turmoil of the world but is rather where warfare is even more intense and where the animal qualities encouraged by a life of battle— strength, fear, and cunning—predominate. The slum and the home are not only battlefields, however, but are also enclosed arenas. Maggie's tenement is in a "dark region," and her apartment, "up dark stairways and along cold, gloomy halls" (12, 15), is like a cave. Crane's description of the Johnson children eating combines both the warfare and cave images into one central metaphor of primitive competition for food: "The babe sat with his feet dangling high from a precarious infant chair and gorged his small stomach. Jimmie forced, with feverish rapidity, the grease-enveloped pieces between his wounded lips. Maggie, with side glances of fear of interruption, ate like a small pursued tigress" (19–20). By means of this double pattern of imagery, Crane suggests that the Johnsons' world is one of fear, fury, and darkness, that it is a world in which no moral laws are applicable, since the Johnsons' fundamental guide to conduct is an instinctive amorality, a need to feed and to protect themselves.

Once introduced, this image of the Bowery as an amoral, animal world is maintained throughout *Maggie*. Mr. Johnson dies, Jimmie assumes his position, and the Johnsons' family warfare continues as before. Maggie and Jimmie go to work, and each finds that struggle and enclosure mark their adult worlds. Jimmie becomes a belligerent truck driver, imprisoned by his ignorance and his distrust. He respects only strength in the form of the red fire engine that has the power to crush his wagon. Maggie works in a prisonlike sweat shop where she is chided into resentment by her grasping employer. Theirs are lives of animal struggle and of spiritual bleakness in which they only faintly realize their own deprivation. Maggie sits with the other girls in her factory workroom in a vague state of "yellow discontent," and Jimmie, the brawling teamster, "nevertheless . . . , on a certain starlit evening, said wonderingly and quite reverently: 'Deh moon looks like hell, don't it?'" (40).

The moral values held by the Johnsons are drawn almost entirely from a middle-class ethic that stresses the home as the center of virtue, and respectability as the primary moral goal. It is a value system oriented toward approval by others, toward an audience. In the opening chapter of the novel, Jimmie hits Maggie as Mr. Johnson is taking them home. Mr. Johnson cries, "Leave yer sister alone *on the street*" (14) (my italics). The Johnsons' moral vision is dominated by moral roles that they believe are expected of them. These roles bring social approbation, and they are also satisfying because the playing of them before an audience encourages gratifying emotionalism or self-justification. The reaction to Maggie's fall is basically of this nature. She is cast out by her mother and brother for desecrating the Home, and her seducer, Pete, rejects her plea for aid because she threatens the respectability of the rough and tumble bar in which he works. The moral poses adopted by the Johnsons and by Pete have no relation to reality, however, since the home and the bar are parallel settings of warfare rather than of virtue.

The key to the morality of the Bowery is therefore its self-deceiving theatricality. Those expressing moral sentiments do so as though playing a role before a real or implied audience. Crane makes the dramatic nature of Bowery morality explicit in scenes set in dance halls and theatres. In a dance hall, an audience of Maggies, Jimmies, and Petes listens enraptured to a song "whose lines told of a mother's love and a sweetheart who waited and a young man who was lost at sea under the most harrowing circumstances" (61-62). Later, Maggie and Pete see plays in which the

> heroine was rescued from the palatial home of her
> guardian, who is cruelly after her bonds, by the hero

with the beautiful sentiments. . . . Maggie lost herself
in sympathy with the wanderers swooning in snow
storms beneath happy-hued church windows. And a
choir within singing "Joy to the World." To Maggie
and the rest of the audience this was transcendental
realism. Joy always within, and they, like the actor,
inevitably without. Viewing it, they hugged themselves
in ecstatic pity of their imagined or real condition.
(70)

The audience identifies itself with maligned and innocent
virtue despite the inapplicability of these roles to their own lives.
"Shady persons in the audience revolted from the pictured villainy
of the drama. With untiring zeal they hissed vice and applauded
virtue. Unmistakably bad men evinced an apparently sincere ad-
miration for virtue" (71).

This same ability to project oneself into a virtuous role is
present in most of the novel's characters. Each crisis in the Johnson family is viewed by neighbors who comprise an audience that
encourages the Johnsons to adopt moral poses. In the scene in
which Maggie is cast out, both Jimmie and Mrs. Johnson are
aware of their need to play the roles of outraged virtue in response
to the expectations of their audience. Mrs. Johnson addresses the
neighbors "like a glib showman," and with a "dramatic finger"
points out to them her errant daughter (132–33). The novel's
final scene is a parody of Bowery melodrama. Mrs. Johnson
mourns over the dead Maggie's baby shoes while the neighbors
cry in sympathy and the "woman in black" urges her to forgive
Maggie. In the midst of her exhortations, "The woman in black
raised her face and paused. The inevitable sunlight came stream-
ing in at the windows" (161). Crane in this scene connects the
sentimental morality of melodrama and the sanctimoniousness
of Bowery religion. Both the theatre and the mission purvey moral
attitudes that have no relation to life but that rather satisfy
emotional needs or social approval. The heroes and heroines of
melodrama cannot be confronted with reality, but the church is
occasionally challenged. When it is, as when the mission preacher
is asked why he never says "we" instead of "you," or when

Maggie seeks aid from the stout clergyman, its reaction is either nonidentification with reality ("What?" asks the preacher) or withdrawal from it (the clergyman sidesteps Maggie). It is as though the church, too, were a sentimental theatre that encouraged moral poses but that ignored the essential nature of itself and its audience.

Both of these central characteristics of the Bowery—its core of animality and its shell of moral poses—come together strikingly in Mrs. Johnson. There is a bitter Swiftian irony in Crane's portrait of her. Her drunken rages symbolize the animal fury of a slum home, and her quickness to judge, condemn, and cast out Maggie symbolizes the self-righteousness of Bowery morality. In a sense she symbolizes the entire Bowery world, both its primitive amorality and its sentimental morality. It is appropriate, then, that it is she who literally drives Maggie into prostitution and eventual death. Secure in her moral role, she refuses to allow Maggie to return home after her seduction by Pete, driving her into remaining with Pete and then into prostitution. Maggie is thus destroyed not so much by the physical reality of slum life as by a middle-class morality imposed on the slums by the missions and the melodrama, a morality which allows its users both to judge and to divorce themselves from responsibility from those they judge.

Crane's characterization of Maggie can now be examined. His description of her as having "blossomed in a mud puddle" with "none of the dirt of Rum Alley . . . in her veins" (41) is not "realistic," since it is difficult to accept that the slums would have no effect on her character. Zola's portrait of Nana dying of a disfiguring disease that symbolizes her spiritual as well as physical corruption is more convincing. Crane's desire, however, was to stress that the vicious deterministic force in the slums was its morality, not its poor housing or inadequate diet, and it is this emphasis that controls his characterization of Maggie. His point is that Maggie comes through the mud puddle of her physical environment untouched. It is only when her environment becomes a moral force that she is destroyed. Maggie as an expressionistic symbol of purity in a mud puddle is Crane's means of enforcing his large irony that purity is destroyed not by concrete evils but by the very moral codes established to safeguard it.

But Maggie is a more complex figure than the above analysis

suggests. For though her world does not affect her moral nature, it does contribute to her downfall by blurring her vision. Her primary drive in life is to escape her mud puddle prison, and she is drawn to Pete because his apparent strength and elegance offer a means of overcoming the brutality and ugliness of her home and work. Her mistaken conception of Pete results from her enclosed world, a world that has given her romantic illusions just as it has supplied others with moral poses. Her mistake warrants compassion, however, rather than damnation and destruction. She is never really immoral. Throughout her fall, from her seduction by Pete to her plunge into the East River, Crane never dispels the impression that her purity and innocence remain. Her weakness is compounded out of the facts that her amoral environment has failed to arm her with moral strength (she "would have been more firmly good had she better known why" [115]), while at the same time it has blinded her with self-destructive romantic illusions ("she wondered if the culture and refinement she had seen imitated . . . by the heroine on the stage, could be acquired by a girl who lived in a tenement house and worked in a shirt factory" [72–73]).

There is considerable irony that in choosing Pete, Maggie flees into the same world she wished to escape. Like Mrs. Johnson, Pete desires to maintain the respectability of his "home," the bar in which he works. Like her, he theatrically purifies himself of guilt and responsibility for Maggie's fall as he drunkenly sobs "I'm good f'ler, girls" (150) to an audience of prostitutes. And like Maggie herself, he is eventually a victim of sexual warfare. He is used and discarded by the "woman of brilliance and audacity" just as he had used and discarded Maggie. In short, Maggie can escape the immediate prison of her home and factory, but she cannot escape being enclosed by the combination of amoral warfare (now sexual) and moral poses that is the pervasive force in her world.

In his famous inscription to *Maggie*, Crane wrote that the novel "tries to show that environment is a tremendous thing in the world and frequently shapes lives regardless." But he went on to write that "if one proves that theory one makes room in Heaven for all sorts of souls (notably an occasional street girl) who are not confidently expected to be there by many excellent people."[3] The second part of the inscription contains an attack on the "many excellent people" who, like Maggie's mother, immediately equate a fallen girl with evil and hell. Crane is here not so much expressing a belief in heaven as using the idea of salvation and damnation as a rhetorical device to attack smug, self-righteous moralism. The entire novel bears this critical intent. Crane's focus in *Maggie* is less on the inherent evil of slum life than on the harm done by a false moral environment imposed on that life. His irony involving Mrs. Johnson, for example, centers on the religious and moral climate that has persuaded her to adopt the moral poses of outraged Motherhood and despoiled Home.

Maggie is thus a novel primarily about the falsity and destructiveness of certain moral codes. To be sure, these codes and their analogous romantic visions of experience are present in Maggie's environment, and are in part what Crane means when he wrote that environment shapes lives regardless. But Crane's ironic technique suggests that his primary goal was not to show the effects of environment but to distinguish between moral appearance and reality, to attack the sanctimonious self-deception and sentimental emotional gratification of moral poses. He was less concerned with dramatizing a deterministic philosophy than in assailing those who apply a middle-class morality to victims of amoral, uncontrollable forces in man and society. *Maggie* is therefore very much like such early Dreiser novels as *Sister Carrie* and *Jennie Gerhardt*, though Dreiser depends less on verbal irony and more on an explicit documentation and discussion of the discrepancy between an event and man's moral evaluation of an event. *Maggie* is also like *The Red Badge of Courage*, for the later novel seeks to demonstrate the falsity of a moral or romantic vision of the amorality that is war.

Crane, then, is a naturalistic writer in the sense that he believes that environment molds lives. But he is much more than this, for his primary concern is not a dispassionate, pessimistic tracing of inevitable forces but a satiric assault on weaknesses in social morality. He seems to be saying that though we may not control our destinies, we can at least destroy those systems of value which uncritically assume we can. If we do this, a Maggie (or a Jennie Gerhardt) will at least be saved from condemnation and destruction by an unjust code.

Writers who seek greater justice, who demand that men evaluate their experience with greater clarity and honesty, are not men who despair at the nature of things. They are rather critical realists. Like William Dean Howells, Crane wishes us to understand the inadequacies of our lives so that we may improve them. Although Crane stresses weaknesses in our moral vision rather than particular social abuses, there is more continuity between Howells's critical realism and Crane's naturalism than one might suspect. This continuity is not that of subject matter or even of conception of man and society. It is rather that of a belief in the social function of the novel in delineating the evils of social life. If one sees such a writer as Crane in this light, the often crude and outdated determinism of early American naturalism lessens in importance. One begins to realize that American naturalism, like most vital literary movements, comprised a body of convention and assumption about the function and nature of literature that unprescriptively allowed the writer to use this shared belief as the basis for a personally expressive work of art. Crane's fiction is therefore permanently absorbing and historically significant not because he was a determinist or fatalist writing about the slums or about the chaos of war. His fiction still excites because his ironic technique successfully involves us in the difference between moral appearance and reality in society. His fiction is historically important because his expression of this theme within the conventions of naturalistic fiction reveals the relationship between critical realism and naturalism. But his fiction is perhaps even more significant historically because he revealed the possibility of a uniquely personal style and vision within naturalistic conventions. Our writers have responded to the critical spirit and the fictional sensationalism and freedom of naturalism without a sense of being burdened by doctrinaire precepts and forms. And it is no doubt this invigorating freedom within continuity that has been one of the principal reasons for the strength and influence of the naturalistic movement in America, from Crane and Dreiser to our own times.

1965

TEN

Self-Censorship and the Editing of Late Nineteenth-Century Naturalistic Texts

One of the still unresolved cruxes in textual theory and practice is the degree to which editors should restore to modern eclectic editions material that the author himself has cut or revised under either direct or oblique pressure. Proponents of such restoration argue that censorship of this kind violates the artistic integrity of the literary work in question. The textual editor who seeks to achieve, as G. Thomas Tanselle puts it, "the reconstruction of the text intended by the author," is thus obligated to attempt to distinguish between revision that is indeed authorial in the sense of refining the writer's intention and revision that is the result of a self-imposed censorship undertaken to make a work more acceptable or salable in the marketplace.[1]

Self-censorship has no doubt existed since the beginning of commercial publication or even before. One can imagine some ancient court minstrel thinking twice about a witticism involving the royal family as he tuned his lute. But for a number of reasons, the issue is far more prominent in the editing of fiction since the mid nineteenth century, and it has recently become especially

133

prominent in the editing of several major turn-of-the-century American novels. One obvious reason for this greater prominence is the inevitable clash between writers of fiction increasingly committed to portraying all phases of life and examining critically all beliefs and a standard of decorum, reflected in the attitudes of editors and publishers, prohibiting the public expression of such material. If you wish us to print your war novel *One Man's Initiation*, John Dos Passos was told in 1919 by his publisher, Allen and Unwin, you will have to remove any mention of prophylactics. It would have been futile for Dos Passos to argue that prophylactics were in fact widely used by American soldiers and that he was attempting to write a true account of the war in France. He made the change and the novel was published without the allusion.[2]

But perhaps the principal reason that the problem of self-censorship has begun to occupy such a major place in the editing of nineteenth- and twentieth-century fiction is the availability of manuscript evidence demonstrating or suggesting that self-censorship occurred. For a number of causes, ranging from changes in publishing procedure to increased authorial self-consciousness, writers have increasingly preserved prepublication drafts of their work. Whereas a manuscript version of a major work by Melville or Poe is a relative rarity, we have for most of the giants of twentieth-century American fiction a cradle-to-grave genealogy of their principal novels. In brief, the problem of self-censorship is before us because as we move toward the editing of more recent authors there is more of it and because the evidence that it occurred has been preserved.

On the surface, the problem would appear to be readily solvable in most instances. In that of *One Man's Initiation*, for example, we have available Dos Passos's correspondence with his publisher and an unrevised set of galleys for the novel that contain the passages Dos Passos agreed to change. There is incontrovertible proof that self-censorship occurred, and we have the material necessary to restore the novel to a version reflecting Dos Passos's vision of truth rather than his desperate desire to publish his first novel. Indeed the job has already been done, since Cornell University Press published in 1969 an unexpurgated edition of *One Man's Initiation* derived from the unrevised galleys.

But, in fact, many examples of possible self-censorship are

not so clear cut, and it is to several of these that I wish to devote most of my attention. The works I will discuss are Frank Norris's *McTeague* (1899), Stephen Crane's *The Red Badge of Courage* (1895), and Theodore Dreiser's *Sister Carrie* (1900). I have several reasons for selecting these works, not the least of which is that I have myself prepared editions of all three and am therefore familiar with their textual history. But also the three works are almost ideal "test cases" for the study of the general problem of authorial self-censorship. Each is an early work by a writer unknown at the time of publication and therefore particularly susceptible to pressure. Each is also a radical work in the context of its own era, both in subject matter and theme. For each there was significant revision that can be viewed as the product of self-censorship, and for each there is available the material needed to reconstruct the novel to achieve a version that reflects the author's intention before the supposed self-censorship began. Finally, *The Red Badge of Courage* and *Sister Carrie* have recently been edited in accordance with the belief that self-censorship did indeed occur. These radical new editions—*The Red Badge* in the new *Norton Anthology of American Literature* and *Sister Carrie* in the Pennsylvania Dreiser edition—are offered not merely as prepublication versions of the novels that are of interest to scholars, but as replacements of the texts that have been in currency for over eighty years.[3] The problem of the restoration of texts that have suffered from self-censorship is thus, in the form of these editions, upon us with a vengeance, and it behooves us to look closely at this problem.

Before examining the textual history of each of these three novels in greater detail, it might be best to take up some general issues involving authorial self-censorship. One obvious problem facing an editor who wishes to reject an authorial revision is that this practice violates the editorial principle that it is an author's final intentions that should be preserved in the text of an eclectic edition. Recent editors have responded to this problem in a variety of ways. So, for example, James Meriwether, in his discussion of the revisions forced upon Faulkner by his editors, claims that it is Faulkner's early versions of his works, before revision, that represent his "final intentions" because Faulkner had "little power to insist that his publishers carry out his intentions."[4] A related response, one adopted by Hershel Parker in a notable essay and by James L.W. West in the Pennsylvania *Sister Carrie*, is to insist on a distinction between the author as writer and editor.[5] As a writer, an author often expresses his final intentions in earlier versions because as an editor undertaking revisions, he is subject to various pressures or makes various ill-considered changes that pervert those intentions.

This desire to preserve Greg's emphasis on final intentions while seeming to fly in the face of that emphasis by the choice of earlier discarded versions of a text is not as perverse as it seems. In fact, it constitutes the triumphant entry of Greg's rationale of copy text into the field of editing nineteenth- and twentieth-century texts for which there is substantial manuscript material, for the basic thrust of Greg's rationale, given its origin in the editing of sixteenth- and seventeenth-century printed works, is to encourage a distrust in later versions of a text. I once remarked elsewhere, and only half-facetiously, that Greg's rationale, both in his stress on the choice of the earliest possible copy text and in his demand that later substantive variants prove their validity, is fundamentally puritan in character.[6] A text, like any other thing, is prone to corruption at the hands of men and must be constantly scrutinized for evidence of such decay. I would now add that the rationale contains as well an element of Romantic Neoplatonism. In the allegory of the journey of the text inherent in Greg's rationale and explicit in the practice of most modern textual scholars, a text emerges from its author's imagination trailing clouds of glory. Then, shades of the prison-house of unauthorized, ill-advised, and self-censored change close down upon it. In this allegory, manuscripts have a special sanctity or holiness, a condition that supports Morse Peckham's belief that we tend to create a hagiography for an author, which turns the work closest to the author into sacred documents.[7] Within this now almost religious allegory of the journey of the text, the editor becomes something of a priest. Confronting the inevitably corrupt thing that is the published text, he cleans it of its worldliness and restores it to its original purity.

No wonder, then, that there has been a rush recently toward the restoration of major novels to earlier states because of the adverse effect of self-censorship upon them. The reasons contributing to the undertaking of this task are numerous and powerful. Greg, when applied to these more recent conditions and problems, fully sanctions the effort. Also, the restored text, if a major revision of a major novel, is potentially an advantageous commercial venture, as witness the Pennsylvania *Carrie* and its simultaneous publication as a Penguin paperback. The attempt even brings textual scholarship into the mainstream of recent criticism, for what could be a more radical deconstruction of a text than to indeed reconstruct it from an earlier version and thus set all previous criticism on its head? It is with an understanding of these recent powerful impulses toward the rescuing of texts from the effects of self-censorship that I would now like to turn to the three examples of possible self-censorship, which I will discuss at some length.

Norris's revision of *McTeague* after its first printing offers a clear-cut example of authorial response to public reaction. The initial printing of the novel by Doubleday and McClure in February 1899 contains a brief incident at a variety theater in which little August Sieppi wets his pants. A number of reviewers commented on the vulgarity of the incident, and in the second printing of the novel, which followed shortly after the first, the passage was revised into a description of McTeague searching for his hat.[8] Since Norris was employed at that time as a reader for Doubleday and McClure and since the revised passage is unmistakably in his vein, the revision is no doubt his. The revision was incorporated into all later editions of *McTeague* until 1941, when the Colt Press of San Francisco republished the first printing. Since that time, editions of *McTeague* with any pretense toward textual accuracy have also used the first printing.

Crane's *The Red Badge of Courage* is a far more complex and ambiguous example of assumed self-censorship. Crane's first complete holograph draft of the novel contains a number of significant sections that are not in the first printing. These include a complete chapter—chapter 12 of the holograph—in which Henry Fleming seeks to philosophize about his condition, and a number of important passages in the last chapter in which Henry sums up his response to his initial experience of battle. Crane himself revised the holograph, the typescript, and proof, and at one or more of these prepublication stages, he cut these sections in which Henry's superficial and self-serving rationalization of his behavior is made glaringly apparent.

The existence of these passages has been widely known since 1952, when R. W. Stallman included a number of them in his *Stephen Crane: An Omnibus*, and since that time, numerous scholars and critics have referred to them and have included them in various ways in editions of the novel—occasionally in bracketed passages but more recently in appendixes or notes. In 1973, a facsimile of *The Red Badge* holograph was edited by Fredson Bowers. (The typescript and galley are not extant.) During the last several years, Hershel Parker, Henry Binder, and Steven Mailloux (the last two are former students of Parker's) have claimed that the 1895 Appleton first edition of *The Red Badge* was self-censored by Crane in his prepublication revisions to make the novel more palatable to his audience—more specifically, to his Appleton editor, Ripley Hitchcock—by eliminating some of Henry's more blatant weaknesses and thus suggesting more positively the possibility that Henry had indeed grown and matured in battle. Parker, Binder, and Mailloux made this claim in a number of articles, and Binder has edited the holograph of *The Red Badge* and offered it, in a frequently repeated phrase, as "the novel that Crane wrote" both in *The Norton Anthology* and in a separate publication.[9]

For Dreiser's *Sister Carrie*, the holograph draft of the novel also differs considerably from the first printing. In describing Carrie's and Hurstwood's natures and adventures, particularly in the Chicago portion of the novel, Dreiser was initially more explicit and expansive in presenting their sexual experience and in philosophizing on their condition. The draft ends with Hurstwood's death and lacks the concluding epilogue on Carrie found in the first printing. Revision in this instance occurred principally after the novel was put in typescript. At this point, encouraged and aided by his wife, Sallie, and his close friend Arthur Henry, Dreiser cut some thirty-six thousand words from the novel and revised the ending. At a later stage in the prepublication history of the novel, both Dreiser and an editor at Doubleday, Page removed some profanity and changed into fictional names a number of names of real places and persons.

The holograph of *Sister Carrie* has been available ever since H.L. Mencken presented it to the New York Public Library in

1937, and the revised typescript has been in the Dreiser Collection of the University of Pennsylvania since the collection was formed through the gifts of Dreiser and Mrs. Dreiser in the 1940s. Many scholars have examined and commented upon these two prepublication states. In 1981, the University of Pennsylvania Press published, under the textual editorship of James L.W. West, an edition of *Sister Carrie* based largely on the holograph. West's claim is that under pressure from Sallie and Henry to make the novel more respectable and thus more salable (as well as stimulated by Harper's refusal of the novel because of its unsuitability for its female readers), Dreiser accepted cuts and revisions suggested by Sallie and Henry that substantially weaken the themes of the novel. West's response to this belief is to attempt to differentiate between revisions of *Carrie* clearly attributable to Dreiser alone or clearly correcting mechanical errors and those that derive initially from Sallie and Henry. The first are accepted, the second not.

I will examine these three examples of presumed self-censorship in the context of four "tests" for accepting the belief that self-censorship has occurred and that restoration of an earlier state of the text is required. My purpose will be to discover if these tests can provide both a resolution of the specific question of self-censorship in these works and a general guide for the resolution of supposed instances in other works. In examining these examples and in offering this guide, I hope that it is clear that I am not putting forth a full solution to this complicated problem. Rather, I am seeking to begin a discussion that might eventually move toward some general agreement about the nature of the issue of self-censorship and about various ways of attempting to cope with it.

The first test is that of external evidence. How much do we verifiably know about the circumstances of the genesis of the work in question and in what ways do these circumstances bear on the question of self-censorship? Second, what can be determined or inferred about the motives of the author in making revisions? Here, the textual scholar becomes at once biographer, literary critic, and social historian, since the pursuit of authorial intent involves an effort to unravel various complex personal, literary, and social threads. Third, what are the differences in quality between the unrevised and the revised work? Is one better than the other in ways that are demonstrable through critical analysis? To put the question another way, will we be removing from the canon, because of possible self-censorship, a superior work? And fourth, are there grounds for considering the first published version of a major work—a version that has had currency for over half a century—as a historical artifact that should continue to occupy the role of general reading text even if it has been subject to self-censorship?

McTeague responds most readily and clearly to these four queries, and I will therefore discuss it initially and briefly. The external evidence in this instance is limited but convincing. The reviews were explicit in condemning the pants-wetting incident; Norris was a member of the firm; and he was shortly after the revision of *McTeague* to undertake a similar revision for similar reasons (the toning down of the details in his description of a hip operation between the serial and book publication of *A Man's Woman*). His motives for the revision are equally apparent. Excremental humor, he had no doubt discovered, may be permissible in a Zola but not in the work of an unknown American writer seeking a reputation. (It is of interest in this regard to note that there were no specific objections to the scene in which the lovesick McTeague explores Trina's mouth with his various instruments.) The change was comparatively minor and Norris made it without question, one would think. As far as literary quality is concerned, most critics would agree that the pants-wetting incident is far superior to that of McTeague searching ineptly for his hat. August's anguish and his mother's anger and embarrassment bring the theater-outing scene to a conclusion of mingled farce and catastrophe similar to most of the major climaxes in the novel. McTeague's search for his hat is lame and toneless in comparison. Finally, the revised scene is too brief—about a page of printed text—to have established any weight as an artifact. Without having their attention called to the passage by a note, most readers of the revised text would probably be hard put to recall what McTeague was doing at the close of the theater scene. Thus, on all four grounds—though admittedly without incontrovertible proof as regards external evidence and motive—there is full justification, I believe, in stating that Norris's revision of August's pants-wetting is self-censorship and that the modern textual editor should return the text to its earlier form.

Applying these four tests of self-censorship to *The Red Badge of Courage* produces very different results and opens up as well a number of major issues in the matter of the relationship of an author to his work. First, specific proof of pressure on Crane to revise *The Red Badge* is nonexistent, and outside influence must therefore be adduced through several oblique kinds of evidence. One such bit of evidence is that Crane later acceded to the demand of Ripley Hitchcock, the editor to whom he also submitted *The Red Badge*, that he cut from the revised edition of his novel *Maggie: A Girl of the Streets* profanity and slang and perhaps even an offensive passage on a "huge fat man" whom Maggie solicits toward the close of the novel. But the cutting of *The Red Badge* was of a fundamentally different nature, since it was not undertaken merely to eliminate troublesome language, and other external evidence bearing on revision is entirely negative. There is nothing in the correspondence between Hitchcock and Crane during the revision of *The Red Badge* or in the manuscript itself or in Crane's later comments about the novel to support the position that he revised it under pressure or that he in any way regretted the revision.

Although the question of authorial motive in the revision of *The Red Badge* is extremely tangled, G. Thomas Tanselle, in a recent survey of "the central questions of editing," demands that we engage the problem. "What the scholarly critical editor must do," he writes, "is to consider the motivation underlying textual changes; such an editor must try to disentangle the author's own wishes from the other elements that shaped the published text."[10] In an earlier essay, Tanselle offers as an example of such disentanglement the response by the editor of William Dean Howells's *The Rise of Silas Lapham* to Howells's revision of several passages in the novel between its serial and book publication. Howells's omission of an offensive passage on the Jews was clearly the product of his own second thoughts on the appropriateness of the passage, while his cutting of an allusion to the use of dynamite to resolve social problems was the result of criticism of the remark. The first cut was thus properly accepted by the editor, and the second was properly rejected and the passage restored to its original form.[11]

Tanselle's example, however, is far too simple and clear-cut for almost all the revision of *The Red Badge* and for the greater portion of the cutting and revision in *Sister Carrie*. Authorial motivation in these instances, and in most similar instances of the major revision of a work between early draft and printer's copy, is not reducible to the possible offensiveness of a few passages. Rather, it is often the question of the writer's basic conception of character and theme that is at stake. Disentanglement thus becomes, if it is attempted, an act of surrogate creative imagination as the editor seeks to determine why and how Crane and Dreiser grew dissatisfied with a significant aspect of the novel and undertook a major revision. As a critic, one welcomes such efforts, for the study of the genesis of a work of course often casts light upon it. But the more problematical question for textual scholars is whether efforts of this kind, whatever their interest as literary criticism, are sufficient to overthrow a text that has been established in the canon for some eighty years.

Crane's revision of *The Red Badge* and Dreiser's of *Carrie* also introduce the almost impenetrable issue of whether to some degree self-censorship is not inherent in any act of public authorship. Let us accept, for the sake of the argument, that Crane's motive in revising *The Red Badge* was indeed to "tone it done," to make it more palatable to Hitchcock and to a general American audience by portraying Henry Fleming, who is after all an example of the archetypal American innocent, as less obviously self-aggrandizing and self-deceived. But can it not then also be argued that this kind of translation of initial sentiment into expressive voice is inherent in most acts of communication? Indeed, there is a significant Freudian cast to the communicative act that is particularly pertinent for modern novelists. Crane and Dreiser had as reinforcements of their superego censors the awareness that friends, editors, publishers, and finally general readership would serve as judgmental audiences.

As one moves further into modern literature, the Freudian implications of the literary editor as father-figure and censor against whom the writer tests himself become especially obvious and important. How often, one wonders, has the power and attraction of a Maxwell Perkins or a Saxe Commins lain in the realization of their authors that their excesses would be chastized and corrected while their essential worth would be recognized and applauded? The issue in this instance, in short, is whether in seeking to "disentangle" motives and then rejecting supposed acts of self-censorship, we may not be in fact returning works of art to prepublic states of the untempered id—to states prior to the interaction between self and world that is inseparable from the expressive process. Textual scholars usually wish to see themselves as closely allied to scientists in the rigor of their procedures, but in this effort to discover and rescue the unsullied voice of the artist, they are reaching toward the high romanticism of pursuit of the ideal.

The third test for the rejection of self-censored revision—that of aesthetic worth—also fails to provide a basis for substituting the manuscript version of *The Red Badge* for the Appleton text. Binder, Parker, and Mailloux believe that the Appleton *Red Badge* is an inferior novel because there has been so much critical disagreement about it. Crane's attitude toward Henry at the close of the novel has in particular been interpreted as ranging from ironic condemnation to full endorsement. The manuscript version, however, offers greater evidence of Crane's belief in Henry's inadequacies and is thus a work of greater clarity, honesty, and force. This association of clarity with worth derives, unfortunately, from the simplistic and inadequate notions about Crane and about late nineteenth-century American naturalism of textual scholars who have had little close acquaintance with either. The entire drift of Crane studies during the past several decades has been toward demonstrating that he seeks, not only in *The Red Badge*, but in all his best work to render the essential ambivalence of our knowledge of experience given the sensitive but unreliable recorder of life that is the human consciousness.[12] Neither Henry nor Crane nor we, in short, can really know for certain the "true" meaning of Henry's experience. In addition, the drift of discussions of works written in the tradition of late nineteenth-century American naturalism has been toward demonstrating that they seldom fulfill definitions of naturalism as pessimistic determinism or the like but rather render experience with a profound union of belief and doubt. To see *The Red Badge* as a work of thematic clarity and of cynical contempt for the human condition, as Parker et al. wish us to do through the "restored" text of the novel, is to diminish what has attracted readers to the work from the beginning—a mix of tones, attitudes, and beliefs that is Crane's approximation of the modern vision.

Finally, there is the "artifact" test for *The Red Badge*. I don't wish by this approach to the problem of self-censorship merely to restate Morse Peckham's behavioristic view that a literary text neutrally records what has happened to it and is thus, not an object to correct, but something to study as a kind of archaeological repository of historical change.[13]

Clearly, as in the instance of *McTeague*, I believe that some texts should be corrected if evidence of self-censorship of the kind revealed there can be found. But the question of the text as artifact, as something worth preserving as part of our past, does enter, I think, in the example of *The Red Badge*, where the "restored" text differs so substantially from that of the first edition and where the first edition text has been part of the awareness of educated readers for four or five generations. It should be clear, I hope, that by introducing this problem I am not proposing that the manuscript versions of *The Red Badge* and *Carrie* should not receive attention and publication. In fact, as I noted earlier, these versions have been presented, not merely as aids to criticism and research, but as replacements for the general reader of the Appleton and Doubleday, Page texts. After eighty years of reading one version of a novel, we are to read another.

Let us again assume that there is more external evidence of self-censorship than I have discovered for *The Red Badge* and that the tests of motivation and quality are also more positive than I have found them to be. Would it be justifiable even then to remove from general circulation texts that have engaged a significant proportion of the American literate consciousness for most of the twentieth century? I may be on soft ground in this matter, but my sense of the issue is that I would prefer to continue to have generally read the version of the novel that emerged out of the tensions of the 1890s. It is this version that reengaged a generation of post-World War I writers who sought to find meaning in their own war experience, that lent itself in the 1950s to a religious reading, and that is currently exciting the interest of theoretical critics of several persuasions. The Appleton text is a palimpsest in that when we read it we are also reading a record of our civilization in the different ways that other men at other times have read it. The Norton *Red Badge* is just another new Civil War novel, one not as good as the novel it resembles and without its historical resonance.

For *Sister Carrie*, the question of possible self-censorship becomes almost sublime in its difficulty. There is no doubt that censorship occurred in the unauthorized revision in proof by Doubleday, Page of Dreiser's use of real names for persons and places. But the far more significant and problematical revision is that by Dreiser, Henry, and Sallie in the manuscript and typescript. That all three participated in the revision is incontrovertible; their hands are apparent on the manuscript and Dreiser later recalled Henry's major role in suggesting material to be cut in the typescript. What remains obscure are Dreiser's motives for accepting Henry's proposed cuts and for revising the conclusion of the novel, either on his own (as he claimed) or at the suggestion and with the aid of Henry and Sallie.

Dreiser later stated that the impulse behind cutting was to shorten an already lengthy novel and that he revised the ending in order to close the work with a passage on Carrie, its central figure, rather than with one on Hurstwood, as in the original draft. But it can nevertheless be reasonably argued that Dreiser's schoolteacher wife played the role of public censor in the revision and that Henry, who was far more experienced than Dreiser in the literary marketplace, played that of public buyer, and that in concert their effect on the cutting and revision was to bowdlerize the work of considerable sexuality, to lessen Dreiser's frank condemnation of some aspects of Carrie's and Hurstwood's actions and characters, and in general to make the novel more palatable to popular Victorian taste. This is indeed the claim made by West and his fellow editors of the Pennsylvania edition and is the basis for their restoration of *Sister Carrie* to its holograph state, with the exception of obvious errors corrected by Sallie and Henry and revisions that can be attributed solely to Dreiser.

One of the major weaknesses in this editorial procedure in

the Pennsylvania edition is that it was undertaken without a full application to the problem of Dreiser's method of composition in his other novels. All of the holograph drafts of Dreiser's eight novels were too long for publication. All were cut and further revised by a process Dreiser initially used for the editing of *Carrie* and that he came to rely on. Friends, editors, lovers, and even casual acquaintances read the manuscript and made suggestions for revision. Dreiser, as he did for *Carrie*, would then accept some suggestions and reject others. There was nothing extraordinary, in short, about the cutting of *Carrie* by Henry and Sallie. Dreiser depended on them just as he was later to depend on his literary acquaintances James Huneker, Floyd Dell, and James T. Farrell, his editors T.R. Smith, Louise Campbell, and Donald Elder, and his lovers and secretaries Sallie Kusell and Estelle Kubitz. Any effort to distinguish between Dreiser as writer and editor in the revision of *Sister Carrie* must also confront the fact that Dreiser throughout his career denied through his practice as author that a distinction of this kind could and should be made. Dreiser as a kind of editor-in-chief of his novels received, absorbed, and responded to the editorial suggestions of others, whatever the quality of or motivation behind these suggestions. But the final responsibility was always his, except perhaps in the case of *The Bulwark*, when he was too sick and old to care about what Louise Campbell did to the novel.

Dreiser's revision of the conclusion of *Sister Carrie* must also be seen within the context of his general practice. He always had difficulty with endings and changed, usually radically, six of the conclusions of his eight novels. For *Jennie Gerhardt*, after the novel was read in typescript by a number of friends, he revised the end from a happy to a tragic conclusion and also added a lachrymose epilogue about Jennie parallel to that on Carrie. *The "Genius"* also had its ending radically revised between late typescript and publication. Dreiser appears to be a writer who was often of two minds about the ending of his novels, with the conclusion of an early draft no more than a trying out—on himself and others—of a possible ending. The revised ending of *Sister Carrie*, it should be noted, is not as severe a revision as some, since Hurstwood's suicide is left intact. In a manner characteristic of the endings of most of Dreiser's novels, it concludes on a both cosmic and bathetic note rather than a circumstantial one.

To look more closely once again at the revision of *Carrie*, Dreiser's motives for accepting the suggestions of Henry and Sallie cannot be untangled. On the one hand, he was anxious to have the novel published because he believed in its quality, because he hoped that it would be financially successful and he depended on his writing for his livelihood, and because he had more than the usual degree of authorial vanity. So when Sallie and Henry suggested various verbal niceties or toned down a sexual passage or cut sections of extended analysis of Carrie's and Hurstwood's state of mind, he was perhaps heeding the call of success as defined by them and was engaged in acts of self-censorship. On the other hand, before *Sister Carrie*, Dreiser had never written an extended piece of fiction. Indeed, he had begun writing short stories, at the age of twenty-eight, only the summer before he began *Carrie*. The novel in its first draft is diffuse, overextended, and repetitious. It can reasonably be argued that any professional editor—and Henry had been a newspaper editor for some years—would seek to cut it and that most authors would recognize the legitimacy of these cuts. Moreover, there is no evidence that Dreiser during the remaining forty-five years of his life ever expressed dissatisfaction with the cutting of *Sister Carrie* or a wish to return the novel to its original form. From 1907, the copyright was his, and with some additional expense he could have had the novel reset. When one considers that in 1926, after the great success of *An American Tragedy* made him comparatively wealthy, he undertook to revise *The Financier* because he was dissatisfied with the novel in its 1912 first-edition form, the failure to publish a "true" *Sister Carrie* becomes even more significant.

To sum up where we are in this account of Dreiser's possible motives in the revision of *Carrie*: First, Dreiser's practice in revising *Carrie* did not differ from that in his other novels. If he practiced self-censorship in revising *Carrie*, self-censorship is inseparable from his notion of the act of authorship. Second, he never rejected the revision of *Carrie*. And third, of the over two-hundred block cuts suggested by Henry and accepted by Dreiser, some are of sexual material, but the great majority are of noncontroversial commentary and scene for which a variety of motives could be legitimately advanced. If an editor were indeed to attempt to disentangle the motives behind every such revision, each editor of *Sister Carrie* and of similar works would in effect be creating a new novel somewhat as a child with a selection of cut-out doll clothes can create a large variety of costumes for her doll by varying her selection. No wonder, then, that West in editing *Sister Carrie* rejects this task and opts instead for the practice of assuming that all suggestions made by Henry are tainted by their origin whatever their nature and whatever their effect on the novel. This method solves the problem of motive by ignoring it. West has in effect published the first draft of the novel slightly emended to reflect those later revisions that are entirely attributable to Dreiser. The Pennsylvania edition is thus, not a modern eclectic edition, but in truth principally an old-fashioned diplomatic edition.

But what of the literary worth of the Pennsylvania edition of *Sister Carrie*? Here, too, the matter is inconclusive, and undoubtedly different readers will prefer different versions of the novel. If I were Arthur Henry in the spring of 1900 in New York, and Dreiser were to ask my advice about the first draft of his novel, I would tell him to cut a good deal of the extended authorial commentary and description, to flesh out more fully the character and role of Ames in the last portion of the novel, and to seek to end with some comment on Carrie, the novel's heroine, but to avoid the tremulous key. In short, I find that most of the revision improves the novel and that in particular the removal of thirty-six thousand words contributes to the pace of the work. I might wish to restore a few of the cut passages on Carrie and Hurstwood, but even these frequently don't so much change our conception of the characters as make more explicit certain features otherwise indirectly rendered. Behind the ballyhoo attached to the "discovery" of the "true" *Sister Carrie*, the Pennsylvania edition is simply not that clearly better or worse than the Doubleday, Page version of 1900. The principal impression of most general readers familiar with the first edition will be, I believe, simply that it is longer.

Careful readers of the Pennsylvania edition may well notice, however, an anomaly not present in the 1900 *Carrie* but "restored" by West nevertheless. As Dreiser wrote the Chicago portion of the novel, he depended for his characterization of Carrie and Hurstwood largely on his knowledge of his wayward sister, Emma, and her saloon manager lover, and his description of them has a number of harshly critical notes. When Carrie and Hurstwood reach New York, however, Dreiser projected more and more of himself into their hopes and fears—into Carrie the aspiring artist and Hurstwood the tragic failure. I believe that when Henry and Dreiser reread the novel in typescript, they realized this discrepancy in characterization, and that many of the cuts in the Chicago portion of the novel—the portion indeed that was most cut—were efforts to correct it. By publishing the holograph version of the novel, the Pennsylvania editors may be, as they claim, "restoring Carrie and Hurstwood to their original clarity of outline," but that outline is in fact one Dreiser rejected in the course of writing and revising the novel. To stress, as Dreiser does in the holograph, Carrie's easy susceptibility to sexual temptation and Hurstwood's sexual culpability is to run counter to the elevated sensibility and tragic fate that Dreiser eventually gave his central figures. The belief that self-censorship implies the removal of material offensive to popular taste but necessary for the full aesthetic effect of the novel ignores the situation, as in *Sister Carrie*, in which this material has indeed become unnecessary given the author's evolving sense of the aesthetic effect he wishes to achieve in the novel.

Of the important character of the 1900 edition of *Sister Carrie* as artifact there can be no question. Dreiser's own generation and several thereafter believed that the novel played a pivotal role in the emergence of a modern American literature. And Dreiser's concluding image of Carrie—in the epilogue not present in the Pennsylvania edition—rocking and dreaming at her window, forever seeking and never finding happiness, has become an archetypal symbol of the questing but unfulfilled artistic imagination. As with *The Red Badge*, given the problematical validity of the Pennsylvania edition of *Sister Carrie*, I would opt firmly for the first-edition text as the work I would prefer to examine critically as Dreiser's novel and to have students read. If we are to read *Sister Carrie* as a novel of 1900, I would prefer to read the novel that emerged out of the personal tensions, conflicting motives, and cultural complexities of that moment and that in the eighty years since its publication has accrued a rich public responsiveness and role. I would not care to read a *Carrie* that has in effect been created out of the textual editing controversies and theorizing of the 1960s and 1970s.

What, finally, can I offer as general counsel? First, beware of the siren call of early drafts. They are, more often than not, discarded drafts and are best regarded as aids toward understanding the evolution of the text rather than as replacements of the text. Second, tread very carefully when seeking to distinguish between the author as writer and as editor and among various motives leading to authorially sanctioned revision. Where external evidence of self-censorship is lacking, and where the passages are themselves not clearly objectionable to contemporary taste, give the author's creative imagination in its role of self-critic (rather than of self-censor) the final word. Third, edit a single work for self-censorship only after gaining full familiarity with its author's total work and with the major criticism bearing on the author's total work. Fourth, accept the proposition that texts reflect the vagaries of human nature and experience and that, when other conditions such as external evidence and aesthetic worth are inconclusive, there is some advantage in opting for the established and known vagary rather than a new and perhaps even more dramatic example of human failing.

I will conclude with a brief anecdote and a briefer moral drawn from it. When John Dos Passos was asked later in life about the bowdlerization of *Three Soldiers* that he had accepted some thirty-five years earlier, he responded that he "occasionally regretted it and occasionally not regretted it."[14] Dos Passos's ambivalence and his failure to insist in changed times on a restored *Three Soldiers* may well serve as "a motto and brief description of our now concluded legend." When there is a degree of doubt in question of self-censorship, leave the text alone.

1985

The Twentieth Century

ELEVEN

American Naturalism in Its "Perfected" State

The Age of Innocence *and* An American Tragedy

Naturalism has been a significant literary movement in American for almost a century. From the early work of Stephen Crane and Frank Norris to the recent novels of Robert Stone and William Kennedy, the subject matter and fictional form of naturalism have continually attracted writers of stature.[1] Of course, given the problematical philosophical base of naturalism, and given as well the often sensationalistic contents of a typical naturalistic novel, the movement has also been subject to intense attack. Indeed, one common assertion by those who would deny significance to naturalism in America is to claim that the movement failed to survive its high point in the 1890s—this despite the powerful thread of naturalistic expression in most major American writers, including Hemingway and Faulkner, from the nineties to our own time.

But naturalism, despite this critical hostility, refûses to go away, and thus, willy-nilly, has attracted a historiography over the last thirty or forty years—a historiography that contains several seemingly permanent and irrefutable assumptions about the movement. The difficulty presented by these assumptions, of course, is that they may serve to hinder rather than aid in the identification of works that can usefully be discussed as naturalistic. This screening role often played by the conventional historiography of American naturalism is nowhere more evident than in the almost complete neglect of Edith Wharton in discussions of the movement. In an effort to locate Wharton's major work more clearly and fully within American naturalism, I will initially discuss those beliefs about the history of American naturalism that have prevented a close examination of her most finished novel, *The Age of Innocence*, as naturalistic fiction. I will then take up *The Age of Innocence* and Theodore Dreiser's *An American Tragedy* as "companion" novels, using the more readily identifiable naturalism of Dreiser's work to confirm the naturalism of Wharton's.

One of the major assumptions about American naturalism is that it is a literature that is closely attuned to, and indeed derives from, "hard times."[2] The naturalist, it is believed, grounds his fiction in the social realities of his historical moment and he therefore cannot help being especially responsive to social reality when that reality impinges cruelly on the fates of most men. Or, to put the matter somewhat differently, the naturalistic ethos, which views man as circumscribed by conditions of life over which he has no control, appears to be confirmed during periods of social malaise and individual hardship. The history of American naturalism seems to support this interpretation of the movement. Naturalism first took hold in America during the economic hard times and social turmoil of the 1890s; it achieved a second major flowering during the 1930s depression; and it appeared as a significant force for a third time during the difficult political conditions occasioned by the onset of McCarthyism and the Cold War in the late 1940s and early 1950s. Indeed, many of the archetypal scenes of American naturalism—of futilely looking for work, for example, as do Hurstwood and Studs Lonigan, or of being killed by a bullet or club that is the symbolic equivalent of an all-powerful economic or political force, as are Annixter and Jim Casy—derive from the contemporary social immediacies in which these works are set. Naturalism, in this assumption about its periodicity, is thus like a dermatological condition. Its appearance usually signifies a disturbance elsewhere in the organism. When the patient gets better, the spots disappear.

A second major belief about naturalism is that it is, to use Dreiserian slang, a young man's game, with both modifiers—young and man—operative. A moment's reflection produces evidence that appears to bear out this view. Frank Norris, Stephen Crane, and Theodore Dreiser were all in their twenties when they wrote important naturalistic novels, and John Dos Passos, James T. Farrell, and John Steinbeck were hardly much older when they published major naturalistic fiction in the 1930s. During the years following World War II, it was the very early fiction of Norman Mailer, William Styron, and Saul Bellow—novels such as *The Naked and the Dead*, *Lie Down in Darkness*, and *The Adventures of Augie March*—that are among the most naturalistic of their works. Two observations arise from these facts. The first is that naturalism appears to attract writers in their youth and then fade as an interest. Crane and Norris of course died when still very young, but otherwise all the writers I have named moved on to other kinds of fiction as their careers advanced. Even Dreiser, who wrote naturalistic novels in his 40s and 50s, went on to a very different kind of fiction in his last years in the semimystical allegories of *The Bulwark* and *The Stoic*. The second observation is that naturalism appears to be entirely the province of male authors. Together, the two observations constitute an implicit indictment of the quality and importance of naturalism. The naturalistic novel, it seems, is the product of a masculine late adolescence frame of mind that has overreacted both to the physical in life and to the deep disappointment that life as found is not as it was promised. An underlying premise of this indictment is that writers within the naturalistic movement lack the fine tuning of the imaginative temperament that women authors presumably have from birth and which the male author will gradually achieve, though some—like Dreiser—show an arrested development well into their careers. Naturalism is thus principally the expression of crass, youthful, male authors. To demonstrate the force of this assumption one need only recall the distaste that naturalism as a literary form occasioned among the followers of Henry James once James assumed—in the early 1940s—his position as the consummate artistic and moral sensibility.[3]

A third—and last—major assumption about naturalism as a literary movement is closely related to its presumed origins as a form of social realism written largely by young men. Naturalism, it has been believed for almost its entire history, is not conducive to artistic expression. Initially it was often denigrated as art by claims that it was a kind of photography in verbal form. But when photography itself emerged as a major art, the notebook took its place as a metaphor of the naturalist's unmediated documentation of external experience. The naturalist might have an accurate sense of how to butcher a hog or of the workings of a Model T, but was the expression of this knowledge art? The answer was usually "no." Norris's often heavy-handed symbolism or Dreiser's disastrous ventures into purple prose were also frequently cited as sure evidence of the inadequacy of the naturalist when he sought to push beyond a documentary style. Thus a kind of naturalism/art inverse ratio was established in the historiography of American naturalism. Writers who were obviously self-conscious and innovative literary craftsmen—a Crane or Faulkner—could not be naturalists, while writers who appeared most clearly to have plowed the dull furrows of documentary realism—a Dreiser or Farrell—were consummate naturalists. And in the critical analysis of any one novel, the less naturalism found by the critic the more likely was he to praise the novel for its artistic strength. Naturalism, in brief, was not a technique but a literary bludgeon. And though bludgeons might create an effect, that effect was a different and lesser thing than the one obtained by a genuine work of art.

These historical and critical platitudes about naturalism that I have been describing do indeed have a certain truth. Naturalism has flourished among difficult social conditions, much naturalistic fiction is written by young men, and naturalism of the poorer sort does have its dull and blatant reaches. But the movement is also—and this is my central point—a far more complex critical and historical phenomenon than is implied by these clichés. The naturalistic novel, in other words, can also emerge during good times; it can be written by mature male *and* female authors; and it can express naturalistic themes with great fictional artistry.

Theodore Dreiser's *An American Tragedy* and Edith Wharton's *The Age of Innocence* are major examples of naturalistic fiction that lie outside of these clichés.[4] Both works appeared during the comparatively flush times of the 1920s—*The Age of Innocence* in 1920, *An American Tragedy* in 1925—and both were written when their authors were in full maturity. (Wharton was fifty-eight, Dreiser fifty-four.) And both works illustrate the highest fictional craftsmanship.

Given their obvious differences in subject matter and fictional form, it is perhaps difficult to recall that both *The Age of Innocence* and *An American Tragedy* are also historical novels of a special and essentially similar kind. Wharton's novel is set in upper-class New York of the 1870s. And *An American Tragedy*, though set in the 1920s, is based on a 1906 incident and, even more pertinently, was grounded in Dreiser's preoccupation since the 1890s in a distinctively late nineteenth-century configuration of the American dream of success.[5] Through the dramatization of an unconsummated love affair on the one hand and a sensational murder case on the other, Wharton and Dreiser seek to depict some of the limitations placed on human freedom by the social and moral nature of late nineteenth-century American life.

One way to begin describing what Wharton and Dreiser wish to say about American life of their youth is to realize that beneath the urbane wit of Wharton and the discursive expansiveness of Dreiser the two novels contain a striking similarity of plot. In *An American Tragedy*, Clyde Griffiths, a young man of poor and uncultured background, makes his way to the upstate New York town of Lycurgus, where he is given employment in his uncle's collar factory. There he falls in love with and has a secret affair with Roberta, a fellow worker in the factory who is from an equally impoverished background. But he also meets and attracts Sondra, the daughter of a wealthy local manufacturer. Desperately anxious to push his way upward, and seeing a marriage to Sondra as a means of doing so, Clyde is about to break off with Roberta when she announces that she is pregnant. In *The Age of Innocence*, Newland Archer, a young man from one of the best and oldest New York families, believes himself in love with May Welland, an equally well-bred girl of his set. Their courtship proceeds placidly until Archer encounters Ellen Olenska and finds himself deeply drawn to her. Ellen, though originally from Archer's world, has disgraced herself in an unfortunate foreign marriage and now is merely tolerated in upper-class New York society. Despite the increasing attraction of Ellen, Archer goes through with the marriage to May. But he is restless and bored in the marriage, he and Ellen express their love for each other, and he is about to tell May that he is leaving her for Ellen when May announces her pregnancy. It is on this fulcrum of an unexpected and undesired pregnancy that both novels balance. Roberta's pregnancy forces Clyde into a series of actions with fatal consequences for them both, and May's pregnancy forces Newland into the inaction of an acceptance of his marriage to May. The themes inherent in these events can be examined for signs of a common naturalistic ethos shared by the two novels, an ethos that can also constitute evidence of the existence of a naturalistic fiction that transcends the limitations placed on the movement by its conventional historiography.

By the 1920s, the naturalistic impulse had refined itself into a more subtle representation of the qualifications placed on man's freedom than was true of naturalistic works of the 1890s. Here are no degenerate parents causing foul hereditary streams to run in the veins of their children, as in Norris's *McTeague*. And here, too, are no such melodramatic renderings of social constraint as an East Side slum or the "moving box" of a military unit in combat, as in Crane's *Maggie* and *The Red Badge of Courage*. Rather, the theme of constraint is dramatized within more domesticated and everyday phases of life, and those constrained within these phases are more like the common run of humanity. Both Dreiser and Wharton, in short, have chosen to push American naturalism away from the direction represented by *McTeague* and *Maggie* and more toward that implied by Dreiser's own *Sister Carrie*, in which largely commonplace characters are drawn toward their destinies within the largely commonplace world of American city life.

In *An American Tragedy*, the capacity of the individual to

be shaped by the ordinary world in which he lives can best be illustrated by Clyde's early experience as a bellhop in the Green-Davidson Hotel. Young, inexperienced, and eager for the pleasures and excitement of life, Clyde finds in the gauche luxuriousness of an American middle-class hotel of the 1920s a potential fulfillment of all he desires. In pursuing this fulfillment, he encounters and absorbs codes of behavior and belief that will condition his own actions and values for the remainder of his life. This process begins with his interview for the position of bellhop and his realization that he must make himself pleasing to his superiors within a hierarchical social structure if he is to climb within that structure. "For the first time in his life, it occurred to him that if he wanted to get on he ought to insinuate himself into the good graces of people—do or say something that would make them like him. So now he contrived an eager, ingratiating smile. . . ."[6]

Clyde also quickly encounters another condition of social power—that those in positions of strength exploit those beneath them. So Clyde is confronted during his first day by the convention of kickbacks that runs through the hotel's economic structure—that he must pay a portion of his tips to his watch captain, another portion to those who supply ice water and drinks, while he himself receives money from hotel merchants to whom he brings trade. Yet these instances of hypocrisy and corruption are not questioned by Clyde, despite his moralistic upbringing, because they are a means toward the winning of a secular Eden far more immediate and desirable than any heavenly reward promised by his parents' faith. "What a realization of paradise!" (I, 37), Clyde cries, when he comes to understand that even a tiny part of the opulence of the Green-Davidson can be his.

The Green-Davidson as a microcosm of that aspect of American life in which power functions as deception and exploitation is even more sharply portrayed in the sexual ethic operative in the hotel. Well-to-do perverts and rich society women prey on the usually willing bellhops, and Clyde also learns of "a guy from St. Louis" who brings a young girl to the hotel, runs up a large bill, and then both deserts the girl and fails to pay the bill. In these instances, Clyde can still recoil with shock because of his sexual inexperience. But so powerful is the controlling ethic of the hotel that Clyde will eventually, in his relations with Roberta and Sondra in Book Two of the novel, act out this precise model of deception and exploitation, one in which Sondra now constitutes the Green-Davidson of his desires. For as he said to himself after his full absorption of the meaning of the hotel, "This, then, most certainly was what it meant to be rich, to be a person of consequence in the world—to have money. It meant that you did what you pleased. That other people, like himself, waited upon you. That you possessed all of these luxuries. That you went how, where, and when you pleased" (I, 45).

In *The Age of Innocence*, a parallel metaphor of entrapment within a powerful social institution is provided by the wedding ceremony of Archer and May. The right church for an upper middle-class New York wedding, the perfectly attired and correctly seated guests, the elaborately rehearsed and precisely orchestrated sequence of events—all constitute an acceptance by those participating in the occasion of a rigid code of life. Yet it is a code that is dead and meaningless—both in itself and in particular as it represents for Archer a death of the spirit that is about to engulf him. Whatever is fresh in the spring day is smothered by the smell of camphor from the "faded sable and yellowing ermines" of the "old ladies of both families."[7] Archer has contributed "resignedly" to the gestures that make up the ceremony, gestures that make "a nineteenth century New York wedding a rite that seemed to belong to the dawn of history" (1157). He has provided flowers and presents for the bridesmaids and ushers, has thanked his male friends for their gifts, has paid the necessary fees, and has prepared his luggage—and each of these seemingly inconsequential acts constitutes his tacit acceptance of the more consequential rites and taboos that are at the heart of a middle-class marriage in his culture. For the remainder of his life, in short, he will be expected to play various prescribed roles and make various conventional provisions.

Unlike Clyde's imprisonment within the ethic of the Green-Davidson, Archer is aware of the enclosed world of behavior and value that is about to shut its doors upon him. But despite the pain and confusion of this realization, he is too much a part of this world to even imagine at this point a rejection of it. And so, at the right moment, he provides the ring, repeats the formula of the marriage vows, and is married to May—a girl he does not love because he is now in love with Ellen. And in the carriage, after the ceremony, a "black abyss yawned before him and he felt himself sinking into it, deeper and deeper, while his voice rambled on smoothly and cheerfully: 'Yes, of course I thought I'd lost the ring; no wedding would be complete if the poor devil of a bridegroom didn't go through that'" (1163).

There are, of course, major differences between these two instances. The Green-Davidson is a gross representation of American middle-class life, and Clyde is both oblivious to its excesses and completely taken in by them. The wedding at Grace Church, on the other hand, is subdued and decorous, its social nuances expressed in a low key, and Archer himself is fully conscious both of his own feelings and of the world that is about to enclose him. But the occasions nevertheless also contain an essential similarity, one which constitutes the distinctive character of naturalistic expression in the more sophisticated stage of its development. In both, there are no authorial declamations about the power of environment, and environment itself is rendered not in melodramatic excess but in the form of commonplace institutions at the heart of American middle-class life—a hotel and a wedding. Yet these seemingly neutral institutions, neutral because they are so commonplace, have the power to hold and imprison the individual—to shape his actions, beliefs, and feelings in ways that control his destiny.

Clyde Griffiths is an archetypal example of an individual of this kind. Indeed, his experiences in *An American Tragedy* can be described metaphorically as his immersion in a series of walled social institutions, from the formalized religion of his early youth to the prison where he is executed, institutions that Clyde ineffectually seeks either to escape from or to enter. One such institution is the collar factory of the Lycurgus Griffiths, a factory that, as Dreiser dissects its controlling principle early in Book Two, comes to represent as well the controlling nature of the American economic system as a whole. Clyde, despite being a member of the family, is to learn the business from the bottom up in the basement shrinking room as a factory hand at a low salary. The Griffiths believe that "the nearer the beginner in this factory was to the clear mark of necessity and compulsion, the better" (I, 180). Better because it was of great importance for those starting out on the road of life to gain "a clear realization of how difficult it was to come by money." Within this formula of working hard for little reward, youthful aspirants to success would "become inured to a narrow and abstemious life. . . . It was good for their characters. It informed and strengthened the minds and spirits of those who were destined to rise. And those who were not should be kept right where they were" (I, 181).

It is this bastardized version of a puritan ethic that contributes greatly to Clyde's destruction. He indeed wishes to "come by money"—to be a true Griffiths, to marry Sondra, and to ascend to the paradise of identity and wealth. But he is also driven by the immediate human needs of companionship and love, by needs that take him outside the confines of a "narrow abstemious life" into a relationship with Roberta. And so he eventually finds himself in a terrible dilemma in that he must somehow dispose of Roberta in order to gain the crowning symbol of success, Sondra. He is torn, in other words, between a confining and imprisoning form of duty represented by a pregnant Roberta and a seemingly liberating fulfillment of desire represented by a marriage to Sondra. Unable to find a way out of this dilemma acceptable both to Roberta and himself, he begins to plan her death, a plan that will eventually lead to his own death. Put another way, Clyde is fatally constrained by the moral climate of Lycurgus both as it restricts his freedom within the ladder of success construct and as it limits him to a single acceptable response to Roberta's pregnancy. He seeks in both instances to break out of these constraints—to make love to Roberta and then not to marry her when she becomes pregnant—but his failure to do so successfully is a token both of his own weaknesses and of the power of the institutionalized moral and social walls he is seeking to breach.

Newland Archer's world is as much a system of limitations and prohibitions as is Clyde's. And though Archer in the end chooses to accept rather than to break through these barriers, the effect of the novel, as with *An American Tragedy*, is to demonstrate the power of the socially constraining over individual desire and destiny. Archer's world, as I have noted, is one in which tribal custom, discipline, and taboo are as prohibitive as engraved tablets of the law. But though little is permitted, even less is said. Communication rather—in what is perhaps the first fully intended semiotic novel—is by a system of signs. They all live, Archer reflects, "in a kind of hieroglyphic world, where the real thing was never said or done or even thought, but only repre-sented by a set of arbitrary signs" (1050). The "real thing" in *The Age of Innocence* is Archer's discovery of his love for Ellen Olenska during the course of his courtship, engagement, and marriage to May Welland.

Within the poles of duty and desire in *The Age of Innocence*, May is all that Newland's breeding and world deem most accept-able. She is young, pure, of excellent family, and—for good measure—attractive. She is also, Archer begins to realize, inde-scribably dull, conventional, and predictable. Ellen, on the other hand, is a thoroughly suspect commodity within tribal values. With a dissolute husband and a rumored love affair behind her in Europe, she is clearly shopworn and is available principally as a mistress—as indeed she is so pursued by the wealthy philanderer Beaufort. Moreover, she is bohemian and artistic and emotionally deep. Archer, seeing the long dull road before him which May represents, and fully engaged emotionally for the first time in his life by the pathos and beauty of Ellen's nature, contemplates escape from duty and fulfillment of desire. But at every turn he is silently but effectively anticipated, forestalled, and thwarted. His marriage to May is advanced, Ellen's divorce is blocked by family pressure, and—at a climactic moment—May uses her just-discovered pregnancy to drive off Ellen and hold Newland.

In one of the principal ironic devices of *The Age of Inno-cence*, Archer and Ellen serve as the major spokesmen for and agents of the system of moral and social taboos that keeps them apart. Neither wishes to descend to a clandestine affair; there must be a complete break with their world or nothing. And a complete break, Newland realizes, though it may gain love, will also mean the loss of "habit, and honour, and all the old decencies that he and his people had always believed in" (1259). And so, in the end, when Newland is driven by the imminent loss of Ellen to project a possible escape—to find at last the emotional equivalent of the fresh air he is constantly seeking in stuffy draw-ing rooms and closed carriages—the "old decencies" he speaks for exert their greatest power in the compelling commitment represented by May's pregnancy.

The Age of Innocence, as I have noted, is a novel of inaction rather than, as is true of *An American Tragedy*, one of doing.

Newland and Ellen never consummate their love. And though, in a scene remarkably evocative of *An American Tragedy*, Newland at one point wishes May dead (1251), he does not harm her but rather settles into the placid but empty life with her that he had foreseen. But though it seldom expresses itself either in open prohibition or direct punishment, the social and moral world portrayed in *The Age of Innocence*—the world that Archer describes as a "silent organization" of habit, custom, and assumption—exerts a web of compulsion that powerfully shapes and controls individual belief and behavior in the most vital areas of human experience.

An *American Tragedy* and *The Age of Innocence* share another major characteristic of American naturalism in its fully mature form. In both works, the central figure consciously accepts the premise that he is free. For Clyde, freedom is expressed in his belief that he can fulfill the American dream—that he can move from the basement of the Griffiths factory to the ideal world of an unending summer with Sondra at Twelfth Lake. Indeed, much of the action of the novel emerges out of Clyde's effort to translate his sense of himself—that there is a better life than he has had and that he can gain it—into actuality in the face of his own limitations and an intractable world. In *The Age of Innocence*, Newland even more than Clyde accepts the proposition that he can mold his own life. It is his to choose, he believes almost to the end, whether he will elect to live with May or run away with Ellen. But both Clyde and Newland come to realize that their destinies were shaped outside of their conscious volition. In prison, awaiting execution, Clyde understands—as the world has not—how much his nature had been conditioned by "the ill-fate of his early life and training." And he realizes as well how devoid of any true freedom of choice was the seeming choice between Roberta's "determination that he marry her and thus ruin his whole life" and "the Sondra of his beautiful dream" (II, 392). And Newland, in Paris some thirty years after seemingly freely choosing to remain with May, is told by his son that May, on her deathbed, had spoken of the crisis represented by Newland's attraction to Ellen and of how May had asked Newland not to leave her, had asked him to give up "the thing [he] most wanted." After a long pause, Newland responds to his son, "She never asked me" (1298). May did not have to ask, and Newland was not given a choice, because—with the announcement of her pregnancy—the choice was made for Newland, as May well knew and as Newland now fully realizes, so powerful were the constraints that all of them—including Ellen—fully accepted.

Both novels, therefore, dramatize not only that we live in a contingent universe, that our lives are largely shaped and conditioned by the distinctive social context in which we find ourselves, but also that we continue to share in the myth of the autonomous self that is capable of realizing and choosing its own fate. And in both works as well, though each in its own way, the dynamic aesthetic center of the novel is the tragic irony inherent in the conflict between a character's felt belief in his autonomy and a social contingency that does indeed shape his destiny. Clyde, thinking that he can somehow get out of his scrape and still have Sondra, Newland reaching out for a self-acceptance of his love for Ellen and what this requires of him—both figures are pursuing life as though it were malleable when it is they who have been and are being shaped.

Clyde and Newland are thus neither dumb brutes nor unthinking victims of grossly determining conditions. They are rather close to life as many of us suspect it is. They are less than strong figures who nevertheless wish to believe that they can control their lives and who discover that the ordinary worlds in which they exist—a commonplace factory town and an upper-class community—subtly but nevertheless powerfully are the controlling agents of their fates.

Novels such as *The Age of Innocence* are seldom discussed as naturalistic fiction because of the critic's assumption that if a novel is naturalistic in its central impulse it cannot be a successful novel and because *The Age of Innocence* is clearly successful. But another tack would be to recognize that most literary movements produce in their opening stages ungainly and awkward expressions of the movement—much pre-Shakespearean Elizabethan tragedy, for example—and that American naturalism is no exception to this general rule. The major naturalistic novels of the 1890s are indeed often crude and melodramatic both in theme and form. But in *An American Tragedy* and *The Age of Innocence* the movement comes to maturity both in the discovery of a fuller range of experience available for the representation of naturalistic themes and in the skill of the dramatization of these themes.

1992

TWELVE

Contemporary American Literary Naturalism

*L*iterary Naturalism has had an equivocal career and reputation in America. Though seemingly attuned to American life in its concreteness and circumstantiality, it also runs counter to the predominant strain of optimistic moralism in the American character. In addition, in a country still afflicted with a powerful residue of religious fundamentalism, the sexual sensationalism of naturalism—Trina McTeague, for example, lying naked on her gold coins—has never failed to attract condemnation.[1] Yet, as Willard Thorp noted in 1960, in a study of major tendencies in modern American literature, naturalism in America has "refused to die,"[2] with this refusal made even more singular in the light of its early demise in England and on the Continent.

In my recently published book, *Twentieth-Century American Literary Naturalism: An Interpretation*, I sought to account for the persistence of naturalism in America.[3] After examining the various manifestations of naturalism in American fiction from the 1890s to the early 1950s, I came to the conclusion that a major reason for the endurance of the movement has been its dynamic adaptability. While critics of American naturalism have

167

since the beginning attempted to fix on it a static philosophical center derived from Emile Zola's ideas—materialistic determinism and the like—naturalist writers have refused to constitute themselves into a school. They have rather continued to do what they have always done—to write with distinctive personal individuality about "hard times" in America, hard times in the sense both of economic and social deprivation and of the malaise of spirit arising out of such deprivation. And they have continued as well to impose on this material of national failure conscious efforts to explain—to explain both specific ills and, by extension, the nature of all experience—efforts which move their fiction strikingly toward the symbolic and allegorical in expression. Naturalism has been in America a literature in which the writer depicts man under pressure to survive because of the baleful interaction between his own limitations and the crushing conditions of life and in which the writer also proffers, through his symbolism, an interpretive model of all life. It is a fiction, in brief, that is both powerfully concrete and provocatively expansive. What has varied in the history of naturalism in America is not the writer's commitment to the depiction of the inadequacies of American life. Rather, it is the nature of American life itself—its particular social reality and intellectual preoccupations—that has changed and that has thereby resulted in the varying themes and strategies of the American naturalistic novel—in its dynamic character, in short.

The three periods of hard times in American life since the late nineteenth century that have seen major outbursts of literary naturalism are the 1890s, the 1930s, and the late 1940s and early 1950s. In the 1890s, the shock of the realization that man now had to exist both in a mechanized urban present and in an animal past stimulated an often ideologically fuzzy but fictionally brilliant effort to constitute new myths and symbols of man's condition in the modern world. Whether depicting man as animalistic brute, as a confused soldier in a smoke-obscured battle, or as a searcher for a place of warmth in a cold, anonymous city, the naturalists of this decade were seeking ways to present man as more circumscribed by his nature and by the conditions of life than was usually supposed. During the 1930s, a new generation, responding to the breakdown of the American economic system, continued the search for adequate symbolic constructs to express their concern. But now, responsive as well to the full tide of literary modernism and to the striking example offered by Dreiser's *An American Tragedy* of 1925, they sought—at a moment when the American system and thus the American dream appeared to be at near collapse—to dramatize above all the blighting of the felt inner life by the cultural and economic poverty of America. James T. Farrell's Studs Lonigan, a potentially warm and even poetic young man misshapen by a street ethic, is the archetypal figure in the naturalism of the decade. The naturalism of the late 1940s and early 1950s was far more "cosmic" in tenor, as befits a phase of American history when the euphoria of the immediate postwar years was replaced by the fear and mistrust of the Cold and Korean wars, the McCarthy era, and the birth of an international atomic age. The question raised by such naturalistic novels as Norman Mailer's *The Naked and the Dead* and William Styron's *Lie Down in Darkness* was whether the notion of human freedom had validity within the struggle for power that occurred in such symbolic centers of modern life as the army and the middle-class family.

The permanence and vitality of naturalism in America is, I believe, also due to the presence in it of the modern residue of the tragic impulse. Naturalism, from Hurstwood's decline and death to Dos Passos's "We stand defeated America," has always been a literature of failure. Yet contrary to much received opinion, the naturalist depiction of human and social inadequacy is not equivalent to passive acceptance. The naturalist is not a neutral recorder of futility and fallibility in all their phases. Underlying his fiction is a powerful remnant of the sense that life has meaning and dignity—if not freedom—despite its frequent collapse into chaos and death. So the naturalist will dramatize the pathos of the waste of human potential in the lives of those feeling temperaments, a Clyde Griffiths or Studs Lonigan, who lack the cunning and strength to overcome the structured visions and expectations of their limited worlds. Or he will encourage our sympathy for the Joads of America, men of simple needs, who unsuccessfully attempt to maintain an even keel in an unstable universe. Or he will render the self-driven efforts by a Henry Fleming or a Sergeant Croft to obtain knowledge in a world clouded with ambiguity. These are of course neither conventional tragic sentiments nor conventional tragic heroes. No Hamlets or Lears here. Rather, there is a modern approximation of the essential tragic paradox—that the potentially wonderful creature which is man frequently goes crashing down to destruction and death.

I would like to devote the bulk of my paper to a preliminary and necessarily selective account of what I believe to be a contemporary resurgence of naturalism in American fiction. Since the late 1960s we have again had "hard times" in America. The two initial causes were of course the prolonged and costly and fruitless Vietnam War and the Watergate affair, both of which implied a major breakdown in America's global and national ethical character. These were followed in the mid and late 1970s by the crisis in the American city (the blight, violence, and bankruptcy of New York are indicative), by a severe recession deepening into near-depression, and by the fear that the world, with America's aid, was hastening into a nuclear holocaust.

I will discuss three recent works of fiction as examples of reactions to this new sense of hard times and of yet another phase of American literary naturalism. Each work derives from its writers's distinctive response to a specific inadequacy in contemporary American life, and each is also in a tradition of analogous responses by earlier naturalists to similar conditions. So Joyce Carol Oates's *them* of 1969 is a novel of the deprivation and violence of urban life. Like Crane's *Maggie* of 1893, it seeks to demonstrate, as Crane said of his novel, that "environment is a tremendous thing in the world and frequently shapes lives regardless."[4] So Norman Mailer's *The Executioner's Song* of 1979, like Dreiser's *An American Tragedy*, dramatizes, within a story of crime and punishment, the failure of our social and legal response to human need and desire. And so Robert Stone's *A Flag for Sunrise* of 1981, like Frank Norris's *The Octopus* of 1901 and John Steinbeck's *The Grapes of Wrath* of 1939, explores in the context of national social and political conditions the interplay between religious conviction and determining social reality in American life.

Of course, it is difficult to be more than suggestive in any selective study of a literary tendency or movement. One's specific choices and thus larger theses are always open to question and challenge. Nevertheless, these are three large-scale, important, and compelling works by three major contemporary novelists. Any perceived relationship among the works should therefore throw some light on one of the directions of contemporary American writing.

---

them is probably the best example in contemporary American fiction of the conscious effort by a major writer to recover and renew the themes and fictional conventions of American literary naturalism. The novel details the fortunes of a poor midwestern family, the Wendalls, from late in the Depression to the Detroit riot of the summer of 1967. Almost every characteristic of the naturalistic city novel, from *Maggie* and *McTeague* through *An American Tragedy* and *Studs Lonigan*, is present in *them*. When we first meet Loretta Wendall, the mother of the two principal figures in the novel, Maureen and Jules, she is a young girl whose own mother is dead and whose father is a drunkard. Through a series of brutish husbands, she raises her children without love or guidance in a slum setting of drink, unemployment, petty crime, ethnic prejudice, and violence. Except for the powerful sympathetic bond between Maureen and Jules, the emotions of the family are those of their world—envy, anger, fear, and hate. The novel opens with Loretta's jealous brother shooting her teenage lover while he sleeps in her arms, and it closes with Jules killing a policeman during the Detroit riot. Between these two deaths occur such staples of slum fiction as prostitution and rape, additional murders and attempted murders, alcoholism and drug addiction, and violence of every description. So full and rich is Oates' use of the "classic" matter of naturalistic fiction that one wonders if it is not with tongue in cheek that she claims, in her Author's Note to the novel, that she has not exaggerated the life depicted. "Indeed," she writes, "the various sordid and shocking events of slum life, detailed in other naturalistic works, have been understated here, mainly because of my fear that too much reality would become unbearable."[5]

Although Jules and Maureen Wendall are part of this world of spiritual and material deprivation, they both wish to be something else and something more. Oates appears to have chosen dual protagonists—a brother and sister—to stress that whatever their differences in sex, temperament, and specific experience, Jules and Maureen, because of the general similarity of their lives and fates, constitute one of the paradigms of slum experience. Both are dissatisfied with their lives and make early unsuccessful attempts to escape—Maureen to the library, where it is quiet and there is a chance to dream; and Jules to the streets, where there is at least an illusion of freedom. But for both figures these tentative early efforts reflect a far deeper need—to escape being a Wendall. So when Jules's father dies, Jules, as he recalls his father's life, realizes the danger of himself slipping into that life. The core of his father's life, Jules now knows, was anger. "Anger for what? For nothing, for himself, for life, for the assembly line, for the cockroaches and the dripping toilet. One thing was as good as another" (147). But Jules will not take this road. Instead, "Money was an adventure. It was open to him. Anything could happen. He felt that his father's essence, that muttering dark anger, had surrounded him and almost penetrated him, but had not quite penetrated him; he was free" (147).

Money, in fact, is not only an adventure, a means, but an end in itself. For money is one of the principal attributes of "them"—the middle-class world of wealth and possessions in which, Jules and Maureen vaguely and inarticulately feel, the self is somehow free from all that impinges on it in their present lives. And, they discover, the most available and seemingly effective way to acquire money and admission to the world of "them" is through sex and love. As Dreiser had demonstrated in *Sister Carrie* and *An American Tragedy*, upward mobility is often achieved through the bedroom and the altar. The first two parts of *them* (the novel is divided into three sections) are devoted to two such parallel efforts by Maureen and Jules. In the first section, Maureen, while still a schoolgirl, allows herself to be picked up by an older man. She asks for money for the sex she has with him, sex which she responds to unfeelingly and mechanically. But her step-father sees her with the man, finds the money she has hidden, and in a jealous rage beats her so severely that she remains psychically wounded for many years. In the second section of the novel, Jules becomes deeply obsessed with Nadine, an upper middle-class girl from Grosse Point. Oates tells us about Jules in this stage in a Dreiserian passage:

He thought of himself as spirit struggling with the
fleshly earth, the very force of gravity, death. All his
life he thought of himself in this way. . . .
Of the effort the spirit makes, this is the subject of
Jules's story; of its effort to achieve freedom, the
breaking out into beauty, in patches perhaps but
beauty anyway, and of Jules as an American
youth. . . . (274)

Nadine is like Sondra Finchley, the rich girl of Lycurgus whom
Clyde Griffiths views as a paradise to be gained. Nadine is what
the spirit seeks as beauty because she is escape and freedom and
hope, and she is to be won by a force in Jules that is both love
and, as he tells her, "something deeper" than love because of its
semireligious nature. But Nadine is "them"; she may be desired
and indeed provoke desire, but her response to adoration is
"cold," "steely," "limp," and "numb." When at last she permits
Jules to make love to her, she fails to have a sexual climax. After
spending a day and night with Jules, Nadine, feeling degraded
and defiled, shoots him. Like the class that she symbolizes, she
seems to beckon and offer herself, but in reality she holds herself
back and then seeks to destroy Jules because of her fear that in
being possessed she will become what he is.

The first two sections of *them* thus present us with analogous stories in which Maureen and Jules are almost destroyed by
their effort to scale the walls into the bastion of "them." The
last section of the novel dramatizes their equivocal success in
achieving their goal. Maureen offers the clearest example. At
twenty-six, she decides that she must at last "escape the doom of
being *Maureen Wendall* all my life" (338). To marry—anyone,
so long as he is not of her class and world—is to gain this
new identity. So with an amoral cunning, rather than her earlier
ingenuous selling of herself, she sets her sights on her night school
teacher, a poor graduate student with a wife and children. He
leaves his family for Maureen, they marry and move to the suburbs, and Maureen becomes pregnant. She tells Jules at the close
of the novel, "I'm going to forget everything and everybody. . . .
I'm a different person" (507).

Jules adopts less obvious but fundamentally similar means to at last reach "them." Down and out, he is picked up by some university radicals as an example of the suppressed working class. Through them, he meets a slumming upper-class girl—also from Grosse Point—whom he rapes and turns into a prostitute. During the Detroit riot, he kills a policeman, but after the riot he becomes a spokesman for the radical position. The end of the novel finds him going to California to work in a government antipoverty program. Both Maureen and Jules, it is clear, have adopted the weapons of their world—cunning, shrewdness, and ruthlessness—in order to escape it. They are now angry, but the directionless anger that imprisoned their father is now a means toward freedom because it is a directed anger toward the class they wish to join. Jules's prostitution of the young girl and Maureen's stealing of her husband away from his wife and children are conscious acts of anger and vengeance against the world of "them" that had earlier denied them access. The Detroit riot, with its destruction of property and attack on order, becomes to Jules a symbol of this new freedom of anger. As he wanders the burnt-out streets, "He was drifting with freedom, intoxicated with freedom. That was what he had tasted in the air . . . freedom. The roofless buildings, already burnt-out, looked up into the sky in a brazen, hopeless paroxysm of freedom" (492).

Of course, though Jules and Maureen have "escaped," they have done so at such cost to themselves and to others that we are left with little sense of victory. The wasted streets of Detroit are apt testimony to the hate forced upon Jules as the price of freedom, he who had earlier tried love. But like Clyde Griffiths, who had also been forced into hate and anger by the inexorable pressure of his desires in the face of an immovable wall of class, Jules—and Maureen—also suggest in the strength of their need the permanence of the condition that is the human spirit seeking relief and fulfillment. Jules and Maureen as an American boy and girl desiring something better in life than to be a Wendall reveal both the terrible hazards accompanying an effort of this kind and its vitality. To reach "them" by the means Jules and Maureen use at the close of the novel is not estimable, Oates appears to be saying, but to be seeking still, after their earlier crushing defeats, is a revelation of the inexhaustible strength of man's quest for a better life.

Something of the same ambivalence characteristic of the naturalistic tragic ethos is present in Oates's own role in *them*. One of Maureen's teachers in night school is Oates. Maureen is deeply envious of Oates's career, marriage, and home, and when Oates gives her a failing grade in the course, Maureen is bitter and angry. "You failed me" (335), Maureen writes Oates, playing upon her grade and the deeper failure of Oates to respond adequately to Maureen's nature and needs. But though Oates did not reach out to Maureen—as few of us are capable of doing—she did shape an account of her that constitutes an attempt to understand and thus to make at least partial restitution. So, as in much tragic art, the writer, through his creation of an art object, testifies both to his helplessness in the face of the human dilemma and to his efforts to understand and to help others toward understanding.[6]

Norman Mailer's *Cannibals and Christians*, a collection of miscellaneous pieces published in 1966, contains a poem entitled "The Executioner's Song."[7] Throughout the poem Mailer plays on the various meanings of the verb "to execute." The song of the executioner who dispatches criminals is also that of the artist who executes in the sense of to perform. In particular, the artist, like the executioner, seeks to "kill well and bury well"—to bring a work of art from its sources in life to its paradoxical "dead" form as an art object. And like the executioner, the artist also sits in judgment on his subject. As the executioner claims in a central passage of the poem,

> If I could execute neatly
>   (with respect for whatever romantic imagination
>   gave passion to my subject's crime)
>   and if buried well,
>   (with tenderness, dispatch, gravity
>   and joy that the job was not jangled . . .)
>   well, then perhaps,
>   then might I rise so high upon occasion

as to smite a fist of the Lord's creation
into the womb of that muse
which gives us poems. . . .

The poem strikingly anticipates Mailer's effort, over ten years later, to tell the story of Gary Gilmore, a criminal executed for murder in 1977. Like Dreiser in *An American Tragedy,* which is also a massive account, based on documentary sources, of a sensational story of crime and punishment in America, Mailer in *The Executioner's Song* seeks to execute well—to recreate Gilmore's life with respect for the "passion" of the inner man, and to communicate through expressive form the complex and mixed emotions—the tenderness and gravity—of a tragic event.

Gary Gilmore would seem to be as unpromising a subject for a tragic work as was Chester Gillette, the prototype of Clyde Griffiths. The product of a broken and poor home, Gilmore had begun in adolescence his lifelong pattern of lengthy periods in prison followed by brief respites on the "outside." By April 1976, when he was released from a federal penitentiary in Illinois, he had spent eighteen of his thirty-five years behind bars. On parole in Provo, Utah, he has within a few months of his release again drifted into a life of drinking, drugs, theft, and flare ups of violence. He has also begun to live with Nicole Baker, a nineteen-year-old girl who has been married three times (the first at fourteen) and has two children. After an intense but brief period of love, Nicole leaves him because of his fecklessness and rages. Needing money to pay for a pickup truck he covets, and angry at Nicole, Gilmore commits robberies on consecutive nights, on both occasions killing an unarmed man needlessly and in cold blood. He is apprehended, tried for murder, and sentenced to be shot. At this point, Gilmore attracted national attention by refusing to appeal his conviction. Because of a Supreme Court ruling, no one had been executed in America for over ten years. Thus, the legal and moral issues raised by Gilmore's willingness to die, as well as the sensationalism inherent in a prospective execution after so many years, made him "news." Reporters and publicists rushed to Salt Lake City to compete for his story. Despite last minute appeals by the American Civil Liberties Union, Gilmore was executed by firing squad on January 17, 1977, a little over nine months after leaving the penitentiary.

Mailer explains in his Afterword to *The Executioner's Song* that the work "does its best to be a factual account of the activities of Gary Gilmore."[8] But he goes on to note that he has also tried to write "a true life story . . . as if it were a novel"—to achieve accuracy but also "intimacy of . . . experience" (1053). For the factual basis of Gilmore's life, Mailer relied on and often used verbatim a large body of documentary material—court records, Gilmore's letters, published interviews, and so on. He turned most of all to some fifteen thousand pages of transcribed interviews with Gilmore and with those who knew him or were associated with him during his Utah period, from Nicole Baker to friends, family, attorneys, and relatives of the murdered men. In this respect, *The Executioner's Song* resembles Truman Capote's *In Cold Blood* of 1965 and other exercises in the form that has come to be known as the New Journalism or Non-Fiction Novel. The writer seeking to recreate a sensational contemporary event—a crime or disaster—relies heavily on the reporting skills of himself and others but then molds this material into a fictional form that includes the representation of the interior life of the principal figures in the event. But though *The Executioner's Song* resembles *In Cold Blood* in this and other ways, it differs from Capote's and similar works in that Mailer—either as anonymous journalist or named author—is not present in the work. Capote in *In Cold Blood* and Mailer in several of his earlier efforts in the New Journalism help create meaning and form either through their presence in the narrative as participants in the event as it happens or as seekers of meaning in the event after it has occurred. But Mailer as personality or overt authorial presence is completely absent from *The Executioner's Song*. Instead of relying upon himself as focus of meaning and as shaping presence in the narrative, Mailer achieves theme and form in *The Executioner's Song* by his successful and powerful exploitation of two major fictional techniques—the dramatization of the inner life of the figures in the story through free indirect speech, and the division of the work into two strikingly juxtaposed halves.

The Executioner's Song ranks with Zola's *L'Assommoir*, Joyce's *Ulysses*, and the narrative portions of Dos Passos's *U.S.A.* as a work that relies almost completely for its principal fictional effect on the device known as *style indirect libre* or free indirect speech. Mailer shifts his point of view focus frequently in the work—from major figures such as Gilmore and Nicole to a host of minor ones, most of whom appear only briefly. But whoever is the center of interest at any one moment has his or her appearance, actions, thoughts, and feelings reported to us by the narrator in a prose style appropriate to that person. The omniscient narrative voice still performs the traditional function of selecting and ordering that which is presented to us, but the substance of what is presented is in the diction, syntax, and tone characteristic of a specific person or class of persons. Mailer makes this device known to us at the very opening of the work, when Gilmore arrives in Utah. The point of view focus at this moment is Brenda, Gilmore's breezy, good-natured, and forthright cousin, who recalls him as a child. Mailer's reporting of her unspoken recollection is in a slangy, colloquial style appropriate to Brenda's background and temperament: "Gary was kind of quiet. There was one reason they got along. Brenda was always gabbing and he was a good listener. They had a lot of fun. Even at that age he was real polite. If you got into trouble, he'd come back and help you out" (5).

This device pervades the work even, as often happens, when the point of view figure is being depicted externally—when his thoughts and emotions are not being engaged, as when Val Conlin, a used car dealer, is described by the narrative voice as "a tall slim guy with eyeglasses" (136). The "guy" in this passage is of course not Mailer's conventional usage, nor can it be attributed directly to Conlin, who is not the reflective center at this moment. Rather, it is what can be called generically true—that is, it is true to the general usage of Conlin's class and occupation and therefore tells us something both about Conlin's world and, indirectly, about Conlin himself.

This massive exercise in free indirect speech—almost eleven hundred pages which render the minds and feelings of Gilmore and those around him by engulfing us in their habitual language—leads us to believe, in the end, that we know these figures truly as they are because events and people appear before us seemingly directly—in the language of their lives—rather than as shaped through the interpretive medium of an author. Mailer has achieved, though by different means, Henry James's ideal of the representation of experience through the dramatic expression of consciousness.

Free indirect speech can play two not necessarily mutually exclusive roles in a work. Because it distances the narrator from his characters, it can serve a powerful ironic and satiric function, as it does fully in *Madame Bovary* and *U.S.A.* and occasionally in *The Executioner's Song* when Mailer is dealing with the conservative Mormon world of Utah. But its far more prevalent and significant use in Mailer's book is to create that sense of intimacy of knowing that he noted as a goal in his Afterword. Most of all, we come to know Gary Gilmore. At first, we know him as most others initially see him in Utah—a man too anxious to gain too quickly what he wants (money and a good job, a car, a girl) and therefore forcing and bullying and creating resistance and resentment in others that eventually pushes him into criminality. But as Gilmore's portrait deepens through our constant experience of him—both Gilmore himself and the effect he has had on others in the past and present—we come to understand the desperation that underlies his frustrated and failed life and the tormented self-destructiveness behind his actions. Like Perry Smith in Capote's *In Cold Blood*, Gilmore pulled a trigger out of the unrelieved pain, anger, and frustration of a lifetime, emotions which were now hotly renewed by the loss of Nicole.

As he gradually deepens our awareness of Gilmore's tortured life, acute intelligence, and frequently self-deceiving emotionalism, Mailer relies not only on free indirect speech but also on an even more immediate entry into Gilmore's psyche, his prison letters to Nicole. In a characteristic passage, Gilmore writes to Nicole about what his life in prison would be if he is not executed.

> What do I do, rot in prison? growing old and bitter
> and eventually work this around in my mind to where
> it reads that I'm the one who's getting fucked around,
> that I'm just an innocent victim of society's bullshit?
> What do I do? Spend my time in prison searching for
> the God I've wanted to know for such a long time?
> Resume my painting? Write poetry? Play handball?
> Eat my heart out for the wondrous love you gave me
> that I threw away . . . because I was so spoiled and

> couldn't immediately have a white pickup truck I
> wanted? What do I do? We always have a choice,
> don't we? (306)

The choice he makes now, to die, is the consequence of the choice that he knows he did not make earlier, to live with Nicole. Out of our understanding of his realization of the complex depths of his nature, we are ready to accept, by the close of the book, two disinterested judgments on Gilmore as a social and human being. "The system has really failed with this man" (447), comments the district attorney who prosecuted him, while a hard-boiled publicist notes that "Even the people that didn't like him, liked him" (894).

Our deepening engagement in the life and nature of Gary Gilmore has yet another characteristic. As we encounter the resentment of Gilmore's friends and relatives, the love and despair of Nicole, the anger of his victims' families, and the sense of duty fulfilled of attorneys and judges, we realize that the work also seeks to render the full interwoven web of suffering, of fear, of awe, and of self-righteousness that is the consequence of any violent act. There are no anonymous, faceless perpetrators, victims, bystanders, or judges in *The Executioner's Song*. All, from motel desk clerk to office typist, are brought to life by the language that is the color of their natures. And all are caught up in the tragedy of a broken and destroyed life. The work is ultimately not so much about murderers and victims as about the essential tragedy of life.

The tragic character of *The Executioner's Song* also benefits from Mailer's second major technical device in the work, his division of it into two balanced parts, "Western Voices" and "Eastern Voices." Each has its own narrative center: in the first, the crime, concluding with Gilmore's conviction; in the second, the imprisonment, ending with his execution. Each is also an exploration of characteristic "voices"—of the modes of expression that represent habits of thought. Gilmore of course predominates as a "voice"—as a center of attention—in both parts. But in addition to him, the first section dramatizes principally Gilmore's Utah world, the second the largely Eastern (or West Coast Eastern) world of newspaper, magazine, and TV journalists who flock to Utah to merchandise, as one of them puts it, Gary Gilmore's dance of death. Chief among these and the major figure in the second half of the book aside from Gilmore is Lawrence Schiller, a free-lance publicist who, after much wheeling and dealing, succeeds in getting the rights to Gilmore's story.

Schiller, we soon realize, is a complex and ambiguous figure. Shrewd and ruthless, he is also a man of considerable natural warmth. He therefore begins to respond to Gilmore with a deep and disturbing ambivalence. Gilmore on his way to the execution chamber is both a salable commodity and a human being about whom Schiller begins to feel strongly. So Schiller is racked with guilt, and like any man suffering the pangs of conscience he begins behaving erratically—salving his conscience by refusing one deal while in self-torment reaching out to complete another.

Gilmore and Schiller—Western and Eastern voices—represent the complementary halves of the American experience as rendered in *The Executioner's Song*. In social terms, Gilmore's story is an indictment of the American "system" that destroys its repressed classes, Schiller's is an almost mock-epic account of American media hype, of the American middle-class craving for human interest sensationalism. But far more movingly and profoundly, the two stories constitute one of the tragic centers of the American experience—that both the criminal punished by the system and the publicist profiting from the system suffer basically the same anguish and self-hate because of their desire to gain what life—the system—appears to offer them. In the face of the deep moral ambivalence that accompanies desire in America, Gary Gilmore and Lawrence Schiller are brothers in pain.

Robert Stone's *A Flag for Sunrise* is in the tradition of American naturalism represented by Frank Norris's *The Octopus* and John Steinbeck's *The Grapes of Wrath*. Like these large-scale novels of the turn-of-the-century and the 1930s, Stone's work is centered on a fundamental social and ideological crisis of his day—in this instance, the implications for American life of the use of our immense economic and political power to affect the lives of people elsewhere. And like these earlier works, the depiction in *A Flag for Sunrise* of the seemingly universal degradation of modern life is leavened by at least one portrait of a visionary voice and a heroic action.

The novel is set principally in the imagined Caribbean republic of Tecan. Tecan is a heightened model of the nature of American activities in the Third World; in particular, its character suggests that we are doomed to relive our experience in Vietnam again and again. Poor, diseased, and ruled by a corrupt and ruthless military dictatorship, Tecan is controlled by American economic interests and by the CIA, both of which justify their suppression of a native revolutionary movement on the grounds of possible Soviet involvement. Except for its revolutionaries and missionaries, animality is the dominant moral style of Tecan. The novel opens with a police lieutenant demanding absolution from a priest for the mindless murder of a young girl; it closes with the lieutenant again asking the priest for absolution, but now for the brutal murder of a different girl. The lieutenant says to the priest, "I am not an animal . . . I believe there is a spiritual force,"⁹ but his actions belie his belief. Tecan, we soon discover, epitomizes, in exaggerated form, the operative ethic of the world at large. So a CIA agent claims, in his attack on what he calls an indulgence in "moral posturing":

> We're at a very primitive stage of mankind [he says], that's what people don't understand. Just pick up the *Times* on any given day and you've got a catalogue of ape behavior. Strip away the slogans and excuses and verbiage, the so-called ideology, and you're reading about what one pack of chimpanzees did to another. (26)

In this world of Tecan, where "apes" mouth but do not believe in or act upon the old pieties, there come together three Americans whose joint attitudes and fates constitute the modern condition. Justin is already on the scene as a young nursing nun at a small, remote mission on the Atlantic coast of Tecan. She is a woman who has an intense need to believe in the possibility of order and justice, but her faith has been shaken by her years in Tecan, and she is about to laicize. Pablo is an American Coast Guard deserter. He is, as we come to know him as he works his way down the Caribbean, a vile human being—unscrupulous, vicious, and small. He is consumed and made dangerous by a paranoic belief that someone is "fucking with my head" (65). If Justin and Pablo are almost allegorical representations of a vague and formless good on the one hand and an animal malignancy on the other, Holliwell—the third major figure in the novel—constitutes the ambivalent center of man's modern ethical possibilities. An anthropologist who had worked for the CIA in Vietnam and who feels deeply guilty about it, he nevertheless permits himself to be recruited, without openly acquiescing, into investigating reports of revolutionary activity at the Tecan mission. "It would be strange," he thinks to himself, half-cynically, "to see people who believed in things, and acted in the world according to what they believed. It would be different. Like old times" (101). Holliwell is thus the American ethical psyche in its present mixed condition. As Justin notes, though he is tall and well-built, his face "bespoke softness and self-indulgence" (234)—the moral flabbiness of a man of "dry" spirit who believes justice is "only a word" and who "took things as they were" (245). Initially a man of good intentions, he has been dragged into moral compromises and self-evasions by the pressures, fears, and loyalties of life, and now scarcely knows where he stands—whether he has come to Tecan to spy on the revolution or to support it.

The three figures meet and interact at the mission in the days immediately before and during the outbreak of the revolution. Justin has been recruited into the cause and permits the mission to be used as a post, while Pablo is a seaman on a boat running guns for the revolution, guns that are to be landed at the mission. On the day before the fighting begins, Justin and Holliwell become lovers—he impelled to seek her "white goodness" to slake "the hangover thirst of his life" (299), she identifying the possibility of love with hope for the achievement of other ideal constructs. But their lovemaking is a failure. She "eludes" him, and afterwards they are "all separate again in their loneliness and fixedness, illusions of union fled" (379).

At sea, Pablo kills the rest of the gunrunning crew and completes the sale, but because he is wounded and cannot man the boat alone, he is forced to come ashore at the mission. Holliwell, realizing that he is now under suspicion by both sides, confesses his CIA connection to Justin and promises that he will not inform on her. When he is picked up by the police, however, he does indeed implicate her—ostensibly to save her, but also to save himself. When fighting breaks out, Justin, Holliwell, and Pablo are at the mission. Justin decides that the wounded Pablo and the endangered Holliwell must be put to sea in a small boat, where they will presumably drift into safety; she is to remain behind to aid the wounded revolutionaries.

The close of the novel is a reprise and summation of its central themes. Justin is captured and is beaten to death by the police. But in her death there is triumph of a kind. Earlier, after she and Holliwell had made love, she had bitterly repeated the first lines of an Emily Dickinson poem that begins, "A Wife—at Daybreak I shall be—/Sunrise—Hast thou a flag for me?" (380). There were no flags at sunrise for her in the consummation of her earthly love; only regret and anger at her betrayal by Holliwell. But now, in the transforming of belief into meaningful act, she does fulfill the promise of the poem. For as the rest of the poem reveals, the "Wife" of the opening line is the conventional image of the bride of Christ, the Christ who takes to his bosom at death all those who believe in Him. Justin, as a nun, had married Christ once before, but now—as a martyred fighter for justice—the marriage is truly consummated. As though in response to the concluding lines of the poem—"Eternity, I'm coming—Sir/Savior—I've seen the face—before!"—Justin cries at the moment of her death, "Behold the handmaid of the Lord" (416). Meanwhile, adrift at sea, Holliwell recognizes the pure animal evil of Pablo and therefore the danger he presents. He seizes a knife from the dozing Pablo, stabs him, and pushes him overboard. But as Pablo sinks, Holliwell sees in his face not evil but "a brother's face, a son's, one's own. Anybody's face, just another victim of ignorance and fear. Just another one of us . . . " (431).

The naturalistic ethos of the novel is clear. Justin may have her flag at sunrise, but Holliwell—who is rescued—has his life. The lesson of Tecan is that good and evil are both vulnerable, good because of the risks it runs in a largely corrupt world, evil because it is essentially ignorance and fear. Survival is a trick of a shrewd and in the end ruthless moral ambivalence, a quality of mind that is an adaptation to the mix of surface moral coloration and amoral struggle characteristic of all life. Holliwell survives— he has his own flag at sunrise, as he himself ruefully notes—

because of his potent moral flexibility. The man who tells Justin, after she has accused him of betraying her, that he is uncertain in his own mind if he did so but that "When I decide what happened, . . . I'll decide to live with it" (408), outlives the open and decisive moral natures of both Justin and Pablo.

Like other epic naturalistic novels, *A Flag for Sunrise* joins an often sensationalistic plot and a complex of social, political, and religious ideas. And like such works, it dramatizes both the persistence of a visionary ethic and its tragic fate in a world of accommodation to what the apologist for "things as they are" in Frank Norris's *The Octopus* called "conditions"[10] and what Holliwell names "this whirling tidal pool of existence" (244).

The three novels that I have been discussing support the notion that, as in the past, naturalism owes its continued existence to its ability both to draw upon earlier naturalistic expression and to adapt its interests to those of the contemporary scene. Of past naturalists, it is undoubtedly Dreiser who casts the longest shadow over the present moment—in particular the Dreiser of *An American Tragedy*, the Dreiser whose concern was the destructive distinction in American life between a rich and self-satisfied nation, with a rhetoric of opportunity, and the social and moral realities of growing up poor. But also occupying an enduring place in the American literary consciousness are the epic naturalists of the 1930s—Farrell, Steinbeck, and Dos Passos—who sought to render the entire American scene as an admixture of broken promises and an occasional tragic visionary.

The traditional matter, themes, and forms of earlier American naturalistic fiction are thus still with us. Limited and deprived characters still struggle to stay afloat in a world of violent destructiveness, and the novels in which they appear still shape themselves into symbolic expressions of major flaws in the American experience. As in much naturalism of the past, the naturalistic occasion is still that of a closed social and moral world and of a figure seeking some way out. Usually not succeeding, but nevertheless seeking. On the evidence of the works that I have been discussing, however, it would seem that for contemporary naturalism "hard times" are now above all the continued failure, for much of our population, of American urban life, and the continued failure, for all of us, of our role abroad. Indeed, the single richest rein of naturalistic fiction during the 1970s—the Vietnam war novel, including Stone's earlier work, *Dog Soldiers*—derives directly from this second concern.

In form, contemporary naturalism continues—as in the 1930s and late 1940s and early 1950s—to absorb much current fictional experimentation. Mailer's combination of the New Journalism and an absolute reliance on free indirect speech, Oates' turn to the self-reflexive novel, in which she is a character in the novel we are reading, and Stone's poetic symbolism are further evidence of the unwillingness of American naturalists to accept the critical cliché that naturalism is merely a joining of massive documentation and sensationalistic event.

Naturalism thus continues to live in America—not only in the novel but less obviously though still powerfully in documentary narrative (as in Michael Herr's *Dispatches*) and in the film (as in *The Deer Hunter*). I bring the news of its continued existence not in celebration, since its presence is a sure sign that writers have again sensed that "hard times" are here. But like it or not, naturalism is again with us.

1985

THIRTEEN

William Kennedy's *Ironweed* and the American Naturalistic Tradition

W illiam Kennedy's *Ironweed* is a striking example of the continuity of naturalism in American fiction. As I have argued elsewhere,[1] naturalism has been a force in American literature since the 1890s not because writers of different generations have committed themselves to a unified and unchanging body of naturalistic assumptions but because each generation, as well as individual authors within a generation, has explored these assumptions with freedom and originality. It is along these lines that I would like to discuss *Ironweed*. Although the novel appears to be an act of homage to the subject matter and themes that have characterized American naturalism since its beginnings, Kennedy has not written a pastiche imitation; he has rather reshaped the materials of a convention into an expression of his own distinctive vision.

Like much American naturalism, *Ironweed* is set in "hard times"—the Great Depression in this instance—and is peopled

largely by the down and out. The world of the novel is principally
that of missions and flophouses, of men and women sleeping in
the street and in empty lots, of cheap wine and cheaper sex, of
life, in short, moving ever downward to an ugly and meaningless
death. Like John Steinbeck's Joads and John Dos Passos's Mac,
Francis and Helen, the chief figures of *Ironweed*, drift from one
marginal moment to the next. Theirs is also—as is true of Frank
Norris's McTeague, James T. Farrell's Studs, and Joyce Carol
Oates's Jules (in *them*)—a world of permanent violence. Francis's
life has been one of physical destructiveness since he accidentally
dropped his infant son Gerald over twenty years earlier, and he
is haunted in his imagination by those he has killed in the brawls
inseparable from his life on the road. "Bodies in alleys, bodies in
gutters, bodies anywhere, were part of his eternal landscape."[2]
In addition, both he and Helen, like Stephen Crane's Maggie and
Theodore Dreiser's Carrie, have used sex as a survival resource.
And Francis, in one of the most persistent naturalistic strains,
running from McTeague through Studs to William Styron's Milton Loftis (in *Lie Down in Darkness*), is beset by a lifelong
alcoholism. Physically, he and Helen have thus led "polluted"
lives for over two decades, with the disfigurements of his missing
fingers and Helen's distended stomach tumor the specific signs of
their decay.

Ironweed not only recapitulates the archetypal naturalistic
subject matter of the degeneration of the poor and weak, but also
alludes specifically to earlier naturalistic novels. As is true of
Hurstwood in *Sister Carrie*, a violent streetcar strike plays a
major role in Francis's life. As in *Jennie Gerhardt*, Helen's life is
permanently shaped by the years she has given to an older man
who refuses to marry her. And the climactic scene of *Ironweed*—
the raid on a hobo camp by Legionnaires, during which Francis's
friend Rudy is killed and Francis himself kills a Legionnaire—is
strikingly similar to the death of Jim Casy in *The Grapes of
Wrath*.

Ironweed, however, in its conjunction of poverty, drink,
sex, and violence, is a recovery of more than the subject matter
of American naturalism. It also dramatizes within this material,
much of which has its origin in the naturalism of the 1890s, two
major themes introduced by naturalists of following generations.
One such theme is that of a character's anxiety to question the

meaning of his life in the midst of encountering the incapacity to control his life. Stephen Crane had presented in Henry Fleming a bewildered figure seeking after the meaning of his existence while immersed in a seemingly destructive and determined world, a theme caught up by Dreiser in *An American Tragedy* and Richard Wright in *Native Son*. This theme—of ineffectually seeking answers where there seem to be no answers, but nevertheless continuing to seek—dominates such postwar novels as Norman Mailer's *The Naked and the Dead* and Saul Bellow's *The Adventures of Augie March* and continues on in Oates's *them* and Mailer's *The Executioner's Song*. Unlike such earlier characters as Maggie, McTeague, and Hurstwood, the central figures in these later novels do not dully and passively bear their decline into emptiness. They want to know how and why, and their unwillingness to accept easy and obvious polarities—that they are either pawns of circumstance or fully responsible for their fates—is one of the distinctive characteristics of novels in these later stages of American naturalism. Thus, in one example of this theme in *Ironweed*, Francis listens to the once rich but now cracked voice of Oscar the bartender. Francis realizes that for both of them

> life had been a promise unkept in spite of great
> success, a promise now and forever unkeepable. . . .
>   The insight raised in Francis a compulsion to
> confess his every transgression of natural, moral, or
> civil law; to relentlessly examine and expose every
> flaw of his own character, however minor. What was
> it, Oscar, that did you in? Would you like to tell us
> all about it? Do you know? It wasn't Gerald who did
> *me*. It wasn't drink and it wasn't baseball and it
> wasn't really Mama. What was it that went bust,
> Oscar, and how come nobody ever found out how to
> fix it for us? (50)

And so too Helen, even as she is sinking into death, is still seeking to know who she is:

Why was it, really, that things never seemed to
work out?
Why was Helen's life always turning into some
back alley, like a wandering old cat?
What is Helen? (135)

A second way in which *Ironweed* reflects an extension of
earlier American naturalism is in the novel's uniting of place,
time, and memory. The Albany of *Ironweed* is not only that of
the scenes and action of a few days in late October 1938. It
is also the Albany of Francis's childhood, youth, and young
manhood, of the various parts of the city he had lived, worked,
and played in, of the friends, family, and loves of the past as all
of these exist in the timeless present of Francis's memory—indeed, as they are often dramatically projected out of his memory
into the ghosts and voices of a hallucinatory reality. In a refinement of the naturalistic stress on the conditioning or determining
force of the world we find ourselves in, later naturalists—stimulated above all by the example of Faulkner—have made the
burden of the past, a past, as in *Ironweed*, inseparable from place
and family, a powerful constraining agency. And so Francis, from
the opening scene of the novel, which finds him at the cemetery
where his infant son and parents are buried, is constantly haunted
by the errors, failures, and deficiencies of his past life as these are
forced out of his memory by his reimmersion in his Albany world.
Kennedy in *Ironweed* has thus brought to full and artful
expression a central paradox in much American naturalistic fiction. On the one hand, the characters of *Ironweed* live degraded
lives in squalor; they are failed human beings by almost any
standard of measurement. "You're a bum," the junk dealer Ross-
kam, himself a caricature of human grossness, tells Francis again
and again with pleasurable superiority. But Francis and Helen
also possess, as I have suggested, a capacity to live fully and
strikingly in their inner natures—to recapitulate in their memo-
ries the course of their lives and to question their fates. Who am
I and why have I turned out this way, they ask. And in asking
they humanize their condition.
Indeed, it is in his depiction of the human ability to live

richly in the inner life while suffering degradation in all other spheres of existence that Kennedy achieves his most distinctive extension of a conventional literary naturalism. Francis Phelan, it becomes clear in the course of the novel, is caught and imprisoned in the pattern of violence and flight that has been his life since he left Albany over twenty years earlier. Or, in another sense, he is imprisoned in time by his haunted recollections of the many moments in his life in which violence, often accompanied by alcohol, has been followed by flight. During one such rumination, he senses "the workings of something other than conscious will within himself: insight into a pattern, an overview of all the violence in his history, of how many had died or been maimed by his hand . . . " (144–45). Some deep conjunction of temperament and circumstance, in other words, has shaped Francis's life into a repetitive model that he is aware of but cannot escape. As the novel advances, we encounter this paradigm in two powerful forms. Francis constantly relives, in his imaginary conversations with the spirits of those he has killed, its reality in the past. And he is demonstrating once again, in the present action of the novel, its current hold. So the novel reaches an apparent climax when Francis gets drunk in a flophouse, kills a man in a hobo jungle, and, in flight once again, hops a freight out of town—a sequence of events which summarizes the entire fabric of his life.

But at the very moment that Francis is acting out the naturalistic premise that man's prior condition is his fate—a premise that has characterized naturalism from Hurstwood through Studs to Mailer's Gary Gilmore—he is also acting out the contrary premise that man has the capacity to control his destiny despite the pattern which has been his past life. For Francis's return to Albany has also revitalized, through his recollections of his youth, a long dormant side of his character, a side represented by his grace and strength on the baseball field and by the awe and wonder of his initial encounters with sex and love through Katrina Daugherty and his future wife Annie. Thus, during the few days which constitute the present of *Ironweed*, Francis reveals both the power of "pattern" in his life and his potential, through the renewed exercise of his innate sensibility, for redemption into the ability to reshape his destiny.

Francis's first act of renewal comes early in the novel when he seeks to save the drunken Sandra from freezing to death outside the mission. He fails in this effort, as he does in his attempt to nurture and protect Helen as she sinks toward her death. But these ineffectual acts of giving and sympathizing, acts, in effect, of attempting to save rather than to take lives, nevertheless prepare the way for Francis's effort to fulfill the most powerful redeeming emotion that has been stimulated by his return to Albany—his desire to express his guilt for his desertion of his family and to make restitution in some way and thus to return to them and thereby to what he once was. In this attempt, Francis senses, there lies a way of breaking his pattern of isolation in violence and flight. And so, at last, Francis spends his remaining few dollars on a turkey and goes home to his wife and children and to the grandchild, now twelve, whom he has never seen. In this act, he has seemingly achieved the "impossible: for he had always believed it impossible for him, ravaged man, failed human, to reenter history under this roof. Yet here he was in this aerie of reconstitutable time . . ." (169).

The conclusion of the novel thus poses the two principal directions of Francis's life in irreconcilable conflict. The pattern of his life has driven him once more to the nonhistory of the fight at the hobo camp and the freight car out of town. But Francis's recovery of the capacity to give and to sympathize has returned him to time and history, has given him, in other words, the ability to control his life. The last few pages of *Ironweed* coalesce these conflicting directions. Francis, it seems, is on the freight car heading south. I say "it seems" because Kennedy uses the conditional mode throughout these pages—"By dawn he would be on a Delaware & Hudson freight. . . . He would be squatting in the middle of the empty car . . . " (224)—as though to suggest a state in the future that Francis is imagining in the present. One course of action for Francis is therefore the freight—a course which includes the premise that Francis "lived in a world where events decided themselves, and that all a man could do was to stay one jump into their mystery" (224). But another course of action, one that is also expressed in the conditional mode of the passage as a whole, is that of finding a refuge in the attic of his home, a place where he can hide from the police until it is safe for him to descend into the reciprocated love of his family—descent to a cot in his grandson's room, a room with

some space to it.
And it got the morning light too.
It was a mighty nice little room. (227)

There is a temptation, because the sequence of events during the conclusion is that of first the freight car and then the return home, to surmise that Kennedy is positing a full restitution of control to Francis—that he has successfully broken the pattern of his life by an act of conscious will (the first step of which is his casting a bottle of whiskey out the car door) that has itself been activated by the renewal of his capacity for love and compassion. But this supposition simplifies a passage that Kennedy has self-consciously left unclear in order to exploit the suggestive implications inherent in its lack of clarity. One such implication is that Kennedy wishes to leave equivocal the result of a conflict between the patterns that are our lives and our capacity to strike out anew, between timeless repetition and the opportunity for change implied by a life in time. The human condition, in short, cannot be reduced to philosophical absolutes but is rather a blurred mix of various tendencies in human nature and experience, a blurred mix which the novel can seek to mimic in its form as well as to express overtly. Moreover, by dramatizing Francis's return home not as an act that has or is occurring but as one that might occur, Kennedy is also implying—as he has done throughout the novel—that the imagined life has its own significant reality whatever the external context of scene and event in which it exists. Francis has killed men, has lived marginally and poorly, and he is continuing to do so. But he has also acquired (as had Helen) the ability to live fully and well in the imagination. Who is to say, Kennedy thus appears to be suggesting, which is the more "real" existence, since it is Francis's imagination that has sustained him, even in its calling up of the haunted moments of violence in his past, and that has finally driven him to return to his roots and family in Albany? Whether Francis is dreaming about life in a sunny room at home or is in the process of actually fulfilling the dream is, in short, less significant than Francis's power to live richly in his dreams.[3]

Thus, while participating fully in the several naturalistic strains I described earlier, Kennedy also treats his naturalistic material and premises with a freedom and an innovative impulse that, I believe, constitute the "genius" of the naturalistic movement in America. For Kennedy, while investing heavily in naturalistic assumptions on the role of temperament and circumstance in determining man's fate, refuses to complete the purchase. Without rejecting the power of patterns, Kennedy also dramatizes the unresolvable indeterminacies of life given the interaction between patterns and the transforming will and given the ability of the imagination to project, if not to actually create, a better life. And it is indeed in this very vein of speculative uncertainty that there lies the uniqueness and suggestiveness of Kennedy's homage in *Ironweed* to the American naturalistic tradition.

Reviews

FOURTEEN

Harold Kaplan, Power and Order

Henry Adams and the Naturalist Tradition in American Fiction

*H*arold Kaplan's study of the "naturalist ethos" in turn-of-the-century America proceeds in orderly fashion from a discussion of ideas of power in a group of nineteenth-century thinkers (principally Marx, Hegel, Darwin, and Nietzsche) to an examination of these ideas in the work of Henry Adams to further study of their presence in the novels of Frank Norris, Stephen Crane, and the early Dreiser. Kaplan's premise is that a preoccupation with power characterizes late nineteenth-century thought, that Adams both fully and subtly reveals the social and political implications of this preoccupation, and that it is present in grosser and less coherent form in naturalist fiction. A further premise is that the disastrous character of twentieth-century civilization owes much to the "naturalist politics" of a belief in redemption through the violence that necessarily accompanies the exercise of power and the reachievement of order.

There is much that is admirable in this study. Kaplan has

the ability to write with a compressed brilliance about ideas that are widely dispersed in time and place, to proceed rapidly and clearly through a thicket of otherwise diffuse notions to a meaningful insight. *Power and Order* is at its best in Kaplan's capacity to conjoin cogently the beliefs of, let us say, an Emerson and a Dreiser, a Hegel and a Carlyle. We feel here that Kaplan, somewhat as in a *New York Review of Books* essay at its best, is nudging intellectual history into what might be called the aesthetics of ideas in which writer and reader share in the range and play of the ideological imagination.

When Kaplan lowers his sights, however, and writes about a *Sister Carrie* or an *Octopus* or a *Red Badge of Courage* his book begins to disappoint. The difficulty at this point is that he has not defined his stance toward these and other naturalist works of the period. On the one hand, he is a historian whose understanding of the important ideas of the principal thinkers of a period contributes to his understanding of the more oblique presence of these ideas in literary works. This is the conventional stance of the history-of-ideas scholar. On the other, he is a moralist who deplores these ideas because of their pernicious effect on world history and who especially deplores them in the work of writers who diffuse the ideas in confused and half-understood form into the general populace. Whatever the inclination to agree with Kaplan's diagnosis of the destructive effect on world affairs of ideas of power and order since the mid-nineteenth century, and whatever the willingness to reject the ingenuous notion that there can be no significant connection between art and politics, there remains a disinclination to respond favorably to Kaplan's use of apolitical literary works of the 1890s to reach toward moral judgments on recent political history. So, for example, when (on p. 127) Crane's themes in *The Red Badge of Courage* are linked with the need of "naturalist political movements" such as fascism and communism to establish authoritarian regimes, the reader is apt to feel that Kaplan's moral earnestness has led him to transform a multidimensional fictional reality into a single-dimensional political metaphor.

These animadversions are not to say that Kaplan's book is not a welcome addition to the story of literary naturalism in America. His work has the great virtues of taking the movement seriously and of examining it from a fresh perspective. If he has overstressed one element in the fiction of the movement, he has done so with panache and with a strength and clarity that invite further discussion.

1986

FIFTEEN

⌐John J. Conder,
Naturalism in
American Fiction⊢——

The Classic Phase

*J*ohn Conder's study of American literary naturalism is, as he himself announces in his Preface, "a thesis book." His thesis is that theoretical discussions of American naturalism during the last several decades—that is, studies principally by Charles C. Walcutt and myself—have lacked a rigorous philosophical method. More specifically, these studies have failed to stress the deterministic center of all naturalistic fiction and have thus failed to locate the key element of unity in the movement as a whole. To rectify this failure, Conder examines closely the expression of deterministic belief in Crane's *Maggie* and *The Red Badge of Courage*, Norris's *McTeague*, Dreiser's *Cowperwood Trilogy*, Dos Passos's *Manhattan Transfer*, Steinbeck's *The Grapes of Wrath*, and Faulkner's *The Sound and the Fury*. Using the poles of a Hobbesian belief in a fully conditioned, causal universe and a Bergsonian emphasis on the consciousness that can function freely outside of clock time, he finds a general movement in American naturalism from a grimly deterministic Hobbesian fiction (as in Crane and Norris) to novels in which (as in Steinbeck and Faulkner) "true individual identity and freedom" are achieved by the inward man in conjunction with the persistence of deterministic forces in his social world.

Conder's general propositions, despite his claims to the redressing of various balances, are in large part both familiar and acceptable. Few would deny that a significant element in naturalistic expression is the demonstration of the powerful qualifications that both our social moment and our own natures place on an absolute faith in human freedom—whether freedom of thought, feeling, or action. And few would deny that as naturalism persisted as a strain into the twentieth century it was affected by a belief in the relative autonomy (if not complete freedom) of the inner self. In short, it is not Conder's thesis that raises serious questions about his book. Rather, it is his analytical method.

When Charles Walcutt (in the 1950s) and I (in the 1960s) began looking closely at American literary naturalism, we were in part reacting against a critical convention that had been in place almost since the origin of the movement. This convention assumed that American naturalism was an offshoot of Zolaesque naturalism, that Zola was a self-proclaimed determinist, and therefore that American naturalism could best be discussed as a thinly disguised form of discursive philosophy. Based on this assumption and method, almost all criticism of the movement found its philosophy either thin or contradictory and the naturalistic novel itself a suspect species. Indeed the general formula was the more naturalistic a novel the poorer that novel.

Walcutt reacted against this tradition by revealing that the fictional expression of ideas in fiction is far more complex and problematical—both for the theme and form of a novel—than any formulaic conception of these ideas, and I went on to claim that this richness of implication is the source of the fictional strength of the best naturalistic novels. For both Walcutt and me, the key to a meaningful reading of a naturalistic novel was the need to stress that it is a novel and not an oblique form of philosophical argumentation.

It is in his return to an earlier way of discussing naturalistic fiction that I think Conder has gone astray. His methodological assumption appears to be that the pursuit of the deterministic implications of fictional event is a self-sufficient form of literary criticism and literary history, and that one can proceed directly from this activity to the formulation of large-scale interpretive constructs both for the work involved and for its place in literary history. Thus, a novel such as *The Red Badge of Courage* is single-mindedly analyzed for evidence of determinism while Crane's powerful arsenal of stylistic devices that contribute to the effect of indeterminacy in the work—his irony and symbolism and impression—are neglected. *The Red Badge of Courage* undoubtedly does contain a deterministic element, but harm is done both to the novel and to the movement of which it is a part by the reduction of the work to an act of pseudo-philosophical discourse.

Conder's book illustrates a common characteristic in the writing of literary history. After a period of neglect or disparagement, an earlier viewpoint toward a literary movement is recovered and revitalized. *Naturalism in American Fiction* plays this cyclic role with intensity; indeed, there has never been a study of American naturalism that pursues the deterministic strain in the movement with Conder's energy. But specific literary historians can perhaps be forgiven if they hesitate to accept an effort to recover older views when they find themselves part of the rejection of more recent ones. And, less personally I hope, those of any generation who are interested in American naturalism may find that Conder's reading of naturalistic fiction as a form of philosophical determinism contributes only modestly to an understanding of the inner springs of meaning and effect in the works of the movement.

1986

SIXTEEN

Walter Benn Michaels, *The Gold Standard and the Logic of Naturalism*

American Literature at the Turn of the Century

Michaels's book consists of eight essays devoted principally to the work of Dreiser, Norris, and Wharton. What unites
the essays and lends the work interest and importance is Michaels's commitment to the "New Historicism," a recent movement in literary studies associated primarily with the University
of California at Berkeley. Indeed, the book is published as volume
2 in the series The New Historicism: Studies in Cultural Poetics,
under the general editorship of Stephen Greenblatt.

Michaels's historicism is "new" principally in his full acceptance of the concept that literary expression is best examined in
relation to the economic conditions and values of the age in which

it appeared. Of course, literary historians and history-of-ideas scholars have frequently examined fiction for its relation to economic belief, but they have usually confined such discussion to novels that deal specifically with economic matters—*The Pit* would be an obvious example—and they have usually also sought out the author's expressed beliefs as a guide to the study of the economic ideas in his fiction. Michaels's critical strategy differs in two major ways. All experience to his mind is essentially economic in the sense that transactions, contracts, agreements, and so on pervade every phase of life, including deeply personal experience, and thus reflect economic values whether author or character believe so or not. And it is the oblique reflection of this pervasive economic centrality that must be studied because this "truer" metaphoric expression of belief often runs counter to the expressed statements of both author and character.

A typical essay in *The Gold Standard* will therefore initially locate in a fictional text an indirectly expressed allusion to a major economic (and thus also metaphysical and epistemological) issue of the age that also has profound pertinence for the text as a whole. In the title essay, for example, the gold theme in *McTeague* and Vandover's dissipation of his inheritance in *Vandover and the Brute* are used to introduce the late nineteenth-century debate over gold and silver as standards of monetary value. This economic issue of the day is then discussed at great length in order to relate it to the larger philosophical question of a preference for the tangibly real as a principle of transaction over substitutions for or symbols of the tangibly real. Finally, the essay returns to the literary works in question and finds that their deep but largely unconscious participation in this debate reverses commonly held critical beliefs about the works—that in fact most turn-of-the-century naturalistic fiction endorses rather than rejects the popular values of the time.

After several generations either of neglect of turn-of-the-century naturalistic fiction because of its supposed artistic failings or of arid efforts to explore once again questions of free will and determinism in the novels, this methodology has a great deal of excitement and value. The detailed substantiality of the naturalistic text is not merely accepted as a convention of naturalistic expression but becomes a finding place for the underlying beliefs and values that motivated this expression. And the age as a whole is revealed in far greater density of attitude and expression than is usually acknowledged.

Yet *The Gold Standard* also has several troubling characteristics—troubling, that is, especially to someone like myself who experienced in graduate school some of the limitations of the old historicism. One such disturbing characteristic is the absolutism of the economic argument, an absolutism that arises, I believe, out of the present intellectual climate in which the economic foundation of experience is not only an attractive concept in its own right but can also be readily adapted to discussions of power and sexuality in life and art. The danger in this single-minded approach to the literary work is of course the danger of tunnel vision—that one will see only what one wants to see. So, for example, Michaels begins his title essay with Norris's comment in *McTeague* that Trina saved "without knowing why"—"without any thought, without idea of consequence—saving for the sake of saving." Michaels accepts this statement at face value and goes on to make Trina's unexamined miserliness the core of his discussion of the economic theme in *McTeague*. But Norris himself, elsewhere in the novel, makes abundantly clear that though Trina herself might not know why she saves, she in fact saves because of her racial background, because of the generations of Swiss stock from which she descends. I am not here arguing that a reading of *McTeague* as a novel about racial instinct is preferable to one that interprets it in relation to arguments about the gold standard. I am suggesting, however, that Michaels's singleness of interpretive strategy, like that of some older history-of-ideas scholarship that relentlessly pursued a major idea through work after work, can produce distortions of the complexity of theme and motif in the literary work.

Michaels's essays also recall the old historicism in their almost total neglect of the aesthetic nature and value of the literary texts under discussion. *The House of Mirth* and *Vandover and the Brute* are novels that differ immensely in fictional form and worth, but both appear in *The Gold Standard* entirely as grist for Michaels's mill. Indeed, the basic cast of mind underlying Michaels's essays closely resembles that of a 1930s literary historian—that the discovery of a source or an idea in a literary work is itself a tacit announcement of the implicit worth of the work. The richer the work in historical relevance the better it is.

I also have some other complaints about *The Gold Standard*. It is too clever by half—both in its occasionally excessive and obscure playing with ideas and language, in the manner of deconstructionist criticism (see especially pp. 176–81), and in its relentlessly revisionist frame of mind, one that often produces interpretations that run counter to the felt response of several generations of readers to a specific novel. (Michaels, for example, finds that Lily Bart in *The House of Mirth* unconsciously endorses rather than resists a marketplace economy of experience.) But I do not wish to imply by my comments in these last several paragraphs that Michaels's studies and the New Historicism in general are not to be welcomed on the critical scene. To the average academic literary scholar of my generation, almost anything new on the horizon is an improvement over the theoretical deluge of the last decade or so. But less flippantly, it is refreshing to see some of the old naturalistic warhorses—*Sister Carrie*, *McTeague*, and *The Octopus*, for example—discussed in new ways that also have a base in the actualities of the times in which they were written. One may not always agree either with the specific findings of this research or with some of its methods, but there is something "new" of considerable interest going on nevertheless. And one supposes that, as in most major movements in scholarship, there will eventually be a separating out of the chaff in the methodology of the New Historicism, with much profitable residue remaining behind.

1988

SEVENTEEN

⊣Lee Clark Mitchell, *Determined Fictions*⊢

American Literary Naturalism

*A*merican literary naturalism seems to be an "in" subject again after a long period of either neglect or disparagement. Within the last five years major studies by June Howard, John Conder, and Walter Benn Michaels have appeared, and the principal writers of the movement have also been featured in books by Philip Fisher, Robert Shulman, and Amy Kaplan, among others. Almost all of these works derive in one form or another from the recent emphasis in literary studies on the relationship of fiction to the circumstances of its own time, with particular emphasis on the role of class or economic power in conditioning literary expression. It is therefore refreshing to find in Lee Clark Mitchell's *Determined Fictions* a very different approach. Mitchell virtually ignores the philosophical angle of inquiry of a Conder and the economic centering of a Michaels. His book rests rather on the premise that naturalistic writers express their beliefs through their verbal and fictional constructs—through their style, in short—and that it is by means of a close examination of style that the critic can best discover the full dimensions of the denial of the autonomous self and the positing of a deterministic world that characterize the naturalistic ethos. It is such devices of naturalistic fiction as repetition or disruptive grammar or a false moral diction that best express the naturalistic writer's commitment to a deterministic belief. After an introductory chapter in which he seeks to distinguish between a late nineteenth-century realist's conception of the self and that of a naturalist, Mitchell devotes the bulk of his book to a study of the verbal and fictional strategies present in four texts—Jack London's "To Build a Fire," Theodore Dreiser's *An American Tragedy*, Frank Norris's *Vandover and the Brute*, and Stephen Crane's *The Red Badge of Courage*.

Despite this inviting approach—one that openly and successfully challenges the conventional idea that naturalistic fiction is usually verbally inept and structurally unsound—*Determined Fictions* is not an entirely satisfactory performance. One flaw, though not the most important, is that the book lacks a useful center. Aside from Mitchell's return on several occasions to the device of repetition in naturalist texts, little sense of a naturalist stylistics emerges from the very different critical strategies adopted by Mitchell for the examination of four very different prose and fictional styles. In the end, the book is principally a collection of four essays, some of which are more successful than others.

A far more significant weakness in *Determined Fictions* is that the value of each essay is almost inversely proportional to the degree that Mitchell depends in it on a close reading of prose style, the aspect of his study that initially promised to be the most innovative. Thus his most convincing essay, on *An American Tragedy*, is devoted principally to Dreiser's ironic doubling of event and characterization, whereas his interpretation of Crane's prose style in *The Red Badge* falls into the common trap of much prose analysis of finding that otherwise thematically neutral characteristics of style confirm themes that it is believed are present in the work as a whole. So, for example, after citing a passage from the novel that consists of a series of very short sentences describing Henry in the midst of a group of retreating soldiers, Mitchell says, "The choppy syntax here once again seems to exclude an organizing will, and powerfully evokes the consciousness of someone who lacks a self" (p. 114). It would seem to me, however, because I do not begin with the premise that Henry lacks selfhood, that the passage is principally an effort to render an impression of rapid action and that it has little bearing on Henry's lack of a self.

Mitchell's least persuasive essays are devoted to "To Build a Fire" and *Vandover and the Brute*. Here Mitchell adopts a number of reader-response and deconstructionist stances in order to demonstrate that the two works seek to subvert through their verbal stratagems a belief that their central characters share a responsibility for their fates, this despite their authors' constant attachment of blame and therefore of moral responsibility to the figures. I find this argument unconvincing, especially for *Vandover*. To assert that for Vandover "The way that conditions are interpreted and, more specifically, the way one's story gets told determines the fate of an individual far more than does any aspect of conditions themselves" (p. 78) is to ignore what happens in the novel. Vandover may indeed adopt, as Mitchell claims, an inappropriate moral language for his sexual desires, but he is brought low not by this language but by the fact that he sleeps with a syphilitic prostitute and is eventually reduced by general paralysis of the insane to a semivegetative state.

There have been some excellent stylistic studies of specific naturalistic writers—Frank Bergon's of Crane, for example, or more recently Barbara Hochman's of Norris—but Mitchell does not reach this level. Perhaps the underlying cause of much that is unsatisfactory in a book that otherwise often reveals a perceptive literary intelligence is that Mitchell starts out with the premise that a naturalistic writer is fully committed to a determinism that excludes a humanistic sense of selfhood. This method is suspect, I believe, despite the often sophisticated discourse of the analysis, because it tends to simplify naturalistic fiction into a one-dimensional philosophical position. It is no doubt problematical to adduce the nature of a literary work from its permanence, but I myself do not think that the works Mitchell discusses (with the exception of *Vandover*) would still be of interest if they are really about what Mitchell says they are about.

1990

Notes

A Selected Bibliography of American Literary Naturalism

Index

⊣ Notes ⊢

1. The Three Phases of American Literary Naturalism

1. *American Writing in the Twentieth Century* (Cambridge: Harvard Univ. Pr., 1960), p. 180.

2. The best brief discussion of naturalism as a worldwide movement is by Lilian R. Furst and Peter N. Skrine, *Naturalism* (London: Methuen, 1971).

3. This is basically the view of George J. Becker in his influential Introduction to his edition of *Documents of Modern Literary Realism* (Princeton: Princeton Univ. Pr., 1963).

4. An unusually acute endorsement of this conventional notion occurs in Edwin H. Cady's essay "Three Sensibilities: Romancer, Realist, Naturalist" in his *The Light of Common Day: Realism in American Fiction* (Bloomington: Indiana Univ. Pr., 1971).

5. *American Literary Naturalism: A Divided Stream* (Minneapolis: Univ. of Minnesota Pr., 1956).

6. "'Not Men': A Natural History of American Naturalism," *Kenyon Review* 9 (Summer 1947): 414–35; reprinted in expanded form in *Documents*, ed. Becker, as "A Natural History of American Naturalism."

7. "American Naturalism: Reflections from Another Era," *New Mexico Quarterly* 20 (Spring 1950): 50.

8. "Zola as a Romantic Writer," San Francisco *Wave* 15 (June 27, 1896): 3; reprinted in *The Literary Criticism of Frank Norris*, ed. Donald Pizer (Austin: Univ. of Texas Pr., 1964), p. 72.

9. Richard Chase, *The American Novel and Its Tradition* (Garden City, N.Y.: Doubleday, 1957).

10. See the standard literary histories of the period: Warner Berthoff, *The Ferment of Realism: American Literature, 1884–1919* (New York: Free Press, 1965); Jay Martin, *Harvests of Change: American Literature, 1865–1914* (Englewood Cliffs, N.J.: Prentice-Hall, 1967); and Larzer Ziff, *The American 1890s: Life and Times of a Lost Generation* (New York: Viking, 1966). My own *American Thought and Writing: The 1890s* (Boston: Houghton Mifflin, 1972) is an interpretive anthology of the decade.

11. *Stephen Crane: Letters*, ed. R. W. Stallman and Lillian Gilkes (New York: New York Univ. Pr., 1960), p. 14.

12. *The Red Badge of Courage*, ed. Donald Pizer (New York: Norton, 2nd rev. ed., 1976), p. 21.

13. *Sister Carrie*, ed. Donald Pizer (New York: Norton, 1970), p. 56.

14. See Lars Ahnebrink, *The Beginnings of Naturalism in American Fiction* (Cambridge: Harvard Univ. Pr., 1950) for Zola's impact on the young American writers of the 1890s.

15. I refer to Jimmie's awe at the beauty of the moon and Maggie's display of the lambrequin for Pete. (Maggie purchases the lambrequin out of an unconscious sense that beauty is associated with love and that beauty must therefore be made visible if love is to be known.) I discuss the theme of beauty in *Maggie* in my introduction to a facsimile edition of the 1893 *Maggie* (San Francisco: Chandler, 1968).

16. See Frederick J. Hoffman's important posthumous essay, "From Document to Symbol: Zola and American Naturalism," *Revue des Langues Vivantes*, U.S. Bicentennial Issue (1976), pp. 203–12.

17. There is no book-length study of American naturalism in the 1930s, though discussion of individual writers as naturalists occurs in Alfred Kazin, *On Native Grounds* (New York: Reynal & Hitchcock, 1942); Walcutt, *American Literary Naturalism*; Thorp, *American Writing in the Twentieth Century*; and *American Literary Naturalism: A Reassessment*, ed. Yoshinobu Hakutani and Lewis Fried (Heidelberg: Carl Winter, 1975).

18. Richard H. Pells, *Radical Visions and American*

Dreams: Culture and Social Thought in the Depression Years (New York: Harper & Row, 1973).

19. "James T. Farrell," *Talks with Authors*, ed. Charles F. Madden (Carbondale: Southern Illinois Univ. Pr., 1968), p. 96.

20. "Notes on the Decline of Naturalism," *Partisan Review* 9 (Nov.–Dec. 1942): 483–93, reprinted in Rahv's *Image and Idea* (New York: New Directions, 1949) and in *Documents*, ed. Becker, p. 589.

21. Trilling, "Reality in America," *The Liberal Imagination* (New York: Viking, 1950) (Trilling's essay appeared initially in two parts in 1940 and 1946); Cowley, "'Not Men'," reprinted in *Documents*, ed. Becker, pp. 429–51.

22. *American Writing in the Twentieth Century*, p. 144.

23. Bellow was born in 1915, Mailer in 1923, and Styron in 1925.

24. *Advertisements for Myself* (New York: Putnam, 1959), p. 27.

25. See Mailer's "Modes and Mutations: Quick Comments on the Modern American Novel," *Commentary* 41 (Mar. 1966): 37–40, reprinted in Mailer's *Cannibals and Christians* (New York: Dial, 1966), pp. 95–103, and Bellow's "Starting Out in Chicago," *American Scholar* 44 (Winter 1974–75): 73. Mailer in his essay does not specifically state his indebtedness to Dreiser, but such an indebtedness for *The Naked and the Dead* can be inferred from his laudatory discussion of Dreiser's social realism.

26. The first two quoted phrases are by Richard Lehan in his *A Dangerous Crossing: French Literary Existentialism and the Modern American Novel* (Carbondale: Southern Illinois Univ. Pr., 1973), p. xix; the last is by David D. Galloway in his *The Absurd Hero in American Fiction* (Austin: Univ. of Texas Pr., 1966), p. x.

3. American Literary Naturalism: The Example of Dreiser

1. Quoted by Franklin Walker, *Frank Norris: A Biography* (Garden City, N.Y.: Doubleday, Doran, 1932), pp. 222–23.

2. The most characteristic discussions of American naturalism occur in histories of American fiction. See, for example, Harry Hartwick, *The Foreground of American Fiction* (New York:

American, 1934), pp. 3–20; George Snell, *The Shapers of American Fiction, 1798–1947* (New York: Dutton, 1947), pp. 223–48; Frederick J. Hoffman, *The Modern Novel in America* (Chicago: Regnery, 1951), pp. 28–51; and Edward Wagenknecht, *Cavalcade of the American Novel* (New York: Holt, 1952), pp. 204–29. But see also Oscar Cargill, *Intellectual America* (New York: Macmillan, 1941), pp. 82–175, and Lars Ahnebrink, *The Beginnings of Naturalism in American Fiction* (Cambridge: Harvard Univ. Pr., 1950).

3. Charles C. Walcutt, *American Literary Naturalism: A Divided Stream* (Minneapolis: Univ. of Minnesota Pr., 1956), p. 220.

4. Eliseo Vivas, "Dreiser, An Inconsistent Mechanist," *Ethics* (July 1938); revised version, *The Stature of Theodore Dreiser*, ed. Alfred Kazin and Charles Shapiro (Bloomington: Indiana Univ. Pr., 1955), p. 237.

5. Two extreme examples of this position are Randall Stewart, *American Literature and Christian Doctrine* (Baton Rouge: Louisiana State Univ. Pr., 1958), pp. 114–20, and Floyd Stovall, *American Idealism* (Norman: Univ. of Oklahoma Pr., 1943), pp. 134–36.

6. The essays were published originally in 1942, 1947, and 1946 respectively.

7. See, for example, Charles Thomas Samuels, "Mr. Trilling, Mr. Warren, and *An American Tragedy*," *Yale Review* 53 (Summer 1964): 629–40. Samuels finds *An American Tragedy* inept beyond belief.

8. *Sister Carrie*, ed. Donald Pizer (New York: Norton, 1970), p. 56.

9. Portions of the discussion of *Jennie Gerhardt* and *An American Tragedy* which follows appear in different form in my *Novels of Theodore Dreiser: A Critical Study* (Minneapolis: Univ. of Minnesota Pr., 1976). I do not wish by my emphasis on the deterministic thread in naturalism to appear to be supporting a return to a simplistic definition of naturalism as "pessimistic determinism" or some such formula. I have devoted much effort over two decades in various critical studies of individual naturalists as well as in more general essays on the movement as a whole to the position that naturalism is a complex literary movement in which distinctive writers combine in their works distinctive

strains of traditional humanistic values and contemporary deterministic belief. Rather, I seek in this essay to suggest that just as we were long guilty of not recognizing the element of covertly expressed traditional value in most naturalists, so we have also been guilty of an uncritical disparagement of the more readily identifiable deterministic strain in their work.

10. *Jennie Gerhardt* (New York: Harper, 1911), p. 401. Citations appear hereafter in the text.

11. In the Theodore Dreiser Collection, University of Pennsylvania Library; quoted by permission of the University of Pennsylvania Library.

12. *An American Tragedy* (New York: Boni and Liveright, 1925), I, 5. Citations appear hereafter in the text.

4. Dreiser and the Naturalistic Drama of Consciousness

1. Lionel Trilling, "Reality in America," in *The Liberal Imagination* (New York: Viking, 1950).

2. Warren French, *John Steinbeck*, rev. ed. (Boston: Twayne, 1974), p. 40.

3. Sandy Petrey, "The Language of Realism, The Language of False Consciousness: A Reading of *Sister Carrie*," *Novel* 10 (1977): 101–13.

4. See, for example, Walter Benn Michaels's discussion of Carrie and Trina in his *The Gold Standard and the Logic of Naturalism* (Berkeley: Univ. of California Pr., 1987).

5. For a somewhat different discussion of the psychological realism of this scene, see Gordon O. Taylor, *The Passages of Thought: Psychological Representation in the American Novel, 1870–1900* (New York: Oxford Univ. Pr., 1969).

6. Quotations from Chapter XXVII that follow are from *Sister Carrie*, ed. Donald Pizer (New York: Norton, 1970).

7. *Jennie Gerhardt*, ed. Donald Pizer (New York: Viking, 1989), p. 217. Citations from this edition will hereafter appear in the text.

8. For a discussion of Dreiser's development and use of this technique in his short stories of the period, see Joseph Griffin, *The Small Canvas: An Introduction to Dreiser's Short Stories* (Rutherford, N.J.: Fairleigh Dickinson Univ. Pr., 1976).

9. Quotations from Chapter XLVI that follow are from *An American Tragedy* (New York: Boni and Liveright, 1925).

10. In the later stages of Roberta and Clyde's trip to the North Woods, Dreiser in fact returns to a device of *Sister Carrie*, in that Clyde, like Hurstwood, hears inner voices that express his fears and desires. My point, however, is not that Dreiser rejects entirely the melodramatic techniques of his earlier fiction but that he also extends his range beyond them.

5. Nineteenth-Century American Naturalism: An Essay in Definition

1. Richard Chase, *The American Novel and Its Tradition* (Garden City, N.Y.: Doubleday, 1957), p. 186n; George J. Becker, "Modern Realism as a Literary Movement," in *Documents of Modern Literary Realism*, ed. George J. Becker (Princeton: Princeton Univ. Pr., 1963), p. 35. See also the definitions by Lars Ahnebrink, *The Beginnings of Naturalism in American Fiction* (Cambridge: Harvard Univ. Pr., 1950), pp. vi–vii; Malcolm Cowley, "A Natural History of American Naturalism," *Documents*, pp. 429–30; and Philip Rahv, "Notes on the Decline of Naturalism," *Documents*, pp. 583–84.

2. The discussion of naturalism in the next two paragraphs resembles in several ways that by Charles C. Walcutt in his *American Literary Naturalism: A Divided Stream* (Minneapolis: Univ. of Minnesota Pr., 1956), pp. 3–29. In general, I accept Walcutt's analysis of naturalism's philosophical and literary ambivalences. I believe, however, that his discussion of the naturalists' divided view of nature and of their maintenance of the idea of free will by implicitly encouraging their readers to social action are ways of describing these ambivalences historically and socially—by source and effect—rather than as they function within the naturalistic novel itself.

3. Erich Auerbach's *Mimesis: The Representation of Reality in Western Literature* (Princeton: Princeton Univ. Pr., 1953) deals with the representation of these ideas in imaginative literature from antiquity to our own day.

4. Frank Norris, "A Plea for Romantic Fiction," *The Literary Criticism of Frank Norris*, ed. Donald Pizer (Austin: Univ. of Texas Pr., 1964), p. 77.

5. *McTeague*, ed. Donald Pizer (New York: Norton, 1977), p. 177. Citations hereafter appear in the text.

6. I discuss this aspect of Norris's thought at some length in my "Evolutionary Ethical Dualism in Frank Norris' *Vandover and the Brute* and *McTeague*," *PMLA* 76 (Dec. 1961): 522–60.

7. Lionel Trilling, "Reality in America," *The Liberal Imagination* (New York: Viking, 1950).

8. *Sister Carrie*, ed. Donald Pizer (New York: Norton, 1970), p. 367.

9. See William A. Freedman, "A Look at Dreiser as Artist: The Motif of Circularity in *Sister Carrie*," *Modern Fiction Studies* 8 (Winter 1962–63): 384–92; and my own "Nineteenth-Century American Naturalism: An Approach Through Form," which follows.

10. *The Red Badge of Courage*, ed. Donald Pizer (New York: Norton, 2nd rev. ed., 1976), p. 33. Citations hereafter appear in the text.

6. Nineteenth-Century American Naturalism: An Approach Through Form

1. Edwin H. Cady, *The Light of Common Day: Realism in American Fiction* (Bloomington: Indiana Univ. Pr., 1971), p. 45.

2. For other views of the naturalistic symbol and the form of the naturalistic novel, see Charles C. Walcutt, *American Literary Naturalism: A Divided Stream* (Minneapolis: Univ. of Minnesota Pr., 1956); Robert M. Figg, "Naturalism as a Literary Form," *Georgia Review* 18 (Fall 1964): 308–16; and Frederick J. Hoffman, "From Document to Symbol: Zola and American Naturalism," *Revue des Langues Vivantes*, U.S. Bicentennial Issue (1976), pp. 203–12.

3. Richard Ellmann, *James Joyce* (New York: Oxford Univ. Pr., 1959), p. 3.

7. The Problem of Philosophy in the Naturalistic Novel

1. *Vandover and the Brute* (Garden City, N.Y.: Doubleday, Page, 1914), pp. 230–31.

2. Fuller discussions of Norris's ideas about art in *Vandover* can be found in my *Novels of Frank Norris* (Bloomington: Indiana Univ. Pr., 1966), pp. 23–52 and Don Graham, *The Fiction of Frank Norris: The Aesthetic Context* (Columbia: Univ. of Missouri Pr., 1978), pp. 16–42.

3. *Sister Carrie*, ed. Donald Pizer (New York: Norton, 1970), pp. 56–57.

4. *Sister Carrie*, p. 24.

8. Frank Norris's Definition of Naturalism

1. "A Plea for Romantic Fiction," *Boston Evening Transcript*, December 18, 1901, p. 14; "Zola as a Romantic Writer," *Wave*, 15 (June 27, 1896): 3; "Frank Norris' Weekly Letter," *Chicago American Literary Review*, Aug. 3, 1901, p. 5. The first essay was republished in *The Responsibilities of the Novelist* (New York: Doubleday, Page, 1903); the second was partially reprinted in Franklin Walker, *Frank Norris: A Biography* (Garden City, N.Y.: Doubleday, Doran, 1932). The third essay was republished, along with the first two, in *The Literary Criticism of Frank Norris*, ed. Donald Pizer (Austin: Univ. of Texas Pr., 1964). Quotations refer to *The Literary Criticism of Frank Norris*.

2. "Zola as a Romantic Writer," p. 71.

3. "A Plea for Romantic Fiction," p. 76.

4. "A Plea for Romantic Fiction," p. 76.

5. "A Plea for Romantic Fiction," p. 78.

6. "Zola as a Romantic Writer," p. 72.

7. It was not uncommon throughout Zola's career for critics to call him a romanticist because of his sensational plots, though such critics usually intended disparagement rather than praise. See Max Nordau, *Degeneration* (New York: Appleton, 1895), pp. 494–97, and F. W. J. Hemmings, *Emile Zola* (Oxford: Clarendon Pr., 1953), p. 74.

8. "Frank Norris' Weekly Letter," p. 75.

9. This choice of novels is not entirely clear, but perhaps it can be explained by the contemporary reputation of the three works and by the fact Norris was writing for a newspaper supplement. *La Débâcle* was well received in America, while *La Terre* was attacked for its gross sexuality and *Fécondité* was heavily criticized for its excessive polemicism.

10. "Frank Norris' Weekly Letter," p. 75.

11. "Zola as a Romantic Writer," p. 72.

12. See Zola's *The Experimental Novel and Other Essays* (New York: Cassell, 1893), pp. 17–18; Lars Ahnebrink, *The*

Beginnings of Naturalism in American Fiction (Cambridge: Harvard Univ. Pr., 1950), pp. vi–vii; and Charles C. Walcutt, *American Literary Naturalism: A Divided Stream* (Minneapolis: Univ. of Minnesota Pr., 1956), pp. vii–viii.

13. Norris to Marcosson, November 1899, in *The Letters of Frank Norris*, ed. Franklin Walker (San Francisco: Book Club of California, 1956), p. 48.

9. Stephen Crane's *Maggie* and American Naturalism

1. Both R. W. Stallman, in "Crane's *Maggie*: A Reassessment," *Modern Fiction Studies* 5 (Autumn 1959): 251–59, and Charles C. Walcutt, in *American Literary Naturalism: A Divided Stream* (Minneapolis: Univ. of Minnesota Pr., 1956), pp. 67–72, touch briefly on the theme of *Maggie* somewhat as I do. I have also been aided by Edwin H. Cady, *Stephen Crane* (Boston: Twayne, 1980), pp. 104–13; Joseph X. Brennan, "Ironic and Symbolic Structure in Crane's *Maggie*," *Nineteenth-Century Fiction* 16 (March 1962): 303–15; and Janet Overmyer, "The Structure of Crane's *Maggie*," *University of Kansas City Review* 29 (Autumn 1962): 71–72.

2. Stephen Crane, *Maggie: A Girl of the Streets* (New York, 1893); facsimile ed., ed. Donald Pizer (San Francisco: Chandler, 1968), p. [3]. Citations hereafter appear in the text.

3. *Stephen Crane: Letters*, ed. R. W. Stallman and Lillian Gilkes (New York: New York Univ. Pr., 1960), p. 14.

10. Self-Censorship and the Editing of Late Nineteenth-Century Naturalistic Texts

1. G. Thomas Tanselle, "The Editorial Problem of Final Authorial Intention," *Studies in Bibliography* 29 (1976): 182.

2. See *The Fourteenth Chronicle: Letters and Diaries of John Dos Passos*, ed. Townsend Ludington (Boston: Gambit, 1974), pp. 284, 288–89, 294.

3. Stephen Crane, *The Red Badge of Courage*, in *The Norton Anthology of American Literature*, vol. 2, ed. Ronald Gottesman et al. (New York: Norton, 1979). This text, edited by Henry Binder, was also separately issued by Norton in 1982. Theodore Dreiser, *Sister Carrie*, The Pennsylvania Edition, ed. James L. W. West III et al. (Philadelphia: Univ. of Pennsylvania Pr., 1981).

4. James Meriwether, "A Proposal for a CEAA Edition of William Faulkner," in *Editing Twentieth-Century Texts*, ed. Frances Halpenny (Toronto: Univ. of Toronto Pr., 1972), p. 14.

5. See Hershel Parker, "Aesthetic Implications of Authorial Excisions . . . ," in *Editing Nineteenth-Century Fiction*, ed. Jane Millgate (New York: Garland, 1978), pp. 99–119.

6. Donald Pizer, "On the Editing of Modern American Texts," *Bulletin of the New York Public Library* 75 (March 1971): 148.

7. Morse Peckham, "Reflections on the Foundations of Modern Textual Editing," *Proof* 1 (1971): 125.

8. Both the original passage and Norris's revision can be found in my edition of *McTeague* (New York: Norton, 1977), pp. 59–61.

9. See Hershel Parker, Introduction to "Special Number on Stephen Crane," *Studies in the Novel* 10 (Spring 1978): 6–7; Henry Binder, "*The Red Badge of Courage* Nobody Knows," ibid.: 9–47; and Steven Mailloux, *The Red Badge of Courage* and Interpretive Conventions: Critical Response to a Maimed Text," ibid.: 48–63.

10. G. Thomas Tanselle, "Recent Editorial Discussion and the Central Questions of Editing," *Studies in Bibliography* 34 (1981): 63–64.

11. G. Thomas Tanselle, "Problems and Accomplishments in the Editing of the Novel," *Studies in the Novel* 7 (Fall 1975): 340.

12. See, for example, the major studies by Frank Bergon, *Stephen Crane's Artistry* (New York: Columbia Univ. Pr., 1975), and James Nagel, *Stephen Crane and Literary Impressionism* (University Park: Pennsylvania State Univ. Pr., 1980).

13. Peckham, "Reflections," 122–55.

14. *The Fourteenth Chronicle*, ed. Ludington, p. 611.

11. American Naturalism in Its "Perfected" State: *The Age of Innocence* and *An American Tragedy*

1. For an effort to assert this position, see Don Graham, "Naturalism in American Fiction: A Status Report," *Studies in American Fiction* 10 (Spring 1982): 1–16.

2. I myself adopt this approach to the history of American

naturalism in my *Twentieth-Century American Literary Naturalism: An Interpretation* (Carbondale: Southern Illinois Univ. Pr., 1982).

3. For a characteristically antinaturalistic position by a Jamesian, see Charles T. Samuels, "Mr. Trilling, Mr. Warren, and *An American Tragedy*," *Yale Review* 53 (Summer 1964): 629–40.

4. *An American Tragedy* has of course been frequently discussed as a naturalistic novel. For a representative sampling of such commentary, see *Critical Essays on Theodore Dreiser*, ed. Donald Pizer (Boston: G. K. Hall, 1981). Wharton's work, including *The Age of Innocence*, is far less frequently linked with naturalism. Two somewhat limited such efforts are Larry Rubin, "Aspects of Naturalism in Four Novels of Edith Wharton," *Twentieth Century Literature* 2 (January 1957): 182–97 and James A. Robinson, "Psychological Determinism in *The Age of Innocence*," *Markham Review* 5 (Fall 1975): 1–5. In addition, Alan Price has briefly compared two earlier novels by Wharton and Dreiser in his "Lily Bart and Carrie Meeber: Cultural Sisters," *American Literary Realism* 13 (Autumn 1980): 238–45.

5. See my *Novels of Theodore Dreiser: A Critical Study* (Minneapolis: Univ. of Minnesota Pr., 1976), pp. 203–4.

6. *An American Tragedy* (New York: Boni and Liveright, 1925), I, 31. Citations from this edition will hereafter appear in the text.

7. *The Age of Innocence*, in *Edith Wharton: Novels* (New York: The Library of America, 1985), p. 1157. Citations from this edition will hereafter appear in the text.

12. Contemporary American Literary Naturalism

1. Fuller discussions of the conventional American hostility to naturalism can be found in Donald Pizer, "American Literary Naturalism: The Example of Dreiser," *Studies in American Fiction* 5 (May, 1977): 51–63, and Don Graham, "Naturalism in American Fiction: A Status Report," *Studies in American Fiction* 10 (Spring 1982): 1–16.

2. Thorp, *American Writing in the Twentieth Century* (Cambridge: Harvard Univ. Pr., 1960), p. 180.

3. (Carbondale: Southern Illinois Univ. Pr., 1982).

4. *Stephen Crane: Letters* ed. R. W. Stallman and Lillian Gilkes (New York: New York Univ. Pr., 1960), p. 14.

5. *them* (New York: Vanguard, 1969), p. 12. Citations from this edition will hereafter appear in the text.

6. In a 1976 interview, Oates noted that both the Author's Note to *them*, in which she described her relationship to the "real-life" prototype of Maureen, and Maureen's letters to her (pp. 329–40) were in fact fictitious. (See Joanna V. Creighton, *Joyce Carol Oates*, New York: Twayne, 1979, p. 65.) Oates' admission, however, does not affect the thematic function of the Oates-Maureen relationship within the novel itself.

7. (New York: Dial, 1966), pp. 131–32. The poem was initially published in 1964.

8. *The Executioner's Song* (Boston: Little, Brown, 1979), p. 1052. Citations from this edition will hereafter appear in the text.

9. Robert Stone, *A Flag for Sunrise* (New York: Knopf, 1981), p. 13. Citations from this edition will hereafter appear in the text.

10. Shelgrim to Presley, in *The Octopus* (Garden City, N.Y.: Doubleday, Doran, 1928), I, 285.

13. William Kennedy's *Ironweed* and the American Naturalistic Tradition

1. See Donald Pizer, *Twentieth-Century American Literary Naturalism: An Interpretation* (Carbondale: Southern Illinois Univ. Pr., 1982).

2. William Kennedy, *Ironweed* (New York: Viking, 1983), p. 29. Citations from this edition will hereafter appear in the text.

3. This reading of the conclusion of *Ironweed* is also supported by two bits of external evidence. In an interview, Kennedy refused to reply directly to the question as to whether Francis had in fact physically returned home at the conclusion. Of the ending of the novel, he said, "It's not simple realism, nor is it simple mysticism. . . . What these last two or three pages say is what Francis Phelan's condition is when we take leave of him" (Kay Bonetti, "An Interview with William Kennedy," *Missouri Review* 8 [1985]: 71–86). And the film version of *Ironweed*, a version for which Kennedy wrote the screenplay, is also equivocal

in its dramatization of the conclusion. During the freight car scene, Annie appears in hallucinatory form and offers Francis a cup of tea, as though he were at home. The scene than changes to Francis' grandson's room, and Francis speaks the last lines of the novel about the space and light of the room. Francis speaks these lines, however, as a voice-over, not as a physical presence in the room. Thus, the film coalesces dramatically the freight car and Francis's home as simultaneously present in Francis's mind.

A Selected Bibliography of American Literary Naturalism

Omitted are studies that do not address the general character of American naturalism or that are limited to the work of one author.

Ahnebrink, Lars. *The Beginnings of Naturalism in American Fiction.* Cambridge: Harvard Univ. Pr., 1950.

Becker, George J. *Realism in Modern Literature.* New York: Ungar, 1980.

——, ed. *Documents of Modern Literary Realism.* Princeton: Princeton Univ. Pr., 1963.

Berthoff, Warner. *The Ferment of Realism: American Literature, 1884–1919.* New York: Free Press, 1965.

Block, Haskell M. *Naturalistic Triptych: The Fictive and the Real in Zola, Mann, and Dreiser.* New York: Random House, 1970.

Borus, Daniel H. *Writing Realism: Howells, James, and Norris in the Mass Market.* Chapel Hill: Univ. of North Carolina Pr., 1989.

Cady, Edwin H. "Three Sensibilties: Romancer, Realist, Naturalist," *The Light of Common Day: Realism in American Fiction.* Bloomington: Indiana Univ. Pr., 1971.

Cargill, Oscar. *Intellectual America: Ideas on the March*. New York: Macmillan, 1941.

Chase, Richard. *The American Novel and Its Tradition*. Garden City, N.Y.: Doubleday, 1957.

Chevrel, Yves. *Le Naturalisme*. Paris: Presses Universitaires de France, 1982.

Conder, John J. *Naturalism in American Fiction: The Classic Phase*. Lexington: Univ. Pr. of Kentucky, 1984.

Cowley, Malcolm. "'Not Men': A Natural History of American Naturalism." *Kenyon Review* 9 (Summer 1947): 414–35.

Farrell, James T. "Some Observations on Naturalism, So Called, in Fiction," *Reflections at Fifty and Other Essays*. New York: Vanguard, 1954.

Figg, Robert M., III. "Naturalism as a Literary Form." *Georgia Review* 18 (Fall 1964): 308–16.

Fisher, Philip. "The Life History of Objects: The Naturalist Novel and the City," *Hard Facts: Setting and Form in the American Novel*. New York: Oxford Univ. Pr., 1985.

Furst, Lilian R., and Skrine, Peter N. *Naturalism*. London: Methuen, 1971.

Graham, Don. "Naturalism in America: A Status Report." *Studies in American Fiction* 10 (Spring 1982): 1–16.

Hakutani, Yoshinobu, and Fried, Lewis, eds. *American Literary Naturalism: A Reassessment*. Heidelberg: Carl Winter, 1975.

Hoffman, Frederick J. "From Document to Symbol: Zola and American Naturalism." *Revue des Langues Vivantes*, U.S. Bicentennial Issue (1976), pp. 203–12.

Howard, June. *Form and History in American Literary Naturalism*. Chapel Hill: Univ. of North Carolina Pr., 1985.

Kaplan, Amy. *The Social Construction of American Realism*. Chicago: Univ. of Chicago Pr., 1988.

Kaplan, Harold. *Power and Order: Henry Adams and the Naturalist Tradition in American Fiction*. Chicago: Univ. of Chicago Pr., 1981.

Kazin, Alfred. "American Naturalism: Reflections from Another Era," *The American Writer and the European*

Tradition, ed. Margaret Denny and William H. Gilman. Minneapolis: Univ. of Minnesota Pr., 1950.

———. *On Native Grounds.* New York: Reynal & Hitch-cock, 1942.

Krause, Sydney J., ed. *Essays on Determinism in American Literature.* Kent, Ohio: Kent State Univ. Pr., 1964.

Lehan, Richard. "American Literary Naturalism: The French Connection." *Nineteenth-Century Literature* 38 (March 1984): 529–57.

Martin, Jay. *Harvests of Change: American Literature, 1865–1914.* Englewood Cliffs, N.J.: Prentice-Hall, 1967.

Martin, Ronald E. *American Literature and the Universe of Force.* Durham: Duke Univ. Pr., 1981.

Michaels, Walter Benn. *The Gold Standard and the Logic of Naturalism: American Literature at the Turn of the Century.* Berkeley: Univ. of California Pr., 1987.

Mitchell, Lee Clark. *Determined Fictions: American Literary Naturalism.* New York: Columbia Univ. Pr., 1989.

———. "Naturalism and the Languages of Determinism," *Columbia Literary History of the United States,* ed. Emory Elliott. New York: Columbia Univ. Pr., 1988.

Pizer, Donald. *Realism and Naturalism in Nineteenth-Century American Literature.* Carbondale: Southern Illinois Univ. Pr., 1966; rev. ed., Carbondale: Southern Illinois Univ. Pr., 1984.

———. *Twentieth-Century American Literary Naturalism: An Interpretation.* Carbondale: Southern Illinois Univ. Pr., 1982.

Poenicke, Klaus. *Der Amerikanische Naturalismus: Crane, Norris, und Dreiser.* Darmstadt: Wissenschaftlichte Buchgesellschaft, 1982.

Rahv, Philip. "Notes on the Decline of Naturalism," *Image and Idea.* New York: New Directions, 1949.

Seamon, Roger. "Naturalist Narratives and Their Ideational Context: A Theory of American Naturalist Fiction." *Canadian Review of American Studies* 19 (Spring 1988): 47–64.

Seltzer, Mark. "The Naturalist Machine," *Sex, Politics, and Science in the Nineteenth Century Novel,* ed. Ruth Bernard Yeazell. Baltimore: Johns Hopkins Univ. Pr., 1986.

Sundquist, Eric J. "Introduction: The Country of the Blue," *American Realism: New Essays*, ed. Eric J. Sundquist. Baltimore: Johns Hopkins Univ. Pr., 1982.

Taylor, Gordon O. *The Passages of Thought: Psychological Representation in the American Novel, 1870–1900*. New York: Oxford Univ. Pr., 1969.

Thorp, Willard. "The Persistence of Naturalism in the Novel," *American Writing in the Twentieth Century*. Cambridge: Harvard Univ. Pr., 1960.

Trachtenberg, Alan. *The Incorporation of America: Culture and Society in the Gilded Age*. New York: Hill and Wang, 1982.

Trilling, Lionel. "Reality in America," *The Liberal Imagination*. New York: Viking, 1950.

Walcutt, Charles C. *American Literary Naturalism, A Divided Stream*. Minneapolis: Univ. of Minnesota Pr., 1956.

Wilson, Christopher P. *The Labor of Words: Literary Professionalism in the Progressive Era*. Athens: Univ. of Georgia Pr., 1985.

Index

231

DONALD PIZER is Pierce Butler Professor of English at Tulane University. A specialist in late nineteenth- and early twentieth-century American literature, he has published widely in this area, including full-length studies of Frank Norris, Theodore Dreiser, and John Dos Passos. His *Realism and Naturalism in Nineteenth-Century American Literature* (1966; 2nd rev. ed., 1984) is a standard work in the field. He has held fellowships from the Guggenheim Foundation, the National Endowment for the Humanities, and the American Council of Learned Societies.